Kaumudi Marathé is a journalist, chef and teacher. Born in Poona, she has spent more than half her life abroad, but still feels strong ties to her native land. Her love of Indian food, music and history has inspired her to drive across the subcontinent, write about India's temples and document its culinary traditions. She is the author of, among other books, *The Essential Marathi Cookbook and Maharashtrian Cuisine: A Family Treasury*. In fact, her reverence for the food of her homeland sparked a personal rebellion in 2007, in which she made it her mission to bring Indian flavours other than curry to kitchens around the world with Un-Curry (www.un-curry.com), the first organic Indian cooking school, catering company and pop-up restaurant in Los Angeles. Her work appears in *Saveur, Paste, LA Parent* and other publications. She makes time for long-distance running, being a mother to her ballerina daughter, Keya, and hiking in the local Southern California mountains with her partner, Dean, and her Tibetan terrier, Ever.

Also by Kaumudi Marathé

The Essential Marathi Cookbook (2009)
Maharastrian Cuisine: A Family Treasury (1999)
Temples of India: Circles of Stone (1998)

Shared Tables

Family Stories and Recipes from Poona to LA

KAUMUDI MARATHÉ

SPEAKING TIGER PUBLISHING PVT. LTD
4381/4 Ansari Road, Daryaganj,
New Delhi–110002, India

Copyright © Kaumudi Marathé 2017

ISBN: 978-93-86582-02-7
eISBN: 978-93-86582-01-0

10 9 8 7 6 5 4 3 2 1

Typeset in Adobe Garamond Pro by SÜRYA, New Delhi
Printed at Sanat Printers, Kundli

All rights reserved.
No part of this publication may be reproduced,
transmitted, or stored in a retrieval system, in any form or
by any means, electronic, mechanical, photocopying,
recording or otherwise, without the prior
permission of the publisher.

This book is sold subject to the condition that it shall not,
by way of trade or otherwise, be lent, resold, hired out,
or otherwise circulated, without the publisher's
prior consent, in any form of binding or cover
other than that in which it is published.

For some of the heroes in my life

Sudhakar & Jerry,
Who made the most of their lives,

Aditya & Odin Jacob,
Who never got the chance to,

Pramodan,
Whose brief life was well spent,

Sanjiv,
With whom I shared a life,

Melkon,
Who always looks ahead,
&

Dean,
Who makes his life one moment at a time.

Contents

Introduction: Why Not Food?   1

1. Origins   6
2. What's In a Name?   10
3. The Brave Girl   23
4. Tell Me a Story   42
5. Sita Returns to Mother Earth   48
6. Happy-Go-Lucky   52
7. Where the Soul Knows Peace   65
8. The Goddess in the Kitchen   70
9. The Beauteous One   76
10. Prajakta's Tale   83
11. Until Death Do We…   87
12. Carry Your Heart   94
13. Me? Sudhakar…   100
14. Love & Marriage   107
15. Bunny   112
16. Sunday's Child   124
17. Made in Wales   133
18. The Fenugreek of Parents   137

19.	Beth & Jerry	145
20.	246	156
21.	The Kingdom of the Seven Hills	176
22.	Land of Rocks	184
23.	The Year of Magical Thinking	194
24.	Getting the Story	198
25.	To Tell the Truth	202
26.	I Want to Write a Book	212
27.	Tie & Knot	217
28.	Coming to America	222
29.	God's Own Country	229
30.	Mi Casa…	238
31.	Mama	243
32.	Un-Curry	254
33.	The Shared Table	263
	Recipes	271
	Acknowledgements	299

Old paint on a canvas, as it ages, sometimes becomes transparent. When that happens it is possible, in some pictures, to see the original lines: a tree will show through a woman's dress, a child makes way for a dog, a large boat is no longer on an open sea. That is called pentimento because the painter 'repented,' changed his mind. Perhaps it would be as well to say that the old conception, replaced by a later choice, is a way of seeing and then seeing again. That is all I mean about the people in this book. The paint has aged and I wanted to see what was there for me once, what is there for me now.

—Lillian Hellman,
Pentimento

INTRODUCTION
Why Not Food?

I, with my brain and my hands, have nourished my beloved few… I have concocted a stew or a story, a rarity or a plain dish, to sustain them truly against the hungers of the world.
—M.F.K. Fisher, author of *The Gastronomical Me*

I was never going to be a chef.

Exquisite aromas linger in my nostrils after decades. Flavour pixies dance on my tongue, conjuring memories of food that people long gone cooked for me.

Inside, deep inside, there has always been a tamped down greed in my soul, a desire to devour, a need to consume. There is hunger.

I am rather restrained. I don't overeat. I chew each mouthful carefully. My eyes are bigger than my stomach, my friends joke. The sight of a pain au chocolat in a Paris boulangerie or the memory of the exquisite baked onions our friend Danilo made for Sanjiv and me in his tiny apartment in Austin, Texas, when we were newly arrived in America, sets my pulse racing.

In India, I travelled back in time whenever I ate a simple lunch at the house where my father was raised, the kind of food I imagined him eating as a child: flaky chapatis, subtly spiced cabbage, sweet-tart pigeon pea stew, buttermilk with ginger, Marathi pickle (loncha), some sweet, crushed jaggery and ghee.

When I moved to the USA, I searched for the country Hollywood had shown me: the shiny 1950s diner, the Jewish delicatessen in New York, the country store out West. I eagerly looked for the best cup of coffee, the fluffiest pancakes or flapjacks, frothy egg creams and comforting Matzo ball soup, cherry pie and jambalaya, an airy beignet and a spicy gumbo, and always, melt-in-your-mouth Texas barbecue.

I cannot remember a time when food and stories were not interwoven in my mind. As a little girl, my biggest treat was getting a cream horn when Mom and I went to the bakery or a new Enid Blyton mystery when she went book shopping. Blyton's descriptions of English teas in country houses, picnics in meadows, bottles of milk chilled in a river, made me long to live in England. When I was nine in Canada, Laura Ingalls Wilder's romantic description of pouring maple syrup into a cast-iron skillet full of snow to make maple candy, made my mouth water and my imagination fire.

But when I was twelve, the English writer H.E. Bates really began my conscious journey of devouring words of deliciousness. Bates' description of Miss Bentley sensuously peeling a peach, in his short story, *A Month by the Lake,* will live in my mind forever. I see the middle-aged woman, feel the warmth of the Italian summer sun on her tanned skin, and sense the latent emotion contained in her act of peeling and slicing the fruit purposefully, then bringing it to her mouth deliberately, as the man she loved watched. Never before had words or food moved me so deeply.

My voyage continued in my twenties with America's best-known food writer, M.F.K. Fisher's poetic evocations of food in her memoir, *The Gastronomical Me.* In it, she describes her memories of food in America, France and Switzerland in the early twentieth century: how as a girl of eight, she watched her grandmother and mother making strawberry jam at their home in Whittier, California, licking the sticky white foam that collected on the wooden spoon used to stir the pot; how she ate her surfeit of excellent food at a little restaurant in rural France where she was the only guest, held captive by a slightly mad waitress; how, in Aix-en-Provence, she once put together a simple dish of cauliflower florets baked with a little butter and Gruyère and discovered it was memorable because the ingredients were so fine.

These tales were aromatic souvenirs of a voluptuous life. It was Fisher who made me realize what my hunger was. It was a hunger for love and happiness and the innocence that accompanies it.

But if, when I was twenty-one years old, you had told me that I would make a career cooking my love into food, that I would teach people how to cook Indian food in America, I would have stared at you flabbergasted, if not laughed in your face. It was not that my parents would have objected to my cooking for a living. It had nothing to do with caste or upbringing. It was just that I never thought of a culinary career. My plans lay elsewhere.

*

It was 1990 and I was graduating from communications school with honours in journalism. I had the co-editorship of the prestigious class magazine on my CV, an internship at the most historic broadsheet in Bombay under my belt, and a prospective job at the same institution, headed by the charismatic and respected journalist, Janardhan Thakur who had had a distinguished career and who showed an interest in me and my decision to write.

Food? Impossible. Yes, but so many implausible things have happened in my life that today I do not think anything is beyond the realms of possibility. Some of my earliest and strongest memories revolve around food. As I write, my nostrils recall the turmeric aroma of fried pomfret crisping in Vahini's kitchen or Ai Aji shelling tender green harbhara beans on the front stoop of Shree Ram Krupa, with us little ones helping as much as we hindered, popping the sweet young chickpeas into our mouths instead of the bowl.

If my hunger is for love, the manifestation of it, food, is a metaphor for everything life holds: chemistry, physics, medicine, nutrition. We need food to survive. But from a young age, love was given to me tenderly on a plate so I also see food as memory and comfort. It is my muse, my inspiration, my way to give love.

I did start my adult life as a journalist but food was always circling in the air above me. When my then-husband Sanjiv and I moved to the USA in 1996 so he could study urban design, I was not allowed to work for pay on my student spouse visa. So I used the time to explore my adopted country, write freelance, raise a child, and teach myself about food and food history.

I read, I cooked, I experimented, I made notes, I entertained. Each time I made Indian food for guests, they were pleasantly surprised because my cooking tasted nothing like restaurant food. 'You should start your own restaurant,' they said. After eleven years we got our green card authorization and I was raring to start work. What about that restaurant? No, I wanted something more. I wanted Americans to *really* know and understand the complexity and wealth of Indian cooking. I wanted to combine my writing and storytelling skills with my love of my native food and my knowledge of American tastes.

So I launched Un-Curry, a catering-teaching-food writing company. Over the past decade, it's been one hell of a ride. I've written a cookbook. I've cooked for everyone from actors like Timothy Olyphant, John Cryer and Kelly Williams to TV producers like Gary Glasberg, from people like me who just wanted to throw a great party to terminally ill patients like Toni Brown who wanted Indian food for her last birthday supper while she was still physically able to chew. I've taught budding vegans and vegetarians how to cook to satisfy both their diets and their appetites. I've shared my country's history and culture with people who might otherwise have gone on thinking that Indian food is just some stereotype called 'curry'. I've opened eyes, taste buds and hearts.

When I think about it, it strikes me that my work, my sharing, is deeply rooted in the people, places and stories, as well as the foods of my youth. In *Shared Tables* I share some of their deliciousness with you, just as I experienced it through the family moments, meals and anecdotes that shaped the paths my life would take. At the end, I have also shared recipes for some of the dishes I mention along the way. They bring me joy and appear regularly on my table, as if my beloveds are sitting down to share a meal with me.

As they say in Marathi when a meal has been served, 'Basaa.' The word literally means sit but the invitation is to 'sit and feast.' I hope you will.

1. Origins

My Lord, I loved strawberry jam...
Also well-chilled vodka, herring in olive oil,
Scents, of cinnamon, of cloves.
So what kind of prophet am I?

—Czeslaw Milosz, *A Confession*

Under a lapis lazuli sky on a gleaming June morning, a cluster of alabaster skinned, blue-eyed folk with red or blonde hair, some freckled, others not, boarded a ship in Persia bound for the Indies.

Two centuries before Christ was born, legend has it, these ancient people set sail across the Arabian Sea to the Indian subcontinent. Why were they leaving their home? Were they explorers or refugees, fleeing persecution as the Armenians and the Zoroastrians were to do a thousand years later?

The breezes over the water cooled their skins and ruffled their hair. They peered eagerly towards the East where a new land waited, a land where they could settle, a place they could make home. Further and further they travelled, away from the Middle East, away from all they knew. The weather turned sullen. The monsoons were approaching; the winds became tempestuous, blueness gave way to grey skies, which rapidly transformed into looming black canopies.

The ship was buffeted by winds that mocked its sturdiness and pushed it further south than the pilot had intended. Water was lashing down hard, stinging the travellers with its fury. A hundred miles south of the seven islands that would one day be known as Bom Bahia and later Bombay, the good harbour, the ship began to creak and shiver. The rain gods had torn its sails to shreds in their tug of war. The pilot had long since given up the hope of a safe landing and most of the passengers sat huddled together, holding hands and praying for a miracle.

Suddenly there was a crash. Its reverberations shook the ship and the passengers' cries rent the skies. As the ship's hull struck rock, there was a sharp ripping sound. The ship heaved, shook and was torn asunder. Passengers lost their footing and tumbled into the water like angels falling from the sky. Many were dead before their bodies hit the sea; others sank into the water, bobbed up alive, flailed and fought for breath as long as they could. Before long, with the rain weeping tears onto them, all the ancient Persians were dead; cold white bodies floating delicately on the water's surface, prajakta flowers tossed in the waves. They could not have known that their destination was within sight and even within swimming distance. Waiting to welcome them lay a lush, coconut palm-fringed coast, warm and humid, fragrant with jasmine and ginger lilies.

As dawn broke, the local fisherfolk bringing their boats out for the morning's fishing were astounded by the sight of the bodies on the water. Rushing towards them, they discovered that each and every one of the foreigners was dead. The fishermen looked down at them in fascinated horror. They were unlike any people they had seen before. Auburn hair spread out brightly in the stormy green water framed ghostly faces with jutting cheekbones; sapphire, emerald, moonstone eyes stared sightlessly towards heaven. One journey had ended and another was beginning.

Shaking their heads, the fisherfolk decided to honour the strangers by cremating them. Fire was the great purifier in this strange new land. Though the natives could not know it, fire was revered in the land of the travellers too. The villagers built a giant pyre of sandalwood on the sand and gently piled the corpses onto it. Saying a prayer, the headman lit the kindling and the dawn sky glowed brighter as the flames of the mighty fire caressed the sky. Then came the miracle.

The story goes that before the local people's frightened eyes, each of the dead travellers arose. Purified by the flames, reborn, they emerged from the fire, stepping down onto the sand, breathing deeply, hearts pumping blood, eyes glowing with life. These reborn travellers, it is said, were called the Chitpavan, the people who had been sanctified by fire.

They also came to be known as Konkanastha, the people who settled on that Konkan coast and made it their home. They were proud, principled and conscientious. As Brahmins, they became ritualistic. Sharp and incisive of mind, they valued learning and honour above all else. Having lost everything to the sea, they tended to be careful with what they grew or made or earned, gaining a reputation for frugality. They were austere, eschewing meat, onion and garlic in their diet and living by strict codes of ethics and religion.

The phrase 'stiff upper lip' might have been coined for them. Loud laughter, passionate arguments and exuberant smiles were not their forte. Under their cool exteriors, however, beat feeling hearts and genuine caring. Their eyes glowed with kindness and they were motivated by compassion, charity and civic sense and gave back to the community in which they lived.

A little further south along the same western Indian coast, lived a group of dark-haired, brown-eyed, fish-eating priestly folk, the Gaud Saraswat Brahmins. Named after Saraswati, an ancient, lost river, they are said to have inhabited its banks in north India aeons ago. The story goes that the river changed its course and meandered underground where it is said to flow to this day. The tribe emigrated, branching off in different directions across the subcontinent; Kashmir, Garhwal and Maharashtra, where they settled on the shores of the Arabian Sea centuries before the Chitpavans arrived from Persia.

Some time long ago, a tremendous drought swept across the land. It killed whatever plant life might have kept Brahmins alive. Traditionally vegetarian, they suffered from the lack of food. They became so distracted trying to find something to eat that they could not fulfill their responsibility to study the holy texts. The river Saraswati feared for the life of her son, a Brahmin named after her. To help Saraswat, the river said she would send up fish from her subterranean waters so he could eat and continue to study the Vedas. Thanks to his mother, Saraswat was able to keep the Vedic tradition alive until the drought had ended. Then he conveyed his knowledge to 60,000 priests and he and his followers were known as the first Saraswat Brahmins.

The vibrant Saraswats were funloving and worldly, comfortable in their own skins. They were hospitable, social and generous, if somewhat reckless and tempestuous. Relishing a good meal, they devoured meat and fish with gusto despite their Brahmanism and thought they maintained religiosity through prayer and ritual fasting.

These then were my ancestors. To my mind, no two tribes could have been more dissimilar in mindset and temperament, but despite their differences, my mother's people, the Saraswats, and my father's tribe, the Chitpavan, were the intelligentsia of Maharashtra. Both set great store by learning and became prominent in the state, in the fields of science, law, medicine, engineering, education, the arts and social activism.

My life was full of contradictions centuries before I was even conceived.

2. What's In a Name?

Monday's child is fair of face,
Tuesday's child is full of grace;
Wednesday's child is full of woe,
Thursday's child has far to go;
Friday's child is loving and giving,
Saturday's child works hard for its living;
But the child that is born on the Sabbath day
Is bonny and blithe, and good and gay.

—Mother Goose Rhymes

My mother had the weekend covered. Her three children were born on a Friday, a Saturday, and a Sunday.

The Sabbath child, Aditya was bonny and blithe but too good for this world. He died within the first year of life. Saturday's child, Sameer works hard. And me, the eldest? I am Friday's child.

I arrived, unknowing, uncomprehending, discombobulated by a mysterious journey. That night, the moon hung gleaming in the sky like a pearl drop. The colour of clotted cream, luminous as raw silk, its fullness announced that the festival of round-bellied Ganpati, the Elephant God, purveyor of propitious beginnings and remover of obstacles, was nigh. The moon's soft radiance lit my eyes from within and its love covered my mother's arms as she cradled and rocked me to sleep.

By the Hindu lunar calendar, it was the month of Bhadrapad.

According to the more ubiquitous Western calendar, the date was 6 September 1968. The monsoons were receding, the heavens had emptied, the long wet season had turned the hillsides into undulating emerald carpets. Raindrops had cleansed the landscape, clarified the autumn air and magnified every leaf and blossom into purity.

Dad's father, a Sanskrit scholar, suggested the name Kaumudi, moonlight, to mark the auspicious day of my birth. It was old-fashioned, almost too much for a baby. But there was a lot that was too much for the baby that was me. I had to be patient, to grow into everything, my big ears, my saucer eyes, my destiny, and most certainly, my name.

Today I am Kaumudi but throughout my childhood, I identified more with my easy nickname, Bunny. I also had a host of other handles and you can date my relationships by which one people use. I was Banna to my maternal grandfather. I am Bandu and Bunia to older friends, K-Girl or Kay to later ones, and Buno to my journalism professor. When I was very young, my parents called me Moana Marathe when I whined and Butterfingers when I got tween-clumsy. My self-given name was Contrary Mary like the girl in a verse that might have been written about me, though the curl was only metaphorically present and devilish.

> *There was a little girl who had a little curl*
> *Right in the middle of her forehead,*
> *And when she was good, she was very, very good*
> *And when she was bad, she was horrid!*

You see, I'm living my life backwards, contrary-like. I am forty-six. I married young, but I am newly single after two decades of coupledom. I had a child when I was thirty-three, ten years later than the age my parents were when I was born. I only learned to drive at twenty-two, and it was twenty-two years later that I bought my first car. After a childhood of bookwormishness, I discovered running as an adult and ran my first marathon at forty-five.

I spent a lifetime in apartments but I am at last ensconced in a house with a garden, unromantically known in my adopted home—the USA—as a yard. Make no mistake, it is not my own. I still rent, while many women my age have all the accoutrements of well-settled middle-agedom. My childhood was pet-free but I now find myself with two animals, a turtle and a dog, acquired within a year, and they needed more space than an apartment could provide, hence the house. After never having worried about retirement savings, I now discover I have no financial cushion for my old age. Unlike many of my peers, I am only now beginning to contemplate old age.

On the flip side, there are some things I did before my contemporaries, like learning to read, which I was doing by the age of three. In first grade, I was only four years old and I skipped grades throughout elementary school, entering high school at the age of thirteen, two years younger and less physically developed than my classmates. My first byline came when I was eleven and I knew then that I wanted to be a writer. My first book was published when I was twenty-six, the next came three years later, and my third, at the age of thirty-nine. Sometimes I think, now what? I've fulfilled all my major dreams, the last being to have a child. I don't mean to say I have no more goals to work towards. But if it were not for my daughter, I would be content to die anytime the powers that be saw fit. I even know what I want my funeral to be like. Wait, are we already talking funerals? I'm barely born yet.

Ever since I can remember, one of my favourite pastimes has been to look into, around dusk, the windows of homes I am passing. I am captivated by signs of life within, the glow of lamplight, a happy family at peace. I see a table set for dinner, an inviting arrangement of irises in a hall, a bright red mailbox signalling a home where people receive letters and parcels from those who love them. I spy a woman bustling about a kitchen with sparkling countertops and fragrant aromas, a couple peering into a bubbling pot, anticipating a meal together with their guests, uncorking a bottle of wine. I peek into a cozy living room, shelves piled high with books, table lamps creating warm shadows, heads together in intimate conversation barely visible over the back of a couch.

Sometimes I covet the physical spaces or furniture I see, at others I am disenchanted by what is before me, cold fluorescent tube light or blank walls that do nothing to draw their inhabitants in. I am held captive by the sight of other lives in progress, a wondering of what makes up those realities and always, somehow, a yearning to be a part of them, a member of those families, basking in a warm orange-yellow electric glow. I am an observer, a watcher, from afar and up close.

Most of my life, I have been a foreigner, an outsider looking in, never quite belonging, always wanting to fit in. It was quite a burden for a child to not be part of the majority, to always look different. For the first few years of my life, I questioned why I had been put upon this planet. Gradually I embraced my otherness. In time, I realized that what made me other was valuable, it was my signature. My life had given me a perspective unlike that of my peers.

Kipling is infamously misquoted as saying, 'East is East and West is West and ne'er the twain shall meet.' But East and West did meet, collide, conflict, diffuse in me, eventually generating some measure of peace. This equanimity may not have allowed me to come to terms with my Westernness or my Indianness, but it allowed me to take what I could from various cultures and use those disparate facets of my personality and upbringing in my work and social interactions. By my twenties, I had concluded that we are all just citizens of the world, of the human race, and that this belonging is more important and inclusive than any nationality, ethnicity, colour or gender should be.

Otherness, Contrary Maryiness, are only two of many childhood tropes that I've carried forward into adulthood. I can trace nearly everything that happens to me now back to something that affected me as a child, from the moonlight on the day I was born to songs and written words that resonated deeply. The people I encountered made a significant appearance in my life or affected my choices later in unexpected and profound ways. All these early influences helped define who I was and who I was becoming and what I was seeking.

I was an inherent feminist, rather an egalitarian, long before I read Germaine Greer, Camille Paglia, Simone de Beauvoir and Anaïs Nin. I railed innocently against injustice years before I knew about making political choices or statements. When I was ten, I complained vigorously to my father when his college friend referred to a black man as a 'kallu' or 'blackie.' To my mind, this was the same as saying, 'nigger.' The term 'civil rights' was unknown to me but I did not need it to know not to discriminate.

Was this because I was born in a year when political protests raged fiercely the world over and women's struggle for equality was at its peak? Did my father's lifelong angst about the repression of his mother by her in-laws make its way into my bloodstream and fire me up without my even knowing? Or did my story begin even earlier, long before my birth? The more I discover about my ancestors, the more I know I am a compendium of their traits and personalities, a portrait of many individuals and families. Some I know, some I learn about over time, and some will forever be either unknown to me or a complete mystery. Still, each of their brushstrokes has had an effect on my inner and outer canvas.

Superficially, here's the picture: my own moles; natural black marks to ward off the 'evil eye.' My mother's smile, my father's eyes, hair, teeth and build, my maternal grandfather's nose, my paternal grandmother's lips, neck and feet, my paternal grandfather's ears and high forehead, and perhaps my maternal grandmother's oval face. Oh, and oddly, her hips! Or are they Dad's? Age will tell. It's a seemingly implausible mix of media but once you have seen the painting, it seems just as it was meant to be.

Naturally, the portrait, rather like Dorian Gray's, is ever-changing. As a baby, I looked like Dad when he was a baby. When I have short hair, I resemble my mother strongly. I never really saw how my daughter resembled me until she turned five, an age I could remember myself being. And looking at old photographs, I might see my face peeping out from other eras and contexts and genders; my great-grandfather; my father's aunts, or my own cousins, different versions of me.

My brother and I look very little alike, he more Sirsikar, me more Marathe—but obviously siblings. We share parents but we each paint family features and traits in our own unique ways. Dad sits with one foot tilted out from the ankle, as his grandfather did. I always thought he resembled his Marathe grandfather until I recently saw a picture of the other one who died before Dad was born. My father is now the same age as the man in the picture so the resemblance, down to the Adam's apple, is striking but I would not have marked it twenty years ago.

Sam sits just as my father does but tilting the opposite foot. He has the Marathe feet. I know because our uncle's sons, Pramodan and Sudarshan, have similarly shaped feet. Yes, my brother could have watched my father's foot placement but how does that account for Dad's unconscious imitation of a grandfather he had never met?

Until I had my daughter, I hotly debated nature versus nurture, strongly believing that both were equally critical in the development of a child. My husband's father died before our daughter was born but when she was a toddler, she walked just like her grandfather, holding her hands loosely balled into fists as he had done. How could she have known his manner of walking?

And yet, I am also a testament to the idea that people are products of their generation. Nineteen sixty-eight, the year I was born, was a time of political unrest and unrestrained protest, of liberation and independence. Modern India was coming of age twenty-one years after gaining independence from British colonial rule. The Vietnam War was wreaking its havoc and antiwar protests raged across the United States of America. It also happened to be a leap year when a woman had the rare prerogative of proposing marriage to her man.

The world was stunned when Martin Luther King Junior was assassinated on 4 April. A week later, on 11 April, American president Lyndon B. Johnson signed the Civil Rights Act of 1968. A few months later, America fell into turmoil again with the assassination of Robert Kennedy and, halfway around the world, a young man named Sadam Hussein became Vice Chairman of the Revolutionary Council in Iraq, sowing the seeds for turmoil two decades hence.

That year, rather late in the twentieth century, Yale University finally announced it would admit female students to its hallowed halls, but a running shoe especially designed for women was still years in the future. The day after my birth, however, an undergarment would become a symbol for women's liberation and equal rights. The bra was burned by feminists and civil rights activists on 7 September in Atlantic City to protest the Miss America Pageant. Ironically, the first ever black Miss America was crowned there on the same day.

It was at this time that the lines between science fiction and science fact were blurring, setting the stage for the following year's moon landing. The first heart transplant was performed in Europe, the semiconductor company Intel was founded, and Stanley Kubrick's *2001: A Space Odyssey* opened in Washington. As with George Orwell's *1984*, people could not envision that the year mentioned in the title would ever come.

I could not know any of this when, on that September afternoon at 4:08 pm, I was welcomed into this world. The usher was Dr Madhumalati Gune who had delivered my father at the very same laying-in hospital twenty-three years before. My mother Meera had come in, somewhat flustered, the previous afternoon when her water broke. There were no books like *What to Expect When You are Expecting* to guide her, nor had her reserved mother forewarned her about the messy intricacies of pregnancy and childbirth. The head nurse assumed that my mother's small belly meant she was not full term, that she was just being a too anxious, first-time mom. She ordered her to go home.

'Come back when you are really ready to have the baby,' she snapped.

My innocent mother dutifully left, only to find a few hours later that her pain had intensified. The next morning my father Sudhakar brought her back to the hospital, insisting she be admitted. Dr Gune scolded the nurse for being careless and my mother for being a goose. I emerged a dry baby, a true Virgo, ready to ask my god for years to come why I had been put upon this earth.

My mother insists I was the most beautiful, alert newborn she has ever seen. On my first day, Dad snapped his fingers and moved his hand from left to right a foot above my face. I followed his hand intently, as I would do for the next four decades. My paternal grandmother was in the delivery room to help my mother. She did not seem to mind that I was a girl but, after one look at me, said caustically, 'How will she get married?' By her measure, I had dark skin and dark-skinned girls traditionally were already disadvantaged on the marriage market.

My indignant mother replied, 'How did *I* get married?'

My maternal grandfather looked down into my face and fell in love for the second time in his life. 'She's a little blue-eyed doll,' he exclaimed. If love can be sparked simply by the sight of another at a time before consciousness and language exist, when one's world and feelings are just colour and sounds, then a deep and boundless, humming, lilting, rich purple was ignited in me for my grandfather as I blinked up at him. He was my first love and even after language was developed, our connection did not require it.

Poona, the small university town where I was born, is situated in the ghats on India's west coast, about 110 miles southeast of Bombay, which was then the financial and manufacturing capital of the country, and the home of the film industry. Bombay was cosmopolitan and wealthy but also racy and brash. Poona seemed sedate and humdrum by comparison, a genteel town where liberated attitudes flourished and social change emanated. It was a place, where early in the 1900s, it was not uncommon to see women driving cars, energetically climbing the surrounding hills or playing badminton for exercise, learning how to sing or dance in the classical tradition, and forming groups to do charitable works.

Poona had long been known as a centre of learning, the home of the Marathi Brahmin priestly caste and for some centuries, the seat of the state's only Brahmin ruling dynasty, the Peshwa. These rulers were from my father's 'tribe', the Konkanastha. The town was naturally a haven for artists, musicians and writers. Poets and playwrights like G.D. Madgulkar and P.L. Deshpande; actors like Jyotsna Bhole, the first woman in Marathi theatre known to enact a female role in a play; acclaimed singers like Sawai Gandharva and his student, the renowned Pandit Bhimsen Joshi, were either born there or made their home there because it nurtured creativity. One of the greatest Indian classical music celebrations, the Sawai Gandharva Festival was started there by Bhimsen in 1953 in honour of his guru.

My father's paternal relatives had migrated from the village of Devachagothna on the lush Konkan coast three generations before he was born in 1944. They lived in the small town of Sangli until my great-grandfather Chintaman Gangadhar Marathe moved his large family to Poona. His son, my grandfather Shreekrishna Chintaman Marathe (Appa), was a civil engineer who designed and built homes in Erandawane, the newer part of town. He was also for many years the highly respected principal of Poona Engineering College. More than three decades after Appa's retirement, when my architect husband mentioned to a senior engineer colleague in

Bombay that his wife's name was Marathe, the man asked excitedly, 'Is she Professor S.C. Marathe's granddaughter? Does she have those *eyes*?' He had been Appa's student years before and my grandfather's principles, dedication and sparkling blue eyes had made a lasting impression on him.

In Poona, surrounded by others of Dad's Konkanastha ilk, my family name was known, my blue-then-green eyes, pale skin, despite my grandmother's dismay at my skin colour, at birth, so it was, and reddish-brown hair were not uncommon features, and I was encircled by those who had known my father's family for at least a century or were related to us somehow or the other. Though I was then unaware of this cocooning, it must have anchored me, giving me the unconscious assurance that comes from a sense of belonging.

It was an assurance that was short-lived. After I turned two, I never again lived for an extended period where my antecedents were so well known, my roots so intact and my history required no explanation. For the rest of my childhood and most of my adult life, I have been a rolling stone, occasionally gathering just a little moss in my perpetual search for history and a permanent landing place. I would not feel I belonged anywhere, neither East nor West, until 1998 when I moved to Los Angeles where everyone else was a foreigner too.

The moment I was born, my grandfather, Appa, walked to a local astrologer and had my horoscope made according to Hindu custom. Raised in a very ritualistic and strictly Brahmin family, Dad rebelled when he grew up, eschewing organized religion. Neither he nor Mom were superstitious either. They humoured Appa but cannot recall even glancing at the prepared chart. They simply filed it away with my birth records. When they visited me in California in 2012, they had recently unearthed the horoscope and brought it to me, hoping I would be amused.

We sat in my living room and Dad read out the Marathi scrawl. The predictions resulted in a great deal of laughter, thanks to their mix of canniness, absurdity and a desire to please. 'This dark-eyed, stocky child,' the document read, 'will not possess more than average intelligence.' Then, as if to apologize or mollify, it continued, 'But she will be kind. She will be a teacher. She will be very lucky and admired by many. She will write many books.' I liked the bits about being stocky and of average intelligence and writing a lot!

Although I had a horoscope immediately, for eleven days after my birth I had no name. This was not unusual. According to local custom and because of the high rate of infant mortality in India well into the 1900s, parents did not name newborns or celebrate their birth until they were fairly certain their children were going to survive more than a few days. Until that day should come, my parents wanted to address me with some handle other than 'Baby'. In my birth scrapbook, Mom scribbled down a long list of the gifts I received. These included a silver rattle, tumbler and Robert Louis Stevenson's *Garden of Verses*. Dad's English professor, Sujit Mukherjee, and his wife Meenakshi gave me a set of bed linens embroidered with little rabbits and a Margaret Wise Brown book of rabbit stories. It was clear. I was Bunny.

What's in a name? A name can shape who you become, it can prompt you to change who you are. A name defines you, constricts you, liberates you. Some names suit their wearers; others seem completely incongruous. What were their parents thinking? we wonder when we meet a sprite named Agatha or an ogre named Rama. Many of us make do with a moniker we had no part in choosing. Some of us rebel or switch names for specific purposes. While I find it hard to believe that Englebert Humperdinck is a name the performer chose to take, he found that it served him well.

Luckily I didn't need to find another name. I was content with what I had received and it shaped me. Bunny suited me not just because I was fun-loving and liked to jump and hop about till I was about eight or so, but because I was still fairly simple and uncomplicated. The older I got, the more appropriate Kaumudi became. Since I'd the opportunity of time to become familiar with it, I shrugged it on with ease.

Then there are surnames. Just as with first names, some suit, some don't. Some people are best known by their last names, others only by their first. To think of Shakespeare being called Willy is as inconceivable as it is to think of Bhimsen being recognized just as Joshi. When I was about five, I puzzled over why I had my father's surname, Marathe, but not Sirsikar, my mother's.

'Anna,' I said curiously, leaning on my grandfather's knee and looking up into his kind eyes. 'Why don't I have your surname too? After all, I am half from your family, right? I think I should be Bunny Sirsikar Marathe.' There was no reply. So I said comfortingly, 'When I grow up, I will add your name to mine.' Anna's eyes filled with tears.

I didn't keep that promise but I was true to its intent of acknowledging family. By the time I got married, I had decided I would not change my last name to my husband's, that I would live bearing the name I was born into. And when my daughter was born in 2001, the year many people did not believe would ever come, I could not resist giving her my family name too. I wanted her to have choices. As far as first names went, since she was born in the USA and we had lived here for so long, her father Sanjiv and I wanted her to have one that was easy to pronounce locally. Our own names had been butchered for years. When I tell people my first name, they often ask, 'Do you have a nickname that's easier?'

'Yes,' I reply, 'But I only share it with people who have learned how to say Kaumudi first.' I figure that if people can say Kieslowski or Kosciusko, my name is worth an attempt. In all fairness, Americans make more of an effort to say it correctly than Indians, who often find it just as unusual.

I have, over the years, figured out a good way to explain the pronunciation of a name that many Westerners hear as Gowmudee because of its soft K sound, which does not exist in English. 'My name is Kaumudi with a K, emphasis on the first syllable.' In other words, not Gowmudee or Kuh-mood-dee or Cow-mu-dee. The closest I can come to spelling it phonetically in English is: Kuh-ow-mu-dee. Wrap the first two sounds together quickly—Kuh-ow, rush over the next with a short U sound—mu, and soften your tongue and touch it to your upper teeth as you say the last—dee.

We were not going to put our child through such tedium or have her be teased in school because her name sounded foreign. Thankfully, we agreed on Keya, pronounced Kay-yah. It may not sound like it, but it's Indian, a Bengali variant of ketaki, the name of the small white flower of the screwpine or Pandanus tree, which grows along riverbanks in South and Southeast Asia. Keya is a fragrant flower, its essence used in some regional Indian cooking and its aromatic leaves in Southeast Asian cuisines. We decided it was short, easy to say and sounded Western enough to fit in. She loves it and it suits her. Perhaps because it is so Western-sounding however, I also felt the need to give her a more traditional Indian middle name, one that emphatically and clearly asserts her heritage.

Ideally, I wanted to name her after my paternal grandmother whom I called Ai Aji.

3. The Brave Girl

If the sky is tattered, where will you mend it?

—Marathi proverb,
translated by Sudhakar Marathe

Before her marriage, my grandmother Ai Aji's name was Veerbala, the brave maiden. Her life required bravery and courage. So did her death.

Veerbala was born in 1914. India was soon to be on the cusp of independence from British colonial rule and about to take birth as a modern nation. She came from a progressive family of political and social activists. Her grandfather, Vaman Abaji Modak, was a man who believed that social change included the emancipation of women and would lead to political independence. He was an educator, poet and translator, all of which my father would become in the late 1960s, ignorant of his ancestry or the love of language and literature that ran through his veins.

In the late nineteenth century, Indian activists were divided into two groups. One, known as freedom fighters, put their energies into driving the British rulers out of India to free their country from colonial rule. The other, equally keen for freedom from foreign control, also believed that it was critical to free Indians from the limits of their own social conventions so they could move forward progressively before and after independence was achieved. Vaman Abaji Modak belonged to this group.

A nineteenth-century version of my father, Modak was one of the four founders of a social reform organization called the Prarthana Samaj. He and his friends, Mahadeo Govind Ranade, Dr Ramakrishna Gopal Bhandarkar and Atmaram Pandurang, were educated men who had empathy for those less privileged and a vision for the country's evolution. Modak is believed to have said, 'It was most necessary for Hindus to reform socially.' To him and his colleagues, the betterment of women was the key to growth and progress.

The four friends founded the Samaj in Bombay in 1860, a Hindu religious and social reform society that became an influential tool for change in Maharashtra. Its members opposed the strict and outdated tenets of the caste system; worked for the abolition of the institution of child marriage, then prevalent in India; and sought to improve the plight of widows by encouraging their remarriage.

Modak had an illustrious career in his own right too. He was the first Indian to be made principal of an educational institution. In 1872, he took over as headmaster of his alma mater, the renowned Elphinstone High School and College in Bombay. Before him, principals, like other senior staff, were brought out from Great Britain.

While he was fluent in English and Sanskrit, Modak was also very much in love with his mother tongue, Marathi. He is the man credited with elevating it to a language compulsory for school board exams in Maharashtra. Until then, the only such language was English. Modak's persistence in ensuring that Marathi was a language worthy of study paved the way for other regional languages to be given the same consideration. For his contributions to the field of education, the British Crown honoured my great-great-grandfather, giving him the Companion of the Order of the Indian Empire (CIE), one of the first such commendations granted after Queen Victoria founded the order of chivalry in 1878. He then came to be called Rao Saheb and received a letter from

K.M. Chatfield, then the British Director of Public Instruction, thanking him for his services.

> Poona, January 2, 1896
> My dear Mr Modak,
> I was very pleased to see the *Gazette* and I offer you my best wishes and congratulations. You proved to government that with a wealth of talent in the country, it was wholly unnecessary to go outside so often; and your example through a long and distinguished service has had the best influence on the Department and public generally.
> Yours very sincerely,
> K.M. Chatfield

As dedicated as Vaman Abaji was to his work, his life was about more than a successful career. Though he was married at seventeen without his consent, he and his wife Rakhma were happy together. She had been home-schooled and read and wrote Marathi at a time when many young girls received no education. She was also a notable horsewoman and the couple often rode together for pleasure. After he was paralysed or possibly afflicted by ALS (amyotrophic lateral sclerosis), she cared for him patiently and tirelessly for the last four years of his life.

The Modaks had two daughters of whom not much is known and six sons: Ramchandra, Vishnu, Govind, Narayan, Krishnaji and Yashvant. Krishnaji married an energetic woman named Tarabai Kelkar but they divorced due to irreconcilable differences in 1920, when divorce was virtually unheard of. My grandmother's aunt by marriage, and certainly a role model for young girls, Tarabai Modak moved to Dahanu-Kosbad where she began to work with the Warli tribe. She is renowned not only for her work and commitment to the Warlis, but also for spearheading the preschool and Montessori movement in India. Her connection to the Modaks inspired her. After all, her father-in-law, Vaman Abaji, had founded the first high school in the country meant specifically for girls in 1884—the renowned Huzurpagha School in Poona.

Ramchandra, the eldest son, was my grandmother Veerbala's father. He, his second wife Anandi and the extended family supported the arts and had a deep love for music, literature and theatre. Their home was filled with photographs, paintings and books unlike the spare, utilitarian homes of many of their contemporaries. They read together as a family and hosted political meetings and musical evenings.

My grandmother and her five siblings were raised in this rich, vibrant atmosphere and the girls were all educated at Huzurpagha. In the early twentieth century, even in a progressive state like Maharashtra, only upper-caste girls like the Modaks got an elementary education. The majority did not go on to high school or even step out of the house unchaperoned and were frequently married by the age of thirteen or fourteen. Thanks to their grandfather's social reform work, it was not only understood that the Modak girls would go to college, but also that they would not be forced into marriage at any age.

Veerbala's older sister, Vatsala, studied medicine and became one of the first women doctors in India. She never married but devoted her life to medicine, working as a physician in the kingdom of Pratapgarh in Rajasthan. The other sister, Manu, married a wealthy Bombay gentleman named Agte and lived fashionably in the big city. A different fate awaited Veerbala. In her own way, I have discovered, she was also *other*, as I would be half a century later.

Veerbala embarked on a BA in English literature at Fergusson College. One doesn't know what she might have done after getting her degree. She liked to read, she liked to act, she enjoyed music, particularly the sound of tablas. She wore the then-modern, six-yard sari instead of the traditional Marathi navwari or nine-yarder most of her peers wore. Most outrageous of all, a bicycle was her mode of transportation. Townsfolk gasped at her audacity when they saw her riding around town alone.

Born in 1910, my grandfather Appa was already a working civil engineer when Ai Aji started her BA. They had been neighbours of a sort, both living in Sadashiv Peth years before. Families who lived there knew each other to some extent. But when Appa had left home to study engineering in Karachi and Quetta in what is now Pakistan, Veerbala was just a gawky, awkward young teen and he didn't give her a second thought. He boarded the train at Colaba station in Bombay and travelled several days to reach his destination at the semi-arid, northwestern frontier of the British Raj. After graduation four years later, he returned home and was employed by the British army to build bridges and barracks.

Short and wiry, he had a broad forehead, deep blue eyes, ears that looked like giant butterfly wings, a bulbous nose, the kind of mustache then in fashion but which Hitler would soon make infamous, and for such a small man, a surprisingly deep and melodious voice. On a frosty December morning, Appa, ripe for love, was marching smartly down Fergusson College Road in his crisp white cotton shirt and starched khaki shorts. His hobnailed boots clicked sharply on the pavement, but came to a complete and silent halt as a vision on a black bicycle swished past him. It was Veerbala.

Appa felt the breeze of her passing and caught his breath. Now known as the Greta Garbo of Poona, the young woman was cool, seemingly unattainable. Her hair was a soft, glossy brown that matched her sparkling, mischievous eyes. Her nose could slice butter and her skin was as delicate and translucent as Japanese rice paper. When she drank water, it was said, you could see it slipping down her throat. Decades later when I touched her skin, it reminded me of creamy puran poli dough, elastic and well oiled, gently perfumed and tinted by saffron. Her veins showed blue-green through its thinness and I was always fascinated by this network of colour.

She was slender but the leaf-green cotton sari now draped a

tall woman's frame, not the fourteen-year-old girl Appa might have recalled. Her thin arms were attached firmly to the handlebars, the beaten gold bangles on her wrists jingling musically against the metal. Her legs pumped up and down, her long-toed, delicate white feet in their thick-soled leather chappals cheerfully pushed the bicycle pedals. Appa was enthralled.

My grandfather was so enamoured that he joined Fergusson College to court my grandmother. Her shy smile and angelic air captivated him. I have no idea how he won her over, but I do know that before long he had proposed and been accepted. Veerbala left college after only two years of her undergraduate degree and settled down to life as a housewife. It was Appa who completed the four-year course, graduating with a degree in English literature.

In the classic irony of her life, Ai Aji had married a man whose conservative family sucked the joy of living out of her and trapped her in a miserable existence of servitude from which she continually retreated, ultimately finding release in an Alzheimer's-induced detachment and then, mercifully, in death. She was the only daughter-in-law who lived with her in-laws, so she became the person in charge of the entire clan's well-being. In the days of extended families, the clan numbered about a hundred and fifty. Veerbala, the brave girl who had biked all over town alone, was renamed Padmavati, the lotus maiden. Prized and guarded as a rare flower, she was not allowed to even step out of the gate of the family home. Her in-laws thought this would seem like wanton behaviour. For the woman who had grown up with unrestricted freedom, her new family now became her world, the house her purdah.

The protectiveness of her in-laws did not extend to her personal well-being. For the next forty years, Veerbala slaved for the Marathes, handling every household chore, catering to her aging in-laws and cooking three meals daily for a shifting population that numbered eight at the very least and might go up to seventy-five on any given day. She also watered the garden with bucket after heavy bucket of water filled at the tap and carried across its large expanse. And there were her husband, daughter Kunda and three sons, Padmakar, my father Sudhakar and the baby Shrikant, to care for.

How did Veerbala ever have the leisure to sit and converse with her husband, play with her children, read, write or sing, or even smile? I cannot remember her talking very much when I was little but she had a strong presence and her eyes were piercing. When she did address me, it was in English, the language with which I was most comfortable. I recall her gentle smile, tinged with a melancholy I did not then grasp. I found her sharp-boned face very stern. I have more compassion now, and after twenty years of marriage, more empathy. I cannot say that I smile to make up for her but certainly in my mind there is a desire to smile and laugh, to make the most of every moment, because I do not want to end up like her.

I spent the summer of 1991 in Poona, recording my grandfather Appa's memories on audiotape. He told me that the happiest period of Ai Aji's married life was when he was posted to Aurangabad in early 1944 and she was able to accompany him for a few months. I am not sure if her older children, Kunda and Padmakar, went along but my grandmother revelled in being her own woman again, in the freedom to simply be a young wife in love with her husband. It was during this halcyon time that my father was conceived, possibly one of the reasons why he was her favourite. Sudhakar, the honeyed one, a constant souvenir of a brief, joyful idyll, the tender memory of a delayed honeymoon.

Sadly, I have no photographs of Veerbala from that time, but in nearly every picture of her I have seen, there is a far-away look in her eyes. When she was young, she looked happy but reaching towards her future. When she was older, she seemed disheartened and sad. This could simply have been the precursor of Alzheimer's. Studying her face over the years, I decided that her expression meant that she would rather have been somewhere else. Her son Padmakar who died young at fifty-nine—of an early onset of Alzheimer's, we thought—also often had that distant look and sad smile.

In pictures of me, from the ages of fourteen to twenty, I am also turning away from the camera's piercing gaze. But I was not sad, only shy, wishing I were elsewhere, getting on with my life. I knew I would one day, someday, but I was impatient for it to begin. Whether that elsewhere was Paris, London, Bombay or Los Angeles, I did not care. I was looking towards my future. I was going to find my home, my people, no matter what it took.

Looking back on my happy and liberated childhood, I see a parallel with Ai Aji's. She too had the 'right' start in life. So what happened? They say that the roots of Alzheimer's are put down during childhood. Moody, depressive, socially disinclined children are less likely to light up the necessary synapses in their brains that will retard the onset of the disease in later life than those who have sunny dispositions. Anecdotal evidence in the Modak family seems to corroborate this.

For years I worried about my father developing early onset Alzheimer's because of the family history. Luckily, Dad was essentially unlike the rest of his family. His optimism, his active, curious and incessantly engaged brain, his love of physical exercise, a gregariousness which was liberated by his profession and my mother, and his wonderful masculine ability to shake off negative experiences that he could not fix, have kept Alzheimer's away.

But in my grandmother's case, perhaps genetic predisposition and temperament made her more vulnerable. Her sad and unfulfilling adult life only exacerbated inherent traits and predispositions. It did not help that diagnoses were rare and treatment or care unheard of in her day. In the Marathe family, which three Modak women had married into, the disease was referred to as the Modak Madness. After all, Alzheimer's was given its official name in the early twentieth century and only recently understood as a form of senile dementia. 'Legend has it,' Padmakar's wife Usha once told Mom, 'that Tarabai Modak cursed the family because she was so unhappy with her husband.' This myth seemed to satisfy curiosity until my generation refused to accept it.

*

After their brief romantic interlude in early 1944, my grandparents returned to Poona, to the family home my grandfather had lovingly designed and built in the 1940s for his parents on his share of the ancestral Marathe land. The bungalow, named Shree Ram Krupa, meaning by Lord Rama's grace, sat serenely halfway down the quiet Eighth Lane between Karve Road and Prabhat Road. Beyond was a jungle, Erandawane, which at the time formed Poona's northwestern boundary. The neighbourhood, which was given the forest's name, was originally planned with Western comforts and modernization in mind and boasted large homes, broad streets, raised sidewalks and street lights. Its character was in stark contrast to the narrow alleys and winding lanes of the historic city core where mixed-use buildings prevailed: old wooden wadas nestled cheek by jowl with shops, post offices, bazaars, theatres and little parks and traffic was a chaotic jumble of pedestrians, cyclists, tongas and vendors with pushcarts.

A mile down Prabhat Road was a new shopping district named Deccan Gymkhana after the local playground where children could play cricket or gulli danda; Dad, as a boy, was on the hututu and langdi teams. To the west was Tilak Tank, a deep stone pool built by the British. The water was an uninviting opaque green but my cousin Madhuri swam there enthusiastically. North of the house was the forest, Dad's boundless playground, and Fergusson College was just a short distance away, to the east.

Across the Mutha River to the southwest, reached by Lakdi Pul, an old wooden bridge, was the old town of Poona where Veerbala's family and some of Appa's relatives still lived. Seven of its neighbourhoods or peths were named after the days of the week: Somwar, Mangalwar, Budhwar (Monday, Tuesday, Wednesday). These names informed people when shops in those neighbourhoods were closed and at any given time, one precinct always had commercial establishments open so people could get their shopping done. Another neighbourhood, Sadashiv Peth, was favoured by the Konkanasthas. If you were a Konkanastha living there, people called you 'Sadashiv Pethi'. Shaniwar Wada, the Saturday Palace, was nearby. One of the residences of the Peshwe, Poona's rulers from the mid-1700s to the early 1800s, the palace sat crumbling majestically, surrounded by vegetable markets and sari shops. Not far away was Tulshi Baug, a garden courtyard surrounded by wooden, two-storey buildings just a room deep. There was a Rama temple at its centre. When Dad and I walked in the courtyard not long ago, he told me how the mixed-use buildings allowed shopkeepers to live modestly and conveniently above their shops. He also showed me where he would come as a child to buy ghee for his mother or terracotta lamps, cotton wicks or hardware.

Unlike those cramped dwellings, Shree Ram Krupa was spacious and Appa had, in the thoughtful and considerate manner characteristic of all the Marathe men I know, paid attention to the needs of the family. He once pointed out to me all its cunning features: indoor toilets, a novelty in those days and a great convenience especially for the family women; a mortar carved into the floor outside the dining room, where Dad and his siblings took turns pounding pohe, semolina and wheat grain for the family's consumption; a wall of cupboards and drawers in the living room which opened outward when needed, one of them converting into a study table; a similar bank of cupboards in the dining room, giving my grandmother storage for snacks and sweets; and deep window ledges that I loved to sit on. They were deep because the walls of the house had been built especially thick to insulate it from the region's dry heat. The stone slab flooring also kept the rooms cool, so you didn't need a fan, even in the dreadful heat of summer.

A long drive bounded the eastern edge of the property. Beyond a wall was a twin house, designed by my grandfather for his sister's family. The lawn made her garden appear immense compared to ours, which was punctuated by fruit trees. To the west of our drive, two large mango trees created a canopy that reached over the front stoop. Underneath, the earth was dry and reddish in the summertime. A bakula tree hung its branches over the drive and rained its tiny, cream-coloured, woody flowers onto it. I remember my grandmother collecting them and using a sharp needle and thread to string them into long-lasting, fragrant garlands that she hung around her porcelain statuettes of Rama, Lakshmana and Sita.

My great-grandfather, Chintaman Gangadhar, spent a lot of time gardening. He and his little grandson, my father, knew what was happening on every square inch of their land. 'No one else spent any time there,' Dad recalls. 'I knew exactly what part of it needed weeding, watering, raking. I knew when the sontakka was about to bloom and I would pick some for my mother. It was her favourite flower. I knew how many fruit were on each tree, when they would ripen. The others did not seem to care. Lucky me. I got all the ripe mangoes and chickoos and guavas to eat.'

Although the house was set back from the road, over the years as the Eighth Lane increasingly became a thoroughfare, smoke and noise were sent through the garden into the front rooms. The back, where Appa and Ai Aji's bedroom was, stayed distant from this polluted progress. It was quiet and calm even in the late 1980s when Appa lived there as a widower. All one could see from his window were coconut palms shading the outdoor pot-and-pan and clothes washing area, and the narrow gate that led to his older brother's home.

But the front stoop was a great place to sit in the evenings when it was cool and pleasant outdoors. It was also where vegetables were cleaned, and transactions made with vendors like knife-sharpeners, fruit and vegetable sellers and the kalai wallah, who tinned brass pots and pans while we watched. We never tired of jumping off the stoop onto the paved path while the grown-ups chatted. Three stone steps led to the heavy front door. Above the door, on an oval clay panel, was the name of the house and a pair of Raja Ravi Vermaesque parrots peering down interestedly at visitors. Whenever I visited, I always waited with bated breath to see who would open the door, my great-uncle Neelkanth, his sweet, diminutive wife Susheela, or my grandfather. If it was Appa, he would say, 'Hunh, yes,' and shake his head from side to side gently, smiling as if he had been expecting me before stepping aside to let me in. Nothing seemed to faze him.

The front door opened onto a central stair leading up to the terrace, part of which had been later enclosed to create another living and dining room, a second kitchen and a large bedroom. My great-uncle's family used this floor. Turning left from the main entrance, you found yourself in the original part of the bungalow. The receiving room was where my great-grandfather Chintaman sat. Known to the family as Anna or big brother, he was a powerful athletic man who towered over his five sons.

From the front room, Anna looked out at his garden and onto the street. There he entertained colleagues, traders and acquaintances who did not go further into the part of the house occupied by the womenfolk. My grandmother would come out to greet guests and say hospitably but with characteristic Konkanastha frugality because every penny counted, '*Ardha cup chaha tari ghya*' ('At least have *half* a cup of tea'). In a few moments, she would serve them a half-filled, strong cup of her badshahi chaha, sweetened by jaggery, rich with milk, and fragrant with cardamom and nutmeg. When my mother Meera was dating my father, she candidly informed Ai Aji that she liked to drink more than half a cup of tea at a time. After that, whenever Meera visited, Ai Aji smilingly put out two fingers. She would then bring two cups of tea and also gave Meera a tin of the supari on which she snacked as if it were trail mix.

Visitors who had the freedom to go beyond the receiving room would take off their chappals and go into an L-shaped passage that brought them to the middle of the house. To the right was the narrow space under the central staircase, a seemingly humdrum spot that we loved. It housed a metal cot and small cupboard for Narahari Laxman Sane, our family retainer. He had lived with and worked for the Marathes at Prabhat Road for over half a century by the time I was born. Those two pieces of furniture may have been the only private space Narahari possessed and of those, certainly the bed was often shared with us, the children of the house who called him Tatya and loved him to bits.

Across from his bed was the door to the main hall or living room, which completed the shorter part of the L of the house. When Dad was growing up, the children laid their beds there each night, unrolling thin cotton mattresses on which they spread cool cotton sheets. During the day, the mattresses were piled up against a wall where they served another, less predictable, purpose for Dad.

Possibly, Appa's khaki trousers and work shirts were sent to the local istriwallah to be pressed with a mighty iron heated from within by hot coals. But there was no money to have the whole family's clothing pressed this way. Growing up, my father's wardrobe consisted of two pairs of khaki shorts held up by braces and two white, short-sleeved cotton shirts. While one set of clothes was on him, the other was being washed and dried. Dad would stretch out his freshly laundered clothes and place them carefully under the bottom-most mattress. A few hours later, his clothes were as wrinkle-free as even the istriwallah could have made them.

The only other clothing Dad owned was a sweater that someone knitted for him. He remembers wearing it in the cold winters until the sleeves were six inches too short and the garment too full of holes to keep him warm. As for shoes, he had none. Chappals were the traditional footwear and, in any case, Dad and his siblings wore theirs only when they were told they had to. Otherwise they preferred to run barefoot and carefree.

The living room sat in state, rather like American parlours, clean and ready for use on special occasions, but shunned on a daily basis for the more cozy parts of the house. Its most memorable feature to me were the stern portraits on the back wall, facing the doorway. One was my great-grandfather, Chintaman Gangadhar, the other was his father, Gangadhar Krishna, whom I thought Dad resembled, down to the mustache! Perpendicular to this 'hall' were two bedrooms. The smaller one in the long part of the L was my grandparents'. Beyond, down another passage, was the dining room to the right, behind which was the kitchen, cleverly designed with windows to the side and front so the lady of the house could see and interact with vendors. To the left was a large bathroom used only for bathing. In those days, toilets were always built separately. I remember this one having the old-style double doors with a sturdy latch that held both together, but was hard for my little hands to manoeuvre shut.

My great-grandparents had the large corner bedroom. Anna died three years before I was born but I heard countless stories of his athletic and mental prowess. He was one of those men you can never imagine having been a child. An authoritarian, a man of discipline and strict scruples, he never gossiped or tolerated pettiness. He was hard on himself and everyone around him. For amusement, he wrestled, and it showed in his mighty physique. 'Even when he was sixty,' Dad says, 'and most men considered themselves old, he exercised every day, stood tall and erect, and was sharp as a tack. Anna was a man to be reckoned with.' His impressiveness was enhanced by a whip he carried around, a memento of his horseback-riding days.

He had worked first as the prime minister of the Kurunwad kingdom and then in the British Civil Service, going as high up its ranks as an Indian could in colonial India. As district collector of the Sangli district, he was the veritable ruler of his kingdom. Magistrate, tax collector, and administrator all rolled into one, he wielded immense power but used it wisely and justly. He understood the communities and tribes he administered, was intimately familiar with the district's terrain and travelled tirelessly on horseback from town to town, sleeping in tents and working at his camp table by the light of a kerosene lamp. He was known for his honesty and integrity and, like Vaman Abaji Modak, was rewarded for his dedication and service with the title of 'Rao Saheb'. To commemorate the honour, his title was inscribed on a grain of rice and presented to him at a special ceremony.

Even while Dad entertained a healthy respect for his grandfather's strength, character and station as patriarch of the clan, he was one of the few people who did not fear him. He had nothing to fear. They were, after all, kindred spirits, sharing a love of nature, hard work and a strict adherence to principles. One day when he was twelve, Dad proudly brought his grandfather his math exam paper. He had done well; 97 per cent was nothing to scoff at. Anna scanned the paper carefully. Looking down into Dad's earnest grey-blue eyes, he asked gruffly. 'Where did the other three per cent go?'

As tough as Anna was, he would not have made my grandmother's life a living hell. This was his wife Saraswati's prerogative, as is common in Indian tales of marriage and in-laws. Everyone called my great-grandmother Akka or older sister. She was the one person in his family whom Dad hardly ever talked about, probably because he had nothing complimentary to say. As the wife of a powerful and well-respected man, Akka became bloated with power and complacent about her place in society. She was selfish, somewhat greedy and inclined to take care of her own, selectively. She cared deeply for her sisters and her daughters and all their offspring, but did not seem to feel kindly towards her sons and unequivocally not towards their children.

Anna's first wife had died in childbirth, along with a stillborn child. Akka was his second wife and the mother of his ten children.

She outlived him by a decade so I did have a chance to meet her. A short, stout, plain woman in her prime, when I knew her towards the end of her life, she was diminutive even to me, a toddler. As she got older, she seemed to spend much of her life on her bed from which she held forth to her admiring relatives who sat on the floor in front of her.

When I think of her son, Appa, in his old age, I see a lean man with soft, snow-white hair and skin glowing pink with good health, prayer beads in his right hand, often saying, '*Shree Ram, Jai Ram, Jai Jai Ram.*' Were his prayers to atone for past sins or was he simply going down the old person's path towards peace and salvation? Akka, birdlike, did not turn to spirituality. She was ritualistic but also very much of this material world, which she had no intention of forgoing. She liked rich food, which was served to her mashed up because she had long since lost all her teeth; she kept tabs on everyone at Shree Ram Krupa, controlling life as best she could; and she enjoyed a good gossip with her daughters who kept her up-to-date on events in the outside world.

My toddler eyes saw a soft, faded blue and white sari wrapped around a tiny, bent woman shuffling about the house, sharp beady eyes watching closely all that was happening. I don't know why Akka was so unkind to her daughter-in-law, my grandmother. I think she must simply have been jealous of my grandmother's beauty and found her personality and breeding incomprehensible. At a time when many Marathi Brahmins still opposed the idea of women being educated, Veerbala came from a family where women were encouraged to learn. Her liberatedness was a mark against her in the Marathe book. Did Akka think Ai Aji was too well educated for a woman? Did she adhere to the notion that a daughter-in-law naturally had to take on all the responsibilities of the home and not think of anything beyond it? Or was she simply a product of her era, blindly following mores and notions and restricted by her own ignorance, living in servitude to convention?

*

My first ever memory has Akka in it. It also rather appropriately revolves around two thoughts that have often preoccupied me—a sense of belonging and food, or at the very least, eating. Whenever we visited Shree Ram Krupa, I had free reign of the place as toddlers seem to do, no rules attached yet to their sovereign plumpness. My one-year-old self wandered in and out of the dining room, which was dark with grey slate floors, cupboards painted a rich brown and set into the walls, and the polished wooden altar where the family deities were. Through a wide arch lay the kitchen, gleaming with highly polished brass and copper pans and tins. I ran about exploring this fascinating world with its pervasive cool calm.

Occasionally I padded into my great-grandmother Akka's room and she asked if I wanted some khau. 'Put out your hand,' she'd say and my chubby paw would stretch out to receive some of the bedaney or khadi saakhar that she kept in jars by her bed. She dropped them from her wrinkled fingers into my waiting palm, making certain she did not touch my skin. Thanking her, I'd go on my merry way, sometimes pausing to show Mom my bounty.

Was I ever told the reason for the lack of contact from Akka? I certainly noted it because the other adults in my world held me tenderly. Over time, I came to the conclusion that it was because my mother was not a Konkanastha, unlike the rest of Akka's family. Mom was a fish-eating Saraswat, which in the minds of many of my Marathe relatives was about the same as not being Brahmin at all. Since I was half-Saraswat, I was virtually untouchable to the fastidious elders. The hypocrisy was laughable. The Marathes did not mind if my mother washed dishes or helped prep vegetables for cooking. Akka would even drink tea made by her. 'She liked me,' Mom smiled. 'We'd chat and she'd laugh at my jokes. But I was not permitted to cook anything when she was going to eat a meal.'

Luckily, my mother took this treatment in her stride, brushing it off with laughter and charming the family with her humour, her giggles and her warmth. Into a sombre, reserved family where smiles were measured, where no one noted or celebrated birthdays or anniversaries or expressed how they felt about each other, my mother infused the Sirsikars' love of celebration, physical affection and their ability to vocalize feelings and give praise where it was due. I do not know a happier person than my mother. The words 'I love you' were not part of the Indian family's lexicon back then and to have uttered them in the Marathe household would have been blasphemy. My mother blasphemed abundantly, thank heavens.

This was the world I inhabited for the first part of my life, being loved by my parents and surrounded by family and it was the world Dad had grown up in, too. Back then, within running distance of his house, were a preschool, an elementary, middle and high school that all the Marathe children attended. My father sprinted there every day, decorously leaving every morning in his uniform, thick leather chappals on his feet. To a young, energetic boy, chappals were an encumbrance so, when he was out of his mother's sight, he slipped them off and hid them in a hedge, picking them up at noon on his way back home.

In Shree Ram Krupa, Dad could be sure of finding a bustle. It was considered a refuge by many: Appa's pregnant sisters, sisters-in-law, maternal aunts, their children, and innumerable other relatives. The house was known simply as the Bangla. 'I am going to the Bangla,' people said, or in my day, 'I am going to Aathvi Gulli (the Eighth Lane).' Out-of-town visitors came to pay respects to my great-grandparents or stay for a night or a week. Those who were hungry came to eat, including poor Brahmin boys who were fed there weekly. Sick relatives recuperated there, indigent ones were supported by Anna and, therefore, by his resident son and daughter-in-law, Veerbala. She was the unsung servant, nursemaid, hostess and heroine of it all.

Little wonder then that when my father was born in November 1944 at the clinic on the wide, tree-lined Jungli Maharaj Road near Deccan Gymkhana, he was angry. India was still a British colony.

Freedom at midnight was almost three years away, but freedom, independence, justice and compassion were infused into that little being before his birth. So was a voice that could not but be heard. When he was brought home, the bungalow resounded with his cries, rippling out into the forest beyond. Susheela Kaku, his aunt, laughed when she told me, 'We all said *Ravana Rao aley...* Mr Ravana, the Demon, has arrived!' We emerge as we are going to be for the rest of our lives. Sudhakar's sense of right and wrong reverberated across the family home.

My father announced loud and clear that he was not going tolerate injustice to anyone, especially not to his mother.

4. Tell Me a Story

It is not the voice that commands the story; it is the ear.
—Italo Calvino, writer

My childhood was filled with stories and I never tired of hearing them.

In my late 1960s- and early '70s-world, an India with little television and no inkling of the Internet era to come, the oral tradition was richly alive. It was my mother who told us most of our bedtime stories. On the rare occasions we could persuade Dad to tell us a story, he would read to us. Rudyard Kipling's *The Elephant's Child* or *How the Alphabet Was Made*; any number of hilarious, slightly bawdy (not by today's standards) Uncle Silas stories by H.E. Bates; Marathi stories he had translated into English; poems that spanned centuries and languages; nineteenth-century journal articles about the hill forts of Maharashtra; *Great Expectations*, *Treasure Island*.

But what we really wanted from him was what Mom regularly gave us; a glimpse into a child-self and into what life was like in that far-off time twenty years before we arrived on this planet and life really began! We begged, 'Please, Dad. Puh-lease, puh-lease tell us about when you were little.'

Very, very occasionally he would agree and we cheered. Putting a chair down between our beds, he would sit down, back erect, foot tilted out for balance, and tell us in his sonorous voice the anecdotes we loved and which ended all too quickly for our liking. While Mom could be wheedled to tell us story after story, Dad doled his out in a miserly fashion, we felt. He believed in the truism from one of my favourite songs: 'And gold would not be precious if we all had gold to spare.'

'One afternoon,' he might begin, 'I came home from school and saw that the hallway was littered with my aunts' chappals… as usual.'

'Show us,' we squealed.

Dad pulled his lanky body out of the chair, scrunched down with his back towards us, pushing his behind out exaggeratedly to mimic a woman's hips and backside. We burst into laughter as he toddled away, imitating how his short, plump aunts kicked off their slippers carelessly—flap, flap—and eagerly scurried into Dad's house to visit their mother. The footwear became a mountain as more visitors arrived, blocking the path of anyone else who might need to go in.

Since the only one who did any tidying in the house was Dad's mother, Veerbala, and she was busy in the kitchen when he came home, all he saw was a mountain of footwear. He knew it would fall to his mother to tidy it up when she had a rare moment to spare. Sudhakar's ten-year-old temper combusted. He was a person of his word. 'I had warned them,' he told us, 'that I would throw their chappals away if they didn't stop making a mess in our house.' But back then, who took a child seriously or paid attention to his threats?

'They were never considerate to my mother who had to keep the house tidy,' continued Dad. 'So I gathered up all the chappals and took them outside. The house backed onto the jungle, Erandawane then. If something were thrown there, who would go into the brush in the dark to find it? I took each of those slippers and flung them into the trees one…by…one.' There was a note of satisfaction in his voice.

My brother and I laughed uproariously to think of the incongruity of our strict father ever having been that mischievous child. At the same time, we felt so tender towards the little boy who wanted to cherish his mother. 'Did they ever find their chappals?' we wanted to know.

Dad shook his head. 'Oh no! But were they ever angry.'

Then we chuckled as we imagined the aunts' puzzlement and chagrin when they were ready to depart and could not find their footwear. Meanies, serves them right! we thought.

Dad is the first feminist I ever knew. From the age of five, he had taken it upon himself to ease his mother's burden. Watching her suffer made him determined not to treat his spouse or any other woman in a patriarchal, chauvinistic way. Growing up, his childish energy was channelled into caring for her well-being because it was clear to him that hardly anyone else cared about her. If Ai Aji needed something from the market, he would dash the two miles to Tulshi Baug to get it for her. Every morning, he would wake up early and slip into the garden quietly. He lugged big steel buckets of water around the garden with his little hands so his mother would not have to. He watered the flowering plants first; frangipani, rose, jasmine, prajakta and then the fruiting trees: mango, chickoo, ramphal, sitaphal and coconut, before running all the way to school which began every morning at 6:30.

What did Ai Aji think of Dad, his way of caring for her, his feeling of injustice? Years later, she sat in the front row of the theatre in Poona University and watched him perform the lead role of the Angry Young Man in *Look Back in Anger*. After the performance, she stood apart watching the commotion as students and colleagues crowded around the cast to offer their congratulations. A colleague of Dad's approached her and asked politely, 'What did you think of your son's acting?'

'Oh, he wasn't acting,' she responded dryly, not missing a beat. 'That's just who he is.'

Mom's life and stories were diametrically opposite to Dad's but her sense of justice was just as profound. She grew up in a Westernized army family. Her father's salary was Rs 4,000 a month at a time when some other men of his generation earned Rs 300. So my mother and her three siblings were pampered, growing up with luxuries Dad never dreamt of as a child. My mother was precocious and strong-willed, gregarious and very fair in her dealings. If she was invited to a birthday party, she tried to have her younger sister invited too. If she were not, Mom would bring treats back for her. If she saw a beggar, she gave him money or food. If she saw a child being bullied at school, she advocated for her.

*

While my parents shared family stories and literature, we were also listening eagerly to stories from the two great Hindu epics, the *Mahabharata* and the *Ramayana*, favourites in homes all over India for millennia. Sometimes my maternal grandmother Vahini would tell us those myths but our chief source was Tatya who was very religious and whose love for the two main characters of the *Ramayana*, King Rama and his wife Sita, bordered on the obsessive. He wrote poems about them in his spare time, sitting cross-legged on the floor or a mat in the sitting room or the verandah where there was light, his writing paper and pen-and-nib and ink bottle balanced on his small metal trunk.

On searingly hot summer afternoons while the adults were napping and we had to stay outdoors, we gathered on Tatya's bed under the stairs. 'A story, a story,' we chorused and he always acquiesced though he must have been tired and in need of a nap.

While my cousins listened rapt and unquestioning to the adventures of Rama, his brother Lakshmana and his wife Sita as they wandered the length and breadth of ancient India during their fourteen-year exile from Ayodhya, I was not shy about voicing my objections and I often disagreed with Tatya's blind faith in the virtues of Lord Rama.

I was six or seven when he told, what seemed to me, a gory tale of Rama battling the demoness Shurpanakha. She had fallen in love with Rama but he rejected her because he was already married to Sita. As a woman scorned is wont to do, Shurpanakha turned fierce and came at him with a sword. The way I heard the tale, Rama drew his sword in self-defence, then swiftly cut off her nose.

'What kind of god would cut off someone's nose?' I asked indignantly. 'How can you say he was a good man, Tatya?'

Tatya blinked, disconcerted. 'Rama was the perfect man,' he answered. 'He was an incarnation of god, of Lord Vishnu who came down to earth as a man to rid the world of evil. He always did what was right and needed.' By which he meant that, because Rama was divine, whatever he did *must* be right and needed.

'But…' I objected, my lips beginning to pout.

The rest of my argument was moot as I found myself swept up in my father's arms and whisked off from a debate that could possibly have turned uncomfortable for Tatya. I could hear him begin his narration again as the dissident was carried away. Dad perched me on the gate and held me securely in place.

'Tell *me* what you think,' he requested and he listened to my rant thoughtfully.

I always had the freedom to talk with my father and express my views, whatever they were. He heard and valued different opinions, no matter the age of the opiner, and he didn't talk down to anyone, least of all to a child. That afternoon, we discussed the relative merits of Rama and his brother Lakshmana whom I thought was a much kinder person. It was only years later that I understood I had heard the story wrong. It was, in fact, Lakshmana who cut off Shurpanakha's nose. This knowledge did not change my opinion about either of the brothers in the least. And in that moment all those years ago, Dad helped me to understand that I had a valid point and that it was all right to question what I heard.

'But… It's not easy to change people's minds about god or

religion, Bunny,' he explained. 'You have to understand that Tatya is an old man, set in his ways. What he believes makes him happy. Respect his viewpoint and let's let him be.'

I did not know then that apart from Ai Aji, Dad had been the only person in that house to love and care for Tatya. Nor did I understand Dad's compassion for a tired, overworked man who had given his life for the Marathes and whose only succour was his faith. When Dad was a child, he was the only one Tatya would dare request to pluck his ingrown eyelashes when they grew too long and started to sting his eyes. He helped massage his sore feet, with their twisted toes. Dad understood how important Tatya was to the family and to his mother. Veerbala thought of Tatya as her only friend. He was the one she joked with and he probably shared his personal griefs and longings with her. She relied on him to keep her sane through long days of hard work and insults.

In his mind, she who suffered so much *was* the goddess Sita.

5. Sita Returns to Mother Earth

Our life is an apprenticeship to the truth that around every circle another can be drawn; that there is no end in nature, but every end is a beginning, that there is always another dawn risen on midnoon, and under every deep a lower deep opens.

—Ralph Waldo Emerson, *Circles*

Vaidehi is another name for the goddess Sita who was a brave woman.

My grandmother's name Veerbala did not roll off my tongue easily. It was strong but not feminine. So when my daughter Keya was born, I gave her a more traditional Indian middle name, which started with the letter V from Veerbala: Vaidehi. After my grandmother's death, her closest friend, Tatya, wrote a poem in tribute to her, envisioning her as Vaidehi or Sita who survived her trial by fire and was swallowed up by Mother Earth when King Rama no longer had any use for her. Giving Keya the name Vaidehi connected her to a great-grandmother she had never met, a woman the depth of whose strength and bravery can only be surmised by the few outward signs of her existence.

It was a skin-tearingly dry Poona-winter cold morning in January 1980. Shining white hair neatly parted in the middle and combed back into a tight bun, skin gleaming soft, silken cream, my sixty-five year old grandmother Veerbala pushed her thin gold bangles back on each wrist and gently hoisted the pallu of her rose-pink sari onto her freshly bathed shoulders. In her eyes there was a vacantness as she looked towards the dining room where her gods waited. Her feet did not feel the chill when she stepped across the stone floor to her altar to begin her morning worship. In truth, her body felt not much of anything any more, the life juice dried out of it by work, age and disappointment. She bent down to light a lamp before she would head to the kitchen to make tea and breakfast.

A loose end of her sari gently fluttered over the lamp and collected up a lick of fire. The synthetic fabric began to eat the flame as it ruthlessly snaked up her body. The sari stuck to her skin like a sheath. Veerbala stood there burning, her legendary porcelain skin singeing and crackling as she stood, frozen, mesmerized by the orange flames, uncomprehending, unable to call for help. She sensed no pain. The Alzheimer's had taken care of that already, deadening her synapses. She was lost to us years before she caught fire. I think of her every time I burn myself in the kitchen. The tiniest steam burn or sizzle of a finger or arm from a hot pot makes me jump in agony. What must one's whole body going up in flames be like?

It was fitting that Tatya, who had loved her deeply and done all he could during her life to ease her burden, should be the one to discover my grandmother on that fateful day. Busy with his chores in another part of the house, he suddenly caught a nauseating whiff of burning flesh. He dashed as fast as his gnarled old feet would carry him through the house, ducking into every room to find the source of the stench. Finally he burst into the dining room where he saw my grandmother enveloped in flames. '*Deva, deva,*' he cried and his heart sank and shattered. He grabbed a blanket from the stack of bedclothes nearby and rolled her in it to put out the fire.

My grandmother was taken to hospital alive. She was treated for third-degree burns and stayed alive for three days, frequently calling for my father, her favourite, by the pet name she had given him.

'Sudhan,' Ai Aji cried, 'Sudhan.' No one told her why he never came. He was thousands of miles away in Canada and no one in his birth family had the presence of mind to call and tell him about his mother. Finally, just as the goddess Sita walked through fire to prove her fidelity to Rama and then asked her mother, Earth, to swallow her up, Veerbala returned to the soil after her fiery ordeal.

In those days, transcontinental phone calls were very expensive. Apparently only death justified such an expense or perhaps no one thought Dad would be able to get a plane ticket and reach Ai Aji before she died. When the trunk call was eventually made to Canada on 27 January Veerbala had been cremated and her ashes scattered so Dad did not get to say goodbye to the most important person of his childhood.

I had awoken that cold January morning to a chilling quiet in our home on the top floor of the old yellow Victorian on Hyman Street. No customary bustle in the kitchen, no animated conversation between my parents or music playing on the Canadian Broadcasting Service. It may have been a Saturday since there was also no urgency to get ready for school. I listened for familiar sounds. Our street was usually rather silent. Most of the houses were uninhabited, there was little traffic and we had become adjusted to Canadian quiet after the noise and chaos that is India. But this silence seemed eerie. As it continued, I became curious and tiptoed into the hallway, dread creeping over me.

As a child, I often felt a sinking nausea when I had done something wrong, more the fear of being found out than of regret. What had I done this time? I asked myself. Had Mom and Dad found out somehow? Were they so very angry they were stunned into silence? Being the centre of my childish universe, I could think of no other reason for the chill. I skimmed through a list of possible offences but drew a blank. Inching down the hall, I came to the living room and peered round the door. The sturdy black telephone, small, dark augur of doom, was out of place, balancing on the wide curved arm of the grey Art Deco couch instead of its home on a peg table. My parents' faces and bodies were cast in stone. One of them must have seen me but I did not know that. I was already scurrying back to the bedroom, worried now for my grandfather.

'Please, please, please, let Anna be all right,' I prayed. 'Please let Anna be all right.' I said the words over and over to make them true.

Sam, my seven-year-old brother, was still fast asleep across the room. My tendency was to wake him whenever I had something to share but not today. Dad had taught us to make our beds as soon as we awoke, holding a corner of our quilts in one hand as we got up so we would not forget or delay. I stood on my bed now and started folding the silky quilt silently, hoping that my Anna was alive and well. I had not seen him since our move to Canada and the thought of never seeing him again was intolerable.

Dad came to the door, looking taller and more self-contained than usual. I wonder now what thoughts were racing through his mind. He came in and stood by me. I cannot recall the words he used to tell me about his mother's death but he spoke softly, gently. I did not respond because I did not know what to say. My knees were buckling in relief. I collapsed on my bed, silently thanking god for answering my prayers.

Anna, my grandfather, was safe.

6. Happy-Go-Lucky

When you're smiling, when you're smiling,
The whole world smiles with you.
When you're laughing, when you're laughing,
The sun comes shining through.

—Larry Shay, Mark Fisher & Joe Goodwin,
'When You're Smiling' made popular
by Louis Armstrong

It was not that I did not mourn Ai Aji, but she was then only a grandmother to me. In my mind, she and Appa, Dad's parents, were ancient, white-haired, undemonstrative. I did not understand them or their way of life. Mom's father was another matter altogether. He was the first person I ever loved, the first I laughed with, the first to understand what I said with my eyes.

In his professional capacity, my maternal grandfather was Lieutenant Colonel Sadanand Manjunath Sirsikar or 'Colonel Saheb'. His given name was Sadanand, The Ever-Happy One, but to everyone who loved him, he was simply Anna. He was the second oldest of Dr Manjunath Thimappa Sirsikar and his wife Lakshmi's thirteen children. As Anna's wife, my grandmother became the Vahini or sister-in-law to the Sirsikar clan, so her children and grandchildren called her that too.

Unlike my paternal grandparents, Anna and Vahini's army life had taken them to many parts of India and they socialized with fellow officers, diplomats and political leaders. They were frequent and extravagant hosts and at their home, I met filmmakers, poets, musicians, academics. I peeked around the bedroom door into the vibrant laughter of a dinner party, curious to know what was going on. The lazy fingers of suave, debonair men twirled waxed mustaches delicately, dangled cigarettes or cigarillos and flicked ash nonchalantly as they flirted with elegant women whose buttery-yellow or ruby-red sequined chiffon saris were draped just so, whose impeccable lines of kajal framed almond eyes and foot-high bouffants were accomplishments for a young girl to aspire to.

The ladies were unflustered by the badinage, giving as good as they got, smiling coyly, laughing throatily as I watched in awe. I never aspired to be like them because they felt artificial in contrast to the guileless, grounded reality of Mom and Vahini but I still admired them, occasionally asking my mother as unsatisfied kids are wont to do, why she was not more like them.

Sadanand was the life of every party, charming, flirtatious, full of bonhomie. With good-natured, democratic banter, he could make the most gauche young man feel comfortable, a man of the world. 'You were a sight to see, Pankaj,' he would say, 'In that skirmish in '61.' Turning to the women, he would hold the young man's arm firmly and announce, 'Ladies, this is a war hero indeed.'

And he could transform the plainest Jane into a scintillating beauty. Raising his hands in wonder, he would exclaim, '*Arrey wah*, Mrs Khanna, how you sparkle tonight!' The lady would blush and dissemble while Anna laughingly winked at her. I watched speechlessly at his innate talent with people. How does he do it, how does he know *just* what to say? my five-year-old self wondered.

Those parties were suffused with a certain yellow light, the richness of my grandmother's buttercup-yellow china. I would skip out to the garden to see the glow cast by the lamps. The bungalow shone like a beacon in the pitch-black night and the silhouetted figures moved animatedly like a shadow play. The living room's coziness beckoned and I returned eagerly back in where I belonged.

Recently my partner, Dean, told me, 'You're like a lighthouse. To be in your light is wonderful, when you turn away and someone is left in the darkness, it is very dark indeed.' That is how I imagine darkness was on the other side from Anna's world, chilling and desolate. Luckily, he never let the woman he married feel it. His deepest love and regard were for his chosen one.

'Shakun,' he often said, holding her narrow chin gently in his fingers and staring down at her as she blushed shyly, 'How lovely you are. What a lucky man I am.' And she, secure in the knowledge that she was adored, never forgotten, was content to sit back and watch her husband move through the flocks of partygoers, laughing, joking, teasing. Vahini indulged Anna good-humouredly, playing hostess at his endless parties and accompanying him on his seemingly tireless jaunts through the social whirl of army life.

*

Sadanand, the ever-happy one, was as happy-go-lucky as his name suggested. He was born on 27 February 1917 in Nagpur, the seventh child of an only child. His father was a doctor and his mother a wealthy, willful woman who usually got her own way, either because she had independent means or because she was stubborn while her husband was not. I suspect Anna inherited his father's easy-going nature, as well as his looks.

Anna had dabbled in communism as a young chemistry student at Benares Hindu University in 1935. India was on the verge of revolution and he was going to be a part of it. But, after a while, it became rather dangerous to be a protestor and when British authorities began to notice him and his colleagues, Anna's friend suggested a clever solution that would also appease the British government. 'Join the British army,' he said.

This made sense to Anna. Giving up his youthful political aspirations rather easily, he signed an emergency commission in 1943. It was the start of a long and illustrious army career, spanning the struggle for Indian independence and the shift from British government and army to a new nation and its fledgling armed forces.

He became an ammunitions specialist and worked behind battle lines, leading junior officers and soldiers on active supply, support, back up and other duties. During Partition, he was posted on the western border and helped to safely evacuate migrants in either direction.

He was slated for a promotion to the post of brigadier when in the autumn of 1962, disaster struck. During the Chinese operations, Anna was posted in the North Eastern Frontier Agency (NEFA, today part of the state of Assam), south of the eastern Himalayan mountain range. He and his team were doing a reconnaissance of the Nathula Pass when the snow began to come down hard. The team was stranded waist-deep in snow for three days. By the time they were rescued, Anna's legs had been seriously injured. He developed water on both his knees and had to be airlifted to New Delhi for medical attention. His injuries left him first in danger of having his legs amputated, which fortunately did not happen, and then, with the threat of synovial arthritis, which did.

After his accident, Anna was termed Medical Category C. This meant that he could either be boarded out—leave the army with benefits—or continue to serve, with no possibility of further promotion. Since the army was his life, my grandfather opted to stay, with no hopes of prestigious postings or seniority. So it was that in 1964, for his last posting before retirement, Anna was sent to Maharashtra to command the Ammunitions Depot at Dehu Road. The small cantonment is sixteen miles northwest of Poona, just off the old Bombay-Poona highway. To its north, basking in sunlight, sits the ancient village of Dehu, where the Marathi poet-saint Tukaram lived in the early seventeenth century.

Tuka, as he was affectionately called, lived and preached by the sacred Indrayani, which flowed gently past the exquisite little stone

Vithoba-Rakhmai temple on its banks. His ashes were scattered there. My beloved grandparents' ashes are too and that is where I hope to join them one day.

*

Anna's daughters, my mother Meera and her younger sister Maya, were about to start college when the family moved to Dehu Road. They enrolled at Poona's Fergusson College together. Their older brothers Ramesh and Nishikant had already made the decision to follow Anna into the army and were studying nearby at the officers' institute, the National Defence Academy (NDA) in Khadakvasla. With all his children's futures resolving themselves, Anna thought, why not settle here?

After he retired in 1968, just before I was born, my grandfather bought land near the cantonment, along with two of his colleagues, Colonel Khare and Colonel Dutta. On adjoining properties, the three army-wallahs had exuberant plans for a merry retired life spent in each other's company. Alas, Khare died soon after their homes were constructed and Dutta became so involved in his children's and grandchildren's lives that Anna rarely saw him. But their decision is why, on the edge of Dehu village just skirting the huts and tenements of working class folk, sit three large bungalows like sleeping cats, luxuriating on ample cushions of land.

Anna's west-facing property was just north of the cantonment. All the land across the road was owned by the ammunitions depot, which often tested explosives in the valley, so no construction was permitted there. My grandparents were guaranteed free flowing westerly breezes and an unobstructed view of magnificent sunsets and gentle hill slopes whose roundness became so familiar to me that even if I close my eyes now, I can travel their contours. Every September, when the summer-broiled grasses turn the rolling hills around my home in Southern California golden, I am transported to Dehu's hills; equally golden, softly curving in the same unassuming, gentle way.

Even as a child, I was acutely aware that Anna's bungalow was an architectural folly. It had been well planned but poorly and cheaply built. After retirement, on a three-year assignment commanding the girls' unit of the National Cadet Corps (NCC) in Poona, Anna had no leisure to oversee the construction of the twin houses he had commissioned for his sister and himself. He did not keep tabs on his contractor who fleeced him and dragged construction out far longer than needed. Anna only said, '*Jaoo de.*' Let it go.

Till the 1990s, when Rajiv Gandhi's government 'liberalized' the Indian economy, re-allowed foreign investment, inviting multinational corporations back into the country, and started India on a downward spiral of debt, following the American example, life was not lived on credit. People generally saved all their working lives to buy a home outright when they retired. So it was natural that in the place where Anna and Vahini knew they would live out the rest of their days, they attempted to create welcoming spaces that could accommodate the great flow of daily and overnight guests they were accustomed to. They named the house Manju Lakshmi as a tribute to Anna's parents.

A spacious living room overlooked a hedged-in front garden that muted the sounds of the bullock carts and buses which plied on the main road to Dehu Road railway station. A broad, deep, two-sectioned porch with an inversely pitched roof stood between the twin concrete houses. At its back end was placed a ladder so getting up on the roof to check the level of water in the tanks, always temperamentally delivered by the municipality, was easy. I grew up thinking all houses had ladders positioned against a terrace. Since we had easy access to the roof, we often played 'house' there, every child over the age of two making their way up the ladder without adult supervision.

Each house also had front-facing verandahs along their width, and side verandahs leading off the two larger bedrooms. Off the central porch, a large door opened onto the living and dining area with a cut-out to the kitchen at the back of the house. There was an outdoor tank behind it to store water. A third, slightly smaller bed and bath were at the rear. All the rooms had wide, deep-set windows letting in great quantities of light, especially in the early days when the trees hadn't grown. The ledges were just begging to be sat upon and I took them up on the offer, spending hours there, perched in a corner or just staring out at the dappled light on the foliage.

The back garden was immense and abutted the boundaries of Dehu village. At the far end was a stone building in which servants sometimes lived. A gap was created in the hedge behind them so Colonel Dutta and his family could climb over the low wall for quick visits rather than coming the long way round, by the main road. This was a great convenience for Mrs Dutta, a short, egg-shaped woman whom Botero would have painted gleefully. She joined us nearly every Sunday evening to watch the Hindi movie feature on TV. She would climb painfully through the gap and since walking was nigh impossible for her, roll slowly forward, arms pitched at forty-five degrees to her body, sweat dripping down her forehead. We skipped alongside her, giggling, observing her obesity with intense and innocent curiosity. We had never before seen anyone so huge.

The day Anna's first television arrived was a big day in the village. The year was 1972 and TVs were new to India. Anna-Aji were the first to get one in Dehu and for years theirs was the only one. I hopped around in breathless anticipation all that morning, climbing onto the gate and peering down the road every few minutes to check if the deliverymen were arriving. When the truck finally pulled up, the household, the neighbours, even Tommy and Brownie, the two stray dogs who spent all day in our garden, hovered around it in excitement as the scrawny, young delivery men staggered into the living room under the weight of a humungous black-and-white television set, fronted with faux wooden shutters.

They placed it reverently on a high shelf diagonally across the room from Anna's chair. A cheer went up. To think we could now watch cricket matches, Hindi films, the news, whenever we wanted!

In a manner of speaking. Early television programming was limited to one channel on which shows were aired for only few hours every evening and consisted mostly of stultifying government sponsored fare for farmers or children and *Chaya Geet*, a compendium of Bollywood film songs, screened on Tuesdays and Thursdays. But we were thirsty travellers in a desert oasis and drank it all in. I had always loved moving pictures. Just as I would read anything available, like the ingredients on a cereal box, I would watch anything at all. My big dream was to watch television in colour one day. For now, the highlight of my week came every Sunday evening at 6 pm when a Hindi movie feature was aired. In my mind's eye, I saw technicolour as the actors pranced across our screen.

Mrs Dutta and the villagers trickled in just before show time. Tommy and Brownie kept us company, and once, to my astonishment, a goat wandered in through the always-open door. The Kashmiri carpet was rolled up so the villagers could sit crosslegged on the cool floor. They huddled together, abashed by the privilege of being allowed into the Saheb's bungalow to share a special event. They looked discreetly away from us as we chattered, got our snacks and settled on the divan. When the villagers thought no one was looking, they sneaked fascinated looks at a world that was not their own, peeking at us as if we were aliens.

Vahini sat on the couch, a spot from which she could easily run to the kitchen if she had to. Once Mrs Dutta had made it onto the porch, she had to struggle up a short step, casting one thick foot over it, holding on to the doorjamb with two hands and heaving the rest of her body in. Then she shuffled a few feet to the couch, held onto an arm and plopped down hard next to my grandmother, breathing heavily and wiping the sweat from her face with a handkerchief she pulled out from warm storage in her expansive bosom.

When she was settled and everyone else had found a perch, I waited with bated breath to see who the star of that evening's movie would be. I prayed, crossed my fingers, and took every other superstitious precaution for it to be the 'hero' for my generation; tall, dark, gangly, sexy-voiced Amitabh Bachchan whom I dreamed of marrying someday. But it was almost as exciting if it were Sunil Dutt, the heart-throb of a previous generation. He was Mrs Dutta's cousin and if his name were announced, she would excitedly launch into stories about growing up with Sunil Praji in the Punjab. I wondered whether Sunil Dutt ever paid attention to his adoring cousin once he had risen to the pinnacle of Bollywood fame but the connection gave Mrs Dutta an intense joy, which transmitted itself to us across those airwaves.

When the music started, we all turned wide-eyed, silent and rapt, to the miraculous screen where our favourite actors and actresses pranced and sang and made us laugh, sob and exclaim on the edge of our seats for two hours or more. Every time the villain punched the hero, *dishoom, dishoom*, Vahini gasped, '*Arrey, arrey, bichara!*' She and Mrs Dutta smiled tenderly when the hero and heroine found each other and ended the film in a loving clinch.

A few years after Manju Lakshmi was built, Anna's children, who all lived far away, suggested that he and Vahini have tenants for company as well as to give them a hand as they got older. Anna converted the old dining room into a kitchen-dining area by adding a counter and a wall of cupboards to separate it from the living room. The three rooms at the back, including the old kitchen, were rented out as an independent unit. Drs Joshi and their three children, Yogesh, Rani and Priya, moved in. The kids became our playmates and I told them very tall tales that they swallowed with wide-eyed innocence.

Anna's sister Baiji Gadekar and her husband never moved

to Dehu nor did their family ever use the twin house. So Anna rented it to tall, fiery Gurudas and his gentle, buck-toothed wife, Vishnupriya. They had two daughters: Krishna and Radha, the younger a mischievous, smiling imp who became my best friend and ran around with me everywhere.

*

Life was a perpetual holiday. It cannot always have been summertime but it seemed that way. We ran up and down the hills surrounding Manju Lakshmi, often barefoot and always bareheaded. Carefree and fearless, we scampered like mountain goats on paths beaten through the golden landscape by heavy-hoofed cattle. The house, and so my grandparents, were always in view but I occasionally turned back to make sure and grinned happily, reassured.

We stopped and stared: at colourful creepy-crawlies only a child is small and curious enough to notice, terracotta-roofed cottages, nestled sleepily in the foothills, under the shade of spreading banyan and tamarind trees. I wondered about the villagers who lived in them. Sometimes we would intentionally wander near the cottages to peep in. A woman squatted by the outdoor tap, beating soapy clothes on a washing stone, then rinsing them in a bucket of fresh water. If a door was open, we could glimpse the shadowy interior, with gleaming brass pots and pans arranged along the kitchen walls. I longed to be invited in for a rustic meal of roasted, hand-flattened millet bhakri, freshly churned butter, white and melting on the hot bread.

The sun made its way further up in the sky until it was almost over our heads and the ammunitions depot's barbed wire fence stretched away north and south as far as we could see. Behind it, lay a no-man's land shrouded in mystery. The road that twisted and wound alongside the fence sometimes brought an olive-green army truck noisily shaking and jangling its way down towards the village. The higher we climbed, the smaller trucks and bicycles and people and houses and animals became, much to our delight. The silence was peaceful. And then before we knew it, we had reached the top of the hill. There sprawled the Ayappa temple where Radha's parents worshipped regularly.

I often accompanied them because I liked listening to the congregation singing and, because if I were lucky, we might get to eat a bite at the communal lunch served after prayers. I was neither hungry nor greedy. I just wanted the experience, to taste flavours different from what I knew. It was the same reason I liked being invited to Radha's house when Vishnupriya was cooking Malayalee food, rich with coconut and rice, two of my favourite ingredients.

Often on a Saturday morning, Radha would come and ask if I could go over for breakfast. 'Of course,' I said, jumping up and down excitedly. Now I would get to eat some fluffy idlis or crisp dosas drenched in fresh ghee and topped with crunchy, big-grained sugar. I sat at Radha's dining table, devouring the treats and chatting happily.

Then her father Gurudas came in and his big booming voice and large, masculine physique quelled my enthusiasm. A panic came over me that was just this side of fear. He always seemed angry and impatient, especially with Radha who was ebullient and joyful and spoke her mind frankly. His voice boomed through the kitchen, reprimanding Radha for her 'cheekiness'. Then he saw me and put on an ingratiating smile. I was his landlord's granddaughter and he had to tolerate me.

'Hello Bunny,' he boomed. 'How are you?'

I ducked my head. 'Hello,' I said softly. 'I'm fine, thank you. How are you?' Somehow I did not trust him and I knew Radha hated him too. There was nothing she or I could do about it but I did not like feeling helpless. Vishnupriya, herself made uncomfortable by her husband, sensed my uneasiness. She put her gentle hand on my shoulder and smiled at me.

I smiled back and when Gurudas left the room, my bubbling,

cheerful chatter emerged from hiding, making jokes to make my hostess laugh. Breakfast over, Radha and I rushed outdoors again. We had been holding our breaths and it was liberating to exhale, laugh, play. She was stronger and bigger but I was faster, which she did not like.

Suddenly she said, 'Race ya!' and started off from the back end of the central verandah toward the garden fence.

'Okay,' I accepted the challenge and we pelted across the garden and down a narrow path between the rose bushes. As we neared the finish line, Radha pushed her shoulder into my side and I found myself falling to the ground, my right knee landing on an inconvenient brick. The flesh on my knee split open in a rectangular gash. I sat howling on the ground, mostly I suspect from the unfairness of having lost the race this way. All I ended up with was a little scar that to this day reminds me of my friend. She, a few days later, was not so lucky.

Every Tuesday her parents hosted a prayer meeting. The large living room filled up quickly with twenty or twenty-five devotees. In front of an altar stood Gurudas, the three horizontal, white, sacred marks of a Shaivite freshly painted across his broad brow. His bald head gleamed and his mahogany-coloured barrel chest was bare except for his sacred thread. He tightened his white lungi and sat down cross-legged, heavy brass cymbals in hand. His friend tuned the harmonium and began to play. We wove our way, barefooted, between the singers to the front of the room towards Gurudas, Vishnupriya and Krishna and squeezed in, joining the clapping and singing.

I stared curiously at the adults in rhapsody, eyes closed, faces raised to heaven. Their saintly, holier-than-thou expressions made Radha giggle. Her father glared at her and Vishnupriya shifted agitatedly. But Radha giggled again. Before anyone knew what was happening, Gurudas had turned angrily and hit her on the head with a cymbal. A cracking sound swalllowed the sound of my anguished scream. Radha fell backward and was deathly still, blood gushing from her forehead. Vishnupriya used the end of her sari to staunch the flow. The next few minutes were a blur till Radha opened her eyes.

Her wound healed but left a jagged scar on her temple, a scary caricature of the religious marks on her father's forehead. What broke inside her that night, however, would never be fixed. I had never known a father like Gurudas. He showed me how complicated and strange adults were and how they could suck the joy of living out of a child, But as sad as I was for Radha, I could not help being thankful because on that day I understood how cherished and protected I was.

I was lucky for when I smiled, my world replied by smiling too.

7. Where the Soul Knows Peace

‖ *Words my only jewels*
Words my only raiment
Words my only sustenance
Words my only wealth to give.
Tuka says, witness the word, my God,
With my words alone do I worship him ‖

—*Saint Tukaram of Dehu*, translated by
Sudhakar Marathe

At Anna-Vahini's home in Dehu I was utterly joyous and carefree.

What is home? Having had to make one in so many places, I tend to look for patterns and familiarities wherever I go. As much as a new town excites my wanderlust and my need to explore and discover it, there comes a point when comparing it favourably to my previous home helps me settle in. Sanjiv joked that I always missed terribly the *last* place I had lived. It's true that reminiscing helped me get over homesickness until I felt I belonged in my new environment, but ultimately almost everywhere I have ever lived is home because it is associated with happy memories.

In the 1970s and '80s, if my parents were between jobs, Manju Lakshmi was our landing spot. When we lived in Poona, I spent weekends there and during my teenage years, summertime meant several months' vacation at the Dehu bungalow. My grandparents doted on my cousin Ashoo and me, their oldest grandchildren. They had indulged our whims and fancies when we were babies, surrounding us with smiles and hugs. In our branch of the Sirsikar family, I am spoken of as Anna's favourite. It was not something I thought of much, accepting it with childish matter-of-factness, but the sense of security that came with this knowledge made me very sure about my place in the world. I belonged, I was wanted, I was looked after.

Early in 1970 when I was not quite two, Anna asked his friend, Tatya Khanolkar, to take some professional photographs of the family and especially of Ashoo and me. For the next dozen years, those large colourized photos hung in the middle of the wall in Anna's living room. There we were, greeting people when they entered the house, Ashoo with curly black hair, chubby cheeks, pouty lips and a naughty grin, and me, Bunna, in a round collared, pink cotton dress, hair still blond and sparse, neck crooked shyly, turning slightly away from the camera, the mole in the middle of my left cheek clearly visible, a demure expression in my eyes.

Six grandchildren followed us but perhaps my grandparents' enthusiasm abated or it simply did not occur to them to add pictures of the other grandchildren to the wall. So the two of us stayed there in joint splendour. This irked some of the other grandchildren or their parents. Finally around 1982, when the youngest of us was about to make her appearance, my aunt Maya suggested that her parents display pictures of *all* the grandchildren. To make things easy, she gifted them a framed composite of the remaining six: Neena, Veena, Sameer, Ram, Reena and Arjun. Anna placed the picture on a bookshelf with a mysterious smile. Maya's daughter, Radhu, the baby of the family and fifteen years my junior, was born soon after. When she was a few years old, an individual tabletop photo of her also appeared on the shelf. The younger seven were appeased. The two who had died young—Leena and Aditya—were never displayed.

*

Anna was just fifty-one when I was born, still dashing and debonair but permanently bent at the knees, fingers gnarled, and in more pain with every passing day. I saw a suave gentleman of leisure, in a white bush shirt and black pants, hair parted in the middle, slicked down with Brylcreem as it had been when it was glossy black in the 1940s, cheeks rosy above a neat mustache in the style of the well-known actor Guru Dutt, twinkling brown eyes flashing with good humour and kindness, his feet in Kolhapuri chappals somewhat shuffling as he walked.

When I was very young, I 'drove' his royal-blue LandMaster. Sitting on Anna's lap, I steered a couple of miles down the road to the army canteen where I loved to shop with him—condensed milk, shaving cream, processed cheese (the only kind of cheese you could buy then in India), tomato sauce, goods you could not get at the old-fashioned grocery store—or to the quiet little railway station to pick up one of my parents or a guest arriving from Poona or Bombay.

We would wait in the shade of the arching peepal tree till the train was about to roll into the station, then I would dash to the turnstile to buy a yellow platform ticket that allowed me past the ticket collector and onto the railway platform. I liked to look at the guava seller sitting there and the neatly stacked yellow and green guavas in a wicker basket, imagining what my life would be if I were her. I would peer down the tracks at the train making its inexorable way towards us. The excitement was not just to receive loved ones but a hunger to be part of this magical experience of travelling.

I loved those outings with Anna because I got to be alone with him. Coca-Cola had something to do with it too. Back in those days, I was an aficionado. On the way home from our errands, I knew we were likely to stop at the Officers' Mess where Anna would sit down with a sigh under an umbrella and order a chilled beer. 'What would you like, Banna?' he asked chivalrously, knowing full well what my answer would be.

'A Coca-Cola, please,' I smiled up at him, delighted to get my very own drink in a bottle to slurp through a straw, without having to share with my brother or cousins. My feet dangled inches above the ground and I hugged my bottle to my chest, sucking in the sweetness, carbonated bubbles making their way into my nostrils, dreams of my adult life fizzing through my head. Then we drove back to Manju Lakshmi, me stretched full-length across the rear deck above the back seat, staring keenly at the sunlit road receding into the distance.

At home, Anna changed into his comfortable kurta-pajama and limped back to his bed. Two wide single wooden beds had been pushed together to make a king-sized one for my grandparents, topped by layers of mattresses. They did not fit evenly across, creating a hollow, a lumpy spot about one foot wide. I burrowed there, flattening my body into the dip and lying still, invisible. As a teenager scribbling poetry every day in my journal, I described Anna's home as the only place where my soul knew peace. It was more precisely that dip in the mattress, next to him.

I felt secure. In my nose was the crisp scent of cotton sheets, Vahini's floral Pond's face cream that lingered on her pillow, and the masculine leatheriness of my grandfather. I would lie there as he listened to All India Radio on the large, black radio console under the window, simultaneously reading the morning paper.

Occasionally I would address a comment to him, neither expecting an answer nor particularly caring if I got one, just using words to connect us and reassure myself of his presence and love. A naughty or distracted look from his warm brown eyes, over the top of his glasses, was answer enough.

Sometimes we listened to songs on the radio. My favourites were Marathi hymns. G.D. Madgulkar, whom Dad was later to meet and whose work he translated, had written a popular version of King Rama's story in Marathi. It was called the 'Geet Ramayana' and the great singer Sudhir Phadke had popularized it, recording the entire book of poems in his deep, melodious voice. I knew the first three songs by heart and was thrilled when Anna gave me my very own copy of the book one year so I could learn the rest. Although I hardly consider Marathi my mother tongue, there is a comfort in listening to the 'Geet Ramayana' and other religious Marathi music that I fail to find anywhere else. It is as if the lilting sounds of that soft, sweet language were etched in some primitive part of my brain and heart. I bring them forth in my darkest hours.

We lazed, me because I was a kid on vacation, completely without responsibility; Anna because that was his life as a retired colonel who had never had to do much except bring home the proverbial bacon. Occasionally we caught strains of Vahini's sweet, high-pitched voice in the kitchen. She sang with pathos as she bustled about her work.

> *Jaane woh kaise log the jinke, pyar ko pyar mila...*
> *Hamne to jab kaliya mangi, katon ka haar mila, ah, ah.*
>
> Who were those lucky ones whose love was requited?
> When I asked for rosebuds, I received a garland of thorns.

The garlicky aroma of her patal bhaji, the tart spinach-yoghurt stew that Anna especially liked, wafted to us too, reassuring us that lunch was imminent.

I waited with excitement in my belly.

8. The Goddess in the Kitchen

A good cook is like a sorceress who dispenses happiness.
—Elsa Schiaparelli, fashion designer

I don't know if my grandmother Vahini liked to cook. I asked her many things over the years but it never struck me to ask her that. I had always associated her, one of my first heroes, with good food and the kitchen. Whether it was santosh, her tomato-coconut soup, aptly named 'contentment' in Marathi or crunchy rice flour-coated, pan-fried pomfret fillets, Vahini knew how to satisfy my hunger.

The other great cook in my life, my mother, was fly-by-the-seat-of-her-pants speedy and innovative. Her food was wildly flavoured and inventive but when I was young, I found it capricious. Children find comfort in consistency and tradition. With Mom's cooking, I was often on tenterhooks about what would she would serve forth. Sometimes, I was deeply disappointed because a dish did not match my potent taste memory. Luckily, my unhappy experiences rarely clouded the good ones.

Mom juggled a working woman's responsibilities with her love of cooking. My grandmother, a housewife, was more conventional and had the luxury of being more deliberate, taking time always to ensure that the dish tasted as she thought it should. Not once did I see her taste the food before she served it, she just knew when it was right. I had the assurance that her recipes would taste exactly as they should, as I remembered them, each time she made them. The most valuable lesson I culled from her kitchen manner was this: discover the essence of a recipe's flavour and then work painstakingly through a specific process to achieve it.

From the age of twenty when she became a wife and mother, cooking had been a significant part of Vahini's life. Her crotchety mother-in-law taught her how to make puran poli, churma ladoo, and the fish dishes laced with coconut milk her husband's family liked. Somewhere along the way she discovered she had a knack, even a talent, for this art called cooking. She was an efficient, innovative and creative cook, but didn't take herself too seriously. She knew that whether she liked cooking or not, she was going to have to do it. She might as well make the most of it. Having had four children in a space of five years, much of her twenties and thirties were spent catering to their needs and individual finickiness. One liked eggs, another did not, the third was often ill, the fourth was still a baby. Vahini often put four different breakfasts on the table and all with a smile.

Despite living in a world where servants did the heavy lifting—cleaning the house, doing all the *mise en place* and washing pots and pans—cooking was not easy for Vahini. Unlike some of her contemporaries, she was not a cook in name alone. She did not order servants about and she was not lazy. She liked doing chores herself. I always saw her working side by side with a maid, cutting, stirring, frying, pickling, never content to wait for someone else to complete a task she could do herself. Its a trait Mom and I share with her.

By the time I knew her, my grandmother was in her fifties. When she was young, she had cooked on stoves fired by wood, not as easy to control as gas. Now she had the convenience of propane, which made her all the more prolific. If I needed her, I ran to the big kitchen where she was conjuring up the next magical meal or concocting wine from unlikely fruit. She might be sitting on the green granite counter next to the two-burner stove, resting her feet on a chair as she stirred a bubbling batch of guava jam or dudhi halva for her large brood.

If, by strange chance she was not in the kitchen, I knew where to find her. I would run into the garden and see her picking guavas or moringa pods, gathering roses, jasmine or sacred basil. Failing that, she was delivering the next round of drinks and treats to my grandfather who spent many of his waking hours on the verandah. Except for a ten-minute nap religiously taken every afternoon, my grandmother was on call for all of us from the time she arose at dawn till the time she crashed into bed long after the rest of the household was asleep.

The first day of our summer vacations was marked by a special lunch Vahini cooked for each of her grandchildren as they arrived at Manju Lakshmi. I always asked for santosh served with hot rice and ghee, thinly sliced, deep-fried salted okra rings in yoghurt, and garlicky brown lentils, with fried pomfret in season.

Despite such sumptuous meals, we were constantly in need of sustenance. 'Aji, I'm hungry,' one of us would call. And she would bring out freshly made guava toffee or coconut vadi or crisp, crunchy chakli and watch as we ate, clapping her hands absent-mindedly, tapping her foot and singing, 'Chak-ali, chak-ali' or the name of whatever she was feeding us. For a more filling snack, there were sliced Alphonso mangoes or my favourite, cream-and-sugar sandwiches, made with cream collected daily from the buffalo milk that was delivered fresh each morning and boiled before use. The cream rose thickly to the top of the pan and my grandmother collected it when the milk had cooled. Once she had gathered a week's worth, she churned butter by hand. Soft white clouds of it sat in a cold pool of water to keep fresh. We liked to run our fingers through it as Krishna must have done. Then we'd pick up a lump and put it into our mouths, letting the heat melt it gently on our tongues.

I had no notion how my grandmother made shopping lists or had the vegetable vendor, grocer and mess sergeant fill her orders. I had no idea how tired she was and how tiring her life. All I knew was that there was never any lack of snacks or sweet treats. I got chocolatey Bournvita stirred in my milk morning and evening, a treat not allowed at my own home, I could go to the cupboard any time I wanted to grab a bite to eat, no matter when dinner was. No one ever said 'No' to us.

This generous and unconditional love was the most generous gift my grandmother and her daughter Meera could have given us. They schooled me, not by any dictum but by the selfless, generous way they lived their lives.

> There is always enough food to go around
> Serve what you make with a smile
> Never refuse a child something to eat
> Share what you have
> People are more important than things

Evenings at Dehu during the holidays or on special occasions when our clan gathered on the verandah were especially joyful and full of laughter. We would arrange chairs in a circle around Anna's, with peg tables in between for cocktails and appetizers. Then we spread dhurries to lounge on. Aji and the other women would have cooked up deliciousness all afternoon.

'Bunny, Neena, Sammy,' a voice would call from the kitchen and we'd run to grab platters of sliced cucumbers seasoned with fresh salt, pepper and ground cumin, thinly sliced ham, and hot fried cocktail sausages.

From the kitchen wafted the friendly chatter of my mother, her sister and sisters-in-law as they helped Vahini fry fish or sauté goat's livers that were sprinkled with lime juice, powdered coriander seed and fresh coriander leaves. Appetizers emerged one after another and we enjoyed each taste fresh off the griddle, popping cucumber into our mouths between hot bites. In season, my grandmother boiled peanuts in the shell. We sucked out the liquid before peeling them to reveal glistening baby pink nuts, at once salty-sweet, moist and crunchy.

Loud bursts of laughter cracked in the air as stories and jokes swirled around our heads. The conversation ebbed and flowed from politics and family stories to local news and back. Sometimes we paid attention, other times I looked at my grandfather and just grinned at him, so happy to be alive. When we needed a break from eating, we played a quick round of hide-and-seek or started a game of rummy. As children, we thought nothing more about Vahini than that she was always there when we needed her. To feed us, to play card games with us on hot afternoons when we could not go out of doors and to tell us stories. We sat on the large maroon carpet that my uncle Nishu had sent from his last army posting in Kashmir, along with a sack of walnuts that we seemed to eat endlessly. I curled my toes in the lush pile as my agile grandmother tucked in the loose end of her black-and-white sari and crossed her legs next to us.

'Tell us about when you were a little girl,' I begged.

'*Tyat kay?* (Oh, what's in that?) she asked, brushing off anything to do with her own life story as unimportant.

'I want to know,' I answered. 'I want to know what you were like when you were little.'

Vahini laughed, with the characteristic little pout that came after, signifying her embarrassment.

'*Burah*,' she yielded. 'When I was growing up in Chindwada,' she started, looking at each one of us in turn, 'there were twenty children in that big wada, my uncle's house.'

'Twenty? Why? What was it like living with so many people?'

'There were lots of grown-ups too. My mother, my aunt and uncle…' She paused, counting. 'It was a lot of fun. I was the youngest, the baby. And all the older children looked after me…'

'But where was your father?'

'My father died when I was very little,' she answered quickly, moving on to tell us how many rooms there were in the wada and how she learned to cook from her aunt and how she was never alone.

Unlike my mother who easily shared funny stories of her precocious childhood, Vahini's childhood only came to us if we asked persistently. And there were two stories she never told. The first was how she and Anna had met and fallen in love.

The second was how her father died.

9. The Beauteous One

The autumn comes, a maiden fair
In slenderness and grace,
With nodding rice-stems in her hair
And lilies in her face.
In flowers of grasses she is clad;
And as she moves along,
Birds greet her with their cooing glad
Like bracelets' tinkling song.

—Kalidasa, *Shakuntala*

Shakuntala, bright-eyed and beautiful, was born on 14 October 1919.

She was my mother's mother and she was born in the small town of Chindwada in the kingdom of Indore, which had been ruled by the Holkar kings for centuries. A few months after Shakun's birth, sharp January light slanted over the fields of sugarcane, tinting the grasses bright fluorescent green. There was a chill in the air that had nothing to do with the winter weather. Two young schoolboys chattered as they pushed their way through the tall, sharp leaf stalks on their way home from school. Suddenly they froze, gaping at the sight before them.

There was their handsome young principal, body propped up against the sweet stems of sugar as if he was leaning against the school wall smoking a cigarette. He was staring at them fixedly. A lock of silky, coal-black hair had fallen over his forehead and his mouth was slightly open. He looked surprised to see them.

'Wait,' said one of the boys, 'He is not looking at us at all. Oh my God!' For it slowly dawned on them that the man's eyes were unseeing, his arms hung slackly by his side, and his body drooped unnaturally towards the ground. That was when they noticed the dried blood on the side of his face. They turned to each other in horror, the beginnings of shock and fear washing over them and breaking into the waves of their screams that swished over the fields, bringing other villagers there in a backwash of alarm.

It was 1920 and Shankar Manjrekar's children had just become orphans. His youngest, Shakuntala, was barely three months old when her father was found dead. Had he been murdered or was it suicide? To this day, his death is still a mystery. But he was not the only one who died that day. Life also ended for his beautiful young widow Parvati, twenty-five years old and already mother of four. Her fate was to continue breathing.

When Parvati heard the news of Shankar's death, she screamed, *'Naahi, naahi, naahi.'* Her tiny frame wrenched and writhed as her little sons held her arms. Turning to and fro, she broke her green glass bangles in her struggle to break loose. In the corner of the room, swinging in her little wooden cradle, her baby Shakuntala blinked at the sounds of her screams, unaware that her life had changed forever. At last, Parvati's body stilled. She lay exhausted on the floor as her relatives swooped in to pick up her baby, caress her other children's heads, and start talking in whispers about the funeral.

In Parvati's mind, her baby Shakuntala's birth became connected as strong as an umbilical cord to the memory of Shankar's death. Her grief and resentment became my grandmother's burden all of her ninety-two years. In those days, there were no therapists on whose couch she could or would have lain to share her pain. My grandmother just hefted rejection onto her broad shoulders, fashioned herself a protective armour of aloofness and distance, and immersed herself in hard work and then, after she found him, in her husband's love.

To make up for the parental rejection she had faced, she suffused her children's lives with love and selfless caring. She did not talk to her grandchildren about her father because she had no memories of him. And though she looked after her mother in her old age, she did not talk about her much either because she had no real happy stories to share.

Shankar was only twenty-eight when he died. His untimely death left Parvati without any means of supporting her young family, in an era when upper-caste women could neither work outside the house nor remarry. In the first half of the twentieth century, widows were destined to a life of servitude to anyone kind enough to take them in. Their heads were shaved, the kunku on their foreheads symbolically smeared and never reapplied, their bangles and wedding necklaces set aside for their children, and their colourful saris and tinkling anklets taken away.

You could tell a widow by her shaven head, unornamented arms and neck, and the unembellished, white cotton or brick-red sari she wore, often without the support of a blouse—which also served as a bra in the old days—or petticoat. A widow, whether she was fourteen or thirty-five, was doomed to a life of austerity and celibacy and her lack of protection from a husband meant she was vulnerable, frequently taken advantage of by other men in her household.

Parvati, my great-grandmother, was fortunate that this was not her fate. She wore light coloured saris and no jewellery, but her head was not shorn. She did not remarry, but her brother-in-law welcomed her family into his home with an open and pure heart. Parvati's children—Shakun, Divakar, Kamlakar and the oldest, Vatsala who was eight or nine and married within a few years—grew up in the huge wada that was the Manjrekars' ancestral home in nearby Chindwada.

The house was built as a rectangle, in traditional Marathi fashion, around a courtyard with more rooms than a young child could count or venture into. The brick and wood structure housed receiving rooms, verandahs, bedrooms, offices, kitchen, granary, storerooms, outhouses, and servants' quarters. The fatherless Shakun spent her childhood surrounded by loving adults and nurturing older siblings and cousins. Her older sister was a second, perhaps more affectionate mother to her, and they remained close all their lives. At playtime, she skipped in her purple and pink cotton parkar polkuh to the Bodri stream round which the town was built. She waded in the shallow water and caught minnows in her palms. Sometimes, she ducked into a little Shiva temple by the water's edge to say namaskar. Her father's name, Shankar, was another name for Shiva and standing barefoot on the cold stone floor in the cool, dark sanctum sanctorum, she thought about her father and felt his closeness.

His brother, Shakun's uncle, treated his nieces and nephews as his own children, and the cousins were raised as siblings. Amongst them all, Shakun shone like a precious gem, exquisite with dark doe eyes, fine skin, a regally aquiline nose, and a glowing blush that made any man who saw her want to protect her for life.

When she was fourteen, she was walking down a Chindwada road in the rain one monsoon, with a sturdy black umbrella to keep her dry. She weighed so little that when a heavy wind blew, it lifted her off the ground and carried her a few feet away. But she was not then nor ever a lightweight. Somewhat surprised by her flight, she giggled. Landing firmly on her feet, she continued on her way, undeterred. At eighteen, Shakun had become a statuesque five feet four inches, towering above her classmates. She had a giant's limbs and tall frame on which rested a sprite's delicately boned face. Perhaps her hands and feet, the largest I have ever seen on a woman, made her self-conscious. She liked to melt in the background in any social setting. She did not fuss about clothes and hair, but she had an understanding of her beauty and valued it. Shakun also had a quirky sense of humour and an air of calm that could be read as coldness. There was resignation and a willingness to take what life would dish out. Mostly she often seemed to be waiting, waiting serenely for her Prince Charming to arrive and carry her off into another, sunburst-filled life.

That year, her older brother Kamlakar went off to study at Benares Hindu University in the holy town of Varanasi on the banks of the sacred Ganga. He met a handsome young chemistry senior there named Sadanand Sirsikar who had come from Nagpur. The two became friends and ended up sharing lodgings in the old city. As Kamlakar got to know the vivacious, cheerful young man, a plan started forming in his head. Kama thought his friend was handsome, gregarious and amusing. Sirsikar's future lay shimmering before him and Kamaa decided it was time his friend thought of marriage. He also had a clever notion of how to pay his loving uncle back for all his kindness to Kama's family since Shankar's death. Kama's cousin Pramila was of marriageable age and Sadanand would be perfect for her. Now how to get the two to meet?

One day, he invited Sirsikar out for a cup of chai. 'I was thinking, Sirsikar,' he said, as they stood on a street corner, blowing into terracotta cups of spiced tea to cool them down. 'I'm going home in April. Come spend the holidays. The cousins are fun and there's so much to do. We can go for walks and play tennis and have picnics by the river…oh, and the mangoes will be ripe! It'll be a change from Nagpur.'

Hmm, thought Sadanand, why not? Impulsively he replied, 'That's a good idea. My mother will miss my being home but you know, it sounds like fun, I need a break. Thank you. This semester was gruelling.'

'And so were the protests you took part in,' joked his friend. Sadanand grinned. He had recently joined the university's Marxist party and was taking part in late-night meetings and protest marches against the British rulers of India. 'Yes, I'd love to come to Chindwada with you.'

So, Sadanand and Kama arrived there early one morning and walked in the blazing summer heat from the railway station to the Manjrekar Wada. Kama's mother Parvati greeted them, pulling her son's head down to plant a kiss on his forehead and smiling at Sadanand.

'*Thodasaa chahah ghyal na?*' she inquired formally of her guest. 'Some tea?' Over tea and biscuits, Sadanand met the Manjrekar clan. All the boys' names ended in 'kar': Kamlakar, Ratnakar, Divakar and the girls had names ending in 'a'. Manjula, Nirmala, Kamala. He nodded hello to each as they were introduced.

'And this is Pramila,' said Kamlakar, a certain insistence in his voice, pulling towards him a pretty, round-faced young girl with curly hair in braids.

Sadanand smiled at Pramila but his eyes had become fixed on the girl behind her. She stood, eyes cast down as her brother finally introduced her. 'This is the baby of our family,' said Kamlakar, putting his arm around her. 'Shakun.'

Do you believe in love at first sight? It happened for Sadanand and Shakuntala at that moment. Her soft, shy eyes looked up at the newcomer and saw his smiling brown ones gleaming down at her. His smile, joyful life bubbling and spilling out of it, captivated her instantly. She found herself smiling, no, grinning broadly back at him with uncharacteristic abandon. There was a joy and vibrancy and completion coursing through her that she had never known before. Try as Kamlakar might for the rest of the visit to bring Sadanand and Pramila together, it was futile.

'What is this Prami, Prami you're harping on about?' Sadanand asked him after he had tried in vain for days to put his cousin and his friend together. 'Once you've seen Shakun, you don't see anyone else.'

Kama shrugged in resignation and grinned. Oh well, he

thought. But his desire to repay his uncle was finally fulfilled. Another university friend of his met Prami, fell in love, and married her, making my great-uncle breathe a sigh of relief. The following summer, after a year of correspondence with her love, my grandmother Shakuntala ran away to Varanasi where Sadanand was finishing his master's degree. They lived together in a one-room lodging and Shakun took a job at a local girls' school as a physical education teacher, so she could support them. Soon, Sadanand wrote to his parents about her and their plans to be together.

'Come to Nagpur,' his father wrote back. 'Get married here. And, for God's sake, get a job. You have a wife to support now.'

So my grandfather left his degree unfinished and the young couple packed up and moved to the Sirsikar family home in Nagpur. Sadanand's mother, Lakshmi, treated Shakun like a pariah for living with her son out of wedlock. It was only 1940, after all, and what my grandmother had done would have been considered outrageous anywhere in the world. Then in September 1941, Shakun did exactly as she ought in producing an heir. Ramesh arrived, bouncing, chubby, pink, and best of all, male. My grandmother was forgiven and took her esteemed place in the family as a respected daughter-in-law. I don't know if it was a consequence of age or of her mother-in-law's disapproval, but my grandmother grew more conventional about her own past and never talked to anyone about living with Anna in Benares. What she never hid was her deep and enduring love for her husband, whom she privately called her king, 'Rajan.' Decades of marriage did not sour their love.

I was proud that she had flouted convention to follow her heart to the man she loved.

10. Prajakta's Tale

One must live as if it would be forever, and as if one might die each moment. Always both at once.

—Mary Renault, writer

Every morning, the tree showered down its white petalled, orange-stemmed beauty.

Vahini and Anna's garden in Dehu was a magical wonderland. My grandfather planted coconut palms, tamarind, mango and lemon trees, and the easy-to-climb red and white guava that stood just behind the twin houses. We would scramble up their pale-barked branches, pluck ripe guavas and sit in the trees, biting into the tender fuchsia flesh and inhaling their slightly acrid aroma. We could not reach the fruit on the higher branches but my grandmother would often hitch up her sari and come out to gather them. She climbed surefooted, stepping from branch to branch like a young girl. Grandmas didn't do that, did they? Ours did and we marvelled at her daring and athleticism. We helped her gather guavas in a shallow basket and she whisked it away to turn into candy.

In the garden's early days, Dad was often to be seen, shovel in hand, digging water channels, weeding, plucking off dead leaves, and planting. There were flowers everywhere. We made chains of red and white madhumalati, which burdened their vines on Anna's front verandah. Delicate white and yellow roses grew outside the kitchen window. Vahini gathered fragrant jasmine for her morning puja. There were Krishnakamal, feathery purple petals arranged around the stamen; a circle of dancing cowgirls surrounding the mischievous, flute-playing cowherd god, Krishna. These were the flowers of the passion fruit. The oddly unappealing hard, smooth yellow skins of the fruit yielded pulpy sunset flesh that Vahini transformed into sherbet.

At the southwestern end of the garden was the thin-trunked prajakta. Every morning, Anna woke up and shuffled out to the verandah in his white kurta-pajama, a cane or a grandchild for support. He would take a few turns in the garden to stretch his legs, then head to the prajakta to collect flowers for his beloved. He bent from the waist painfully, inch by inch, arm slowly extending to reach the flowers that had spread an orange and white carpet on the red earth. Tenderly carrying them in his palm, he headed back to his heavy wooden chair. Unable to control his downward motion because of his stiff arthritic knees, Anna simply trusted the chair to hold him. My father had placed it close to the outside wall of the living room so it could not tip over when Anna landed.

The sun was rising and a cool breeze blowing across the plain as my grandfather reached for the *Indian Express* and Vahini brought out his scalding hot tea. He took her hand and placed the flowers in it, looking up at her with his heart in his eyes. She always smiled and blushed. Breathing in the flowers' heavenly perfume, she gently placed them before her silver deities or because they were too tiny to stand in a vase, floated them in water. There is something so beguiling about a man who has been married for forty years giving flowers to his beloved every morning. Not hothouse roses but hand-picked real flowers. Those tiny five-petalled, divinely scented blossoms with the bright orange stems are the ones I want growing in my garden one day. They are the flowers my parents planted in their Hyderabad garden in honour of my wedding. My childish heart had been captivated by the heartbreaking myth I had read about them, and they haunted me wherever I went. When we moved abroad, the scent came along in my nostrils.

Prajakta is the Marathi name for parijat or night-flowering or coral jasmine (*Nyctanthes arbor-tristes*), aptly known in India as a 'heavenly' flower. It is said that Vishnu the Preserver's throne sat under the tree and Hanuman, the monkey god of the *Ramayana*, liked to sleep in its fragrant shade. But it was the cocky mischief-maker Krishna who is said to have brought the tree to earth to please and appease his wife Satyabhama and his lover, Rukmini. He cleverly planted the prajakta at the edge of Satyabhama's courtyard so that the blossoms also rained into her neighbour Rukmini's garden, keeping both women content. But the prajakta story I fell in love with when I was six and at my most romantic, was different.

A long time ago, a young princess named Prajakta, fell in love with Aditya, the dazzlingly handsome sun god. He dallied with her, as gods everywhere are wont to do, and then moved on. The princess was so devastated that she killed herself. It is said that the prajakta tree sprang up from her ashes and that, even in death, the broken-hearted girl is unable to bear the sight of her scornful lover. She rains her sad flowers face-down onto the earth just before the sun rises. The petals are pure white like the love of the princess, the stems as orange as a magnificent sunrise, the fragrance as intoxicating and unearthly as she found the sun god.

After I was married and living in Bombay, I visited my parents in Hyderabad frequently. Each morning I would wake up and head down to their garden where my prajakta stood. Mom and Dad were waiting for me, with hot tea and a handful of fragrant flowers at my spot on the porch steps. I sipped my tea, sniffing the blossoms and admiring the ones Dad especially left under the tree for me to see. Even when I was far away, the prajakta was a part of my life. Dad would send me a daily tally by email of the flowers he counted under the tree each morning, 1,200; 1,750; 1,004. But even if there were only one, it would not matter.

I could smell its perfume in my nose, hold its soft beauty in my hand and know that it was an avatar of my grandparents' intoxicated, undying love.

11. Until Death Do We...

In every frame upon our wall
Lies a face that's seen it all
Through ups and downs and then more downs
We helped each other up off the ground.
No one knows what we've been through
Making it ain't making it without you.

—Train, 'About to Come Alive'

Anna-Vahini's children worried about what would happen to Anna if Vahini died before him.

But my grandfather had a way of taking care of things. He went first, dying as he had lived, swiftly and in the moment. All his affairs were in order and the thought of what mattered most to him was expressed in his last breath. My grandmother's name was on his lips.

'Shakun...' he cried as the heart attack overtook him and stilled his breath forever. He was just seventy-one. My grandmother had run to the living room to phone for Dr Joshi. So in death, Anna was alone, a fact that Vahini never ceased to regret. They had been together almost fifty years and even towards what was the end of their life together, Vahini still blushed when he complimented her, looking into her eyes and telling her how beautiful she was. I do not know more than the periphery of their love. That garden was theirs alone.

But Anna and I were kindred spirits in our own way. We were both rogues and we could communicate without words. We would look at each other across a room full of people and wordlessly share a joke or an observation. We found the same things funny. So closely connected were we that when I was fourteen, I had a premonition that he would die when I was twenty. Every night when I said my prayers, I asked God to give Anna and Vahini long, healthy lives.

We stopped to visit Anna late that August in 1988. My brother Sameer and I had spent a few days in Bombay with my boyfriend Rajeev and our friend Julia Bentley, and were heading back home to Hyderabad. Since our train was not till four that afternoon, we had three hours to visit Anna and Vahini who were staying with my uncle Ramesh at the cantonment in Wanowari, on the southeastern edge of Poona.

We lay on the carpet watching cricket on TV and chatting with Anna while Vahini and my aunt Madhavi cooked lunch. Anna was happy to see us and seemed his healthy, jovial self. Soon after we had eaten, Sam and I drove away, bags piled high in a rickshaw to catch our train at Poona station. There was no reason for us to think that was our last meeting. But I looked out of the rickshaw's open door to wave to Anna where he stood in the doorway, watching us till we were out of sight. I saw him, leaning on his wooden cane with one gnarled hand, waving to me with the other, a sweet smile spread across glowing cheeks and I knew I would never see him alive again. He was saying a final goodbye.

Three weeks later, just after my twentieth birthday, Anna died of a myocardial infarction, pulling the proverbial rug out from under my feet. I was startled a few days after his death to receive a letter from him. He had mailed it the week before he died and it was very much a farewell. He told me how much he loved me and how proud he and Vahini were of me. 'Come September and we remember our pretty little Banna,' he began, going on to tell me to keep pursuing my dreams. He was certain I would get where I wanted to go.

The previous February, Anna threw a great party for his seventieth birthday. The family converged to celebrate him and spend a week together as a family. 'I'd like to give all the grandchildren a gift on my birthday,' he told Mom. 'Something to remember me by, something they can cherish.'

Mom and her siblings put their heads together to come up with ideas. Finally, my grandfather decided to have silver necklaces made for everyone, with a heart-shaped locket. In the centre of it was an Om. As with most transactions Anna made, he was gypped. The necklaces were silver, to be sure, but their quality was suspect. It didn't matter. As soon as he handed them out, we all put them around our necks. I wore mine day and night.

Nineteen and in the second year of my undergraduate degree at St Francis College in Secunderabad, a memento from my grandfather who lived almost 500 miles away was welcome because it connected us so tangibly. The first time the necklace broke, a few months after I'd received it, I was aggravated but nothing more. It just came apart in my hand when I reached up to my neck to touch it.

'I'll have it repaired,' Mom reassured me. So I gave it to her and went to sleep with a bare neck. The next morning, I heard at college that the dear friend of a friend had died in a tragic accident the day before. Our circle was abuzz with the news, the details of the accident and the inevitable gossip that follows in the wake of tragedy.

Mom had the necklace repaired a few days later and put it around my neck again. As with whatever one wears constantly, it became a part of me, its weight on my neck a comforting knowledge and solace. Then a few months later, it broke again. I was standing at the bus stop and was lucky to catch the broken chain links and the little locket as they fell. Sighing, I put them in my pocket, an ominous feeling coming over me as I boarded the bus. The next day, I was still inexplicably despondent as I headed back into the city.

'Hi,' said my friend Elahe morosely when I arrived at St Francis College. Her tone of voice as she walked over to me slowly alarmed me.

'What's wrong?'

'I have some bad news.'

'Oh no,' I replied, my heart sinking. 'What?'

'Veda's father died.'

'What? How could he? What happened?' Mr Srinivasan was in his forties.

'He was in an accident last night. He skidded off his motorbike. I think he died instantly, yaar.' She shook her head. For us, this second death, another accident, was both strange and incomprehensible.

'Oh God. Poor Veda.' It was too much to contemplate. When our group of friends had gathered, we left en masse for Veda's to comfort her and her family. The thought came to my superstitious teenage mind that my necklace was bad luck. Had I somehow caused this to happen?

Going home on the rickety university bus that evening, I had plenty of time to think. I looked at the elephantine boulders and still pools of water that dotted my route out of the city and to the university campus where I lived. They had been there for millions of years. People on the other hand? Gone in the blink of an eye. If my necklace breaks again, I thought reluctantly, it won't be good. It'll be Anna next, I know.

Mom had the chain fixed once more, remarking at how shoddily it had been made. This time I was loath to put it around my neck so I shoved it under my pillow where it lived for a few months. Finally, I pooh-poohed my superstitiousness and clasped it around my neck. A month later, I put my hand up to touch the necklace and it broke in three places. With a feeling of dread, I put it deep into a drawer in my mother's cupboard and tried to forget about it. Around five o'clock the next morning, we got a phone call telling us that Anna had died.

My mother fainted in the hallway, hitting her head on the kitchen doorjamb. We rushed to help her up and then I rushed to town to book train tickets while my parents packed and closed up the apartment. Crying had to wait till I was in my best friend Mona's arms and her kisses on my cheek made me loosen the tears inside. Then, before we knew it, we were on the Secunderabad Express, a night train heading west to Poona where my uncle would meet us and take us to Dehu. I did not want to go to for the funeral, but Mom was reluctant to leave me alone in Hyderabad. Although I inwardly railed at her on our long, painful journey where everyone's thoughts and memories held them captive, when I saw Anna's body, I realized she was right.

Hindu corpses are cremated right after death to prevent their rotting in the heat. My mother asked that her family wait for her to arrive before cremating her father. Almost twenty-four hours after Anna's death, I stepped gingerly into the living room where I had spent so many hours with him. His body lay waiting for us, on huge blocks of ice to slow down its deterioration. The ice was melting into puddles of grief on the floor. The room was filled with relatives who had gathered to pay their respects. Villagers hung about on the main road outside, saying namaskar to the family as they came and went, just waiting for a glimpse of the Colonel Saheb who had been a de facto village elder; kind, magnanimous, a permanent feature on the Dehu thoroughfare.

I had suffered nightmares about death as a child but I was calm and unafraid now. All the scary movies that had kept me awake nights, all the creepy stories about corpses, my years-old fear of ghosts, disappeared in the chill air of my grandfather's living room. Before me was the person I loved, his arms grey-blue-skinned now like Krishna's, his eyes closed as if he were napping. His cheeks were as rosy as ever and he looked peaceful. There was that naughty smile on his face. How could he be smiling? Is that how he had looked as he breathed his last breath? Enjoying the joke? I grinned, my eyes filling with tears as I bent down and kissed him. His stubble was prickly against my lips but his cheeks felt as they always had.

Some kind soul murmured consoling words. 'He has joined his parents,' said the grating voice, 'You know how he loved them.'

You know nothing, I thought, raising my eyebrows disparagingly.

*

Anna might seem to have found peace, but I knew his heart was troubled because he had left behind the one person he wanted to care for, my grandmother. What would happen to her now? I don't really remember what Vahini looked like that day or whether I hugged her or consoled her. I think she was a sliver of herself, a mere shadow from which the image had been taken away. More than likely, I did not say much to her because I was as self-involved as any twenty-year-old and she and I were each cocooned in our own separate grief.

While Vahini was surrounded by those who tried to comfort her and ease her pain—her daughters, her sons and sons-in-law, and her older brother Kamlakar who had introduced her to Anna over half a century before—some wondered why I was so heartbroken. I did not expect them to understand. I was grappling with the realization that this man who had been there my whole life had left me.

Women in India do not customarily go to the cremation grounds for funerals. But I intended to. No one, not even the gaggle of bustling, annoying, opinionated aunts and uncles flapping around my family, demurred. My cousins Reena and Neena went along too, all of us riding in the back of the huge olive-green army truck that came to carry Anna away. I stood right next to his body, touching the skin of his arm and memorizing every detail of every feature of his face.

At the crematorium, I stood a little apart from the rituals taking place. The body was laid on a funeral pyre, wooden logs stacked four feet high. There were salutes, rifles shot in the air. The priests slipped little batons of sandalwood into the pyre to scent it, then it was lit and was quickly ablaze. I watched the bright orange flames that looked like the fragrant Alphonso mangoes Anna lovingly bought for us each summer, I watched those flames feeding on him and the dark grey clouds of smoke rising above them. My tears were a river overflowing its banks, the pain never-ending.

We must have stayed only twenty minutes as Anna's body headed wherever it had to go but it was an eternity. Reena who was only twelve and had been in the house when Anna died, clutched my arm. We drove home in the big, empty truck and for the first time in my life, Manju Lakshmi was without my grandfather. Out of sheer force of habit, I went straight to his bedroom. It was occupied by people sitting on Vahini's side of the bed, talking to her in low whispers. I climbed onto Anna's side, then rolled into my dip. I lay face down, and breathed his pillow, which had his smell on it, intoxicatingly comforting. In its fragrance was Anna, still there for me. I clung to that pillowcase for two years, unwashed, so I could keep him near.

For six months I cried myself to sleep and every night Anna was in my dreams, shuffling along the verandah to the prajakta tree or lying on his bed, listening to the radio, one arm overhead in a gesture I've inherited. He was happy. I felt the stubble on his cheek when I bent to kiss him and tell him how much I loved him. He hugged me and wrapped me in his love, knowing I needed his help to deal with the bitter sorrow of his death. When I gained normalcy and was beginning to feel alive again, looking ahead to my next step in life—journalism school in Bombay—Anna could rest easy. I never dreamt of him again.

As I went on with my life, his soul found its resting place.

12. Carry Your Heart

i carry your heart with me (i carry it in
my heart) i am never without it (anywhere
i go you go, my dear; and whatever is done
by only me is your doing, my darling).

—ee cummings

For my grandmother, it was another story. Her mourning did not end for the next twenty-three years. She lived into the next century, dying at the age of ninety-two in 2011. For fifteen years before that she had not been in control of her own kitchen or even her home, having willingly handed over the 'keys' to her eldest son Ramesh and his wife who retired to Manju Lakshmi in 1996.

Her four children shared the responsibility of looking after Vahini. She stayed with each for three months at a time, but a day came when she didn't want to travel anymore. She had a point. 'Manju Lakshmi is my home. I don't want to live anywhere else.'

She kept the bedroom she and Anna had shared for thirty years but she began to be restricted to it, rarely even able to step out for exercise, the one thing that had kept her vibrant and strong most of her life. And she began to retreat. As happy as she was to see visitors, as regularly as she kept in touch through letters with children, nieces, nephews, grandchildren and her few remaining contemporaries, she was equally happy reading, finishing one or two novels a day, and watching her beloved Hindi films on television.

'*Arre, arre,*' she would call out as the film's hero battled the villain and as the fighting continued, she periodically warned him, 'He's behind you, watch out!' or 'Oh no, he's going to hit you!'

Mom and I visited Vahini as often as possible. Mom reminisced with her mother, helped her exercise, and they played gin rummy together. But Vahini had been going deaf for years and conversations were increasingly one-sided, her talking and the other person listening. Since she was also not much of a talker, this meant conversations were short or stilted.

As for me, as soon as I arrived at Manju Lakshmi, I made a beeline for her bedroom to give her a hug. I stared at her lovely mysterious face and the long, restless fingers that tattooed a rhythm on the arm of her chair, even as she sat calm and still, humming a tune, tapping her right foot gently, waiting for something to happen. She looked forward to my visits and although she did not always remember her other grandchildren and great-grandchildren's names, she never forgot Keya's or mine. My daughter, when she was a toddler, had stroked my grandmother's soft, wrinkled arms in wonder and made it her job to feed Vahini her medicine each morning. 'I want to dive it to you,' Keya said, making my grandmother chuckle.

When I visited, if my grandmother had just woken up, she would move to an armchair and comb her hair as she always did after her nap. She peered into the stand mirror on the octagonal Kashmiri walnut table and combed the still dark but now thinning hair carefully into a minuscule bun. A humourous glint came into her eyes.

'*Devaala me praarthana karthe, takal padaachya aadhi, mala gheyun ja*' ('I pray to God, please take me before I go bald'), she'd say wryly, looking at me. She deliberated with her kunku, making sure it was in just the right spot on her forehead. It was such a beloved ritual that her daughters had asked her not to smear her kunku in a symbolic sign of grieving as some widows did. Tradition be damned. They also insisted she not conform to Hindu convention, wearing white or foregoing her wedding bangles because Vahini enjoyed presenting herself to the world, elegant and put together. Why should the woman raised by a widow have to dress like one too?

In 2011, *Saveur* magazine asked me to travel to India to research and write a story about the food of my in-laws who belonged to the northwestern region called the Sindh, which had become part of Pakistan after the 1947 Partition. I had travelled to India already that spring so this trip was an unexpected treat and an opportunity to write for a magazine I admired. I spent three weeks travelling in Gujarat and Maharashtra for my story, then headed to Poona to visit family. I stopped in Dehu to see my grandmother who had recently been admitted to a 'senior facility,' about ten miles east of her home.

My rental car driver took me down country roads, past the familiar army cantonment and bungalows I had grown up with, past the Ai Appa temple on the hill where Radha and I had scampered, past my grandparents' bungalow. As we passed Manju Lakshmi, I turned and peered into the driveway. I saw where Anna had sat every day, rain or shine, I saw where his old LandMaster used to stand and where my uncle's car was now parked, I saw the trees we climbed. There were no people about and the place looked deserted, lifeless, devoid of the soul it had possessed when it was my grandparents' home. I took it all in one last time and turned my head away resolutely for I would never visit again. There was no reason to set foot there.

On we drove, past the temple at Dehu where Tukaram worshipped, over the Indrayani river, away from the golden hills and tiny villages that I knew. My sweet cousin Reena had come along because she knew I would never find my way there unguided. I turned and looked at her questioningly. Where the hell are we going? my eyes asked. After aeons, we arrived at the outskirts of a tiny village and followed narrow lanes half-covered by the listing wooden balconies of decrepit houses. We turned onto a dirt road and drove to the very end, beyond which stretched fields of sorghum and sugar cane, a landscape I would have admired on any other day.

Reena asked the driver to pull up in front of a modest, pink stucco house with a tiled courtyard. I looked wonderingly again at her and she gently put her hand on my arm. The family knew how devoted I was to my grandparents. I was speechless. My grandmother, once queen of her realm, had been relegated to this no man's land? We walked up narrow stairs together. Evidently this was not a nursing home. A kind ex-lawyer had turned her house into an old folks' shelter for people who could not look after themselves or whose families had abandoned them.

In the front room were three metal cots. A stray dog wandered in. Two wretched old men and a feeble woman sat cross-legged on the beds, leaning against the roughly plastered walls. They stared into space, nothing left to do but await the freedom that death would bring. I choked. My cousin headed towards my grandmother's private room. I peeped in past an old patterned cloth curtain hanging in the doorway. There lay my beautiful Amazon, diminished, shorter now than my four-foot-eight-inch daughter. Lying on her side on a hospital bed covered with her own flower printed cotton sheets, still regal, still alive but uncharacteristically helpless. Around her rose diseased-pink plaster walls. Garish yellow plastic flowers were stuck in a black plastic vase that even its makers could not have imagined was attractive. They blocked from view a photograph of my grandfather on the tiny corner shelf. It was carelessly turned away from Vahini too, so she couldn't not see him. Nor could she reach her books perched at the end of the shelf.

The lawyer-turned-nurse was lovingly chatting with Vahini as she gave her some medicine. My grandmother looked up as Reena cheerfully bustled in. I stood uncertainly in the doorway and watched her swallow the pills. I am not a cryer and I tried for calm. But the tears would not listen. They gushed up and flowed out of me rapidly. Before I knew it, I was sobbing, heaving, hiding my face in my scarf and backing out into the hallway so Vahini wouldn't see or hear me. Watching this proud woman being cared for by strangers who knew nothing about her was more than I could stand. Could Anna, she, or anyone else who loved her have imagined this fate? It took almost ten minutes for my tears to slow and come to a halt. Wiping my face and breathing deep, I swept into Vahini's room.

'Hi, Aji,' I said cheerfully, peering down at her.

Ninety-two and sharp as a tack. 'Hello,' she replied, '*Kashi ahes*? How's Sanjiv? Keya?'

'They're fine, Aji,' I said, 'They send you lots of love. And Keya sent you these.' I handed her a box of dark chocolates. So starved was my grandmother for intellectual stimulation that she started reading the nutritional information on the box. Then she wanted to know what my shirt said.

'Amsterdam,' I smiled, 'where life gets lived. Remember I went there with Sameera and Jagruti for our fortieth celebration?'

She nodded. I looked at her hand on which was a swelling as big as a tennis ball, some kind of water blister. I touched it gently, then touched each of her large hands with their oval nails, staring at them intently. When I looked back at her face, her eyes were telling me multitudes of stories.

'I love you, Aji,' I said, my tears flowing again and dripping onto her soft skin.

And my stone-deaf grandmother replied, an upward lilt to her voice, 'I love you too-oo.'

I will never forget the sound of her voice as she spoke those words, willing me to be cheerful. I smiled down at her. She stared fixedly at me, eyes overflowing with love, telling me all I needed to know for a lifetime. If I had never known Vahini before, I knew her profoundly in that moment.

That was the last time I saw my lovely grandmother. We left not long after, my head working overtime to figure out how to get her out of that place. Could I move to Dehu and look after her? Could anyone? My mother tried to pacify me because I had to return to Los Angeles and my daughter a few days later. When I left, I was still trying to work out the logistics of looking after my grandmother so she could die in the company of someone who loved her.

It was not to be. She had only been waiting to see me. For the last few days of August and the first few days of September, I prayed to my God that Vahini be spared any more suffering. I had never thought I would ask for a loved one to be released from this life. But now I did so fervently. On 6 September 2011, my forty-third birthday, I begged for that one gift again. But she did not want to go on that day. Three nights later, about three or four in the morning, when it was still dark outside, strong gusts of wind pushed the wooden window blinds about in my bedroom in Glendale. They rattled and heaved. I opened my eyes and even as my heart sank, I smiled. It was a breeze that had travelled across the world to bring me a message. Then I fell into a deep sleep, one I had not had for weeks. In the morning, my brother called to tell me that Vahini was gone. Her prayers—and mine—were answered.

Death had parted them in 1988, but Shakun and her Beloved are together once again in some Great Beyond of Peace.

13. Me? Sudhakar...

You take a different view of your actions when you come to understand, when you are made to understand every day that your existence is necessary—you see, absolutely necessary—to another person.

—Joseph Conrad, *Lord Jim*

Fergusson College was a place where people fell in love.

In 1965, my parents fell in love there, not in the gardens, cafeteria or student lounge, but in a dusty classroom over a book; to be precise, over Joseph Conrad's tragic story, *Lord Jim*.

The students in the second year BA English class were interested in the novel, but they were more entertained by the discussions it generated between their teacher and one particular student, a young man named Sudhakar Marathe. Six feet tall, a rarity in his generation, he was so lanky as to be almost one-dimensional. Khaki drainpipe pants encased his thin legs and the black soda-water bottle glasses he wore rested on unusually large ears. Earnest and scholarly, he always strode into class on time and walked right to the back of the large lecture hall. There he took a seat in the last row, from where he could critically survey his teacher and classmates. A lock of silky brown hair fell over his piercing blue-grey eyes and he pushed it back quickly, before opening his copy of *Lord Jim* and looking at his notes, written in an immaculate hand. The other students chatted and joked till their teacher entered the room.

Some boys were gathered near a desk at the front where Meera, a fun-loving twenty-year-old, sat. Her curly, ebony hair bounced around sparkling eyes and a mouth that smiled, even without provocation. Resting her elbow on a friend's shoulder, she chatted easily with everyone around her.

She and Sudhakar had never spoken to each other though. He glanced in her direction briefly and thought he would really like to talk to her one day. He smiled at the laughter, free and generous, which lit up her face. Then he turned back to his notes. The teacher cleared his throat and began to read as the class settled down. Meera continued to whisper with her seatmate but Sudhakar paid close attention to the lecture, frequently raising his hand to ask piercing questions about the plot, the character, Joseph Conrad's style. This was not the norm at a time when a guru's words were still held as the gospel truth. The teacher sighed. This boy was full of thoughts and ideas, not just about the book but about the world at large. 'Yes, Marathe?' he asked and the class turned around as one to hear Sudhakar's question.

Meera mouthed, 'There goes Lord Slim again!' to her friend Neera, her amused laugh echoing through the high-ceilinged classroom. The teacher looked weary. He was not capable of discussing *Lord Jim* the way the young man wanted. After a few weeks of this, anytime Sudhakar raised his hand, his teacher quickly surrendered.

'You can have it, Marathe, you can have it,' he gasped, by which he meant, 'You win, Marathe, I don't understand your questions and I cannot argue with you in any meaningful way. You are right, let's move on, shall we, so I can get through this damn syllabus.'

Meera thought to herself, how interesting and intelligent Sudhakar is. I hope we can get to know each other better. The rest of the class giggled at their teacher's frustration and looked in admiration at my father. They could not have guessed that Sudhakar had only begun studying English when he was in the eighth grade.

Whenever he turned his attention to a subject, he worked tirelessly and enthusiastically to understand and master it, and so it was with learning English. My father read incessantly, an Oxford English Dictionary his constant companion, and he studied grammar, punctuation, style so that he could use the language correctly and precisely. To hear him speak today, you would not be able to tell that English was not his mother tongue, and it was he who taught me, years later, to avoid being sloppy with language, whichever one I chose to speak, to choose my words carefully after understanding what they really meant.

Dad belonged to the third generation of Marathes who attended Fergusson College after it opened its doors in 1885. My great-grandfather, Chintaman Gangadhar Marathe, enrolled in the first class that would graduate from the institution. But along with an education, the Marathes often found their life partners at Fergusson. My uncles, aunts, cousins, nephews and nieces all met their match, as it were, in those hallowed halls. Dad's parents, Veerbala Modak and Shrikrishna Marathe, fell in love on the campus in 1930, and when my parents were classmates thirty-five years later, Sudhakar was the hometown boy, Meera the foreigner.

A vibrant, cosmopolitan, young woman who had spent much of her life in north India, Meera Sirsikar had recently moved to Poona and found the town old-fashioned and staid. She did not speak the local language, Marathi, but was completely at home with English and Hindi. She did not know anyone local and she most definitely was not aware of the town's more conservative mores. Young Poona women wore only saris in the mid-1960s. My mother and her sister were modern in pleated skirts and blouses, or sleek, bespoke churidar-kurtas. They had matching chiffon chunnis on their shoulders, cunningly intricate coloured glass bangles on their wrists, matching chappals for each ensemble, in all colours of the rainbow. The local girls thought Meera and Maya were not as demure as they should be. They broke all sorts of taboos. They wore lipstick, ate ice cream, drank coffee, and talked freely to boys. The army and naval cadets studying at the defence academy nearby with the Sirsikar brothers, buzzed around the girls' fresh prettiness and charm. My mother and her sister attended parties at night—really? rode in cars with boys—oh my! and, it was whispered, even danced with them!

Meera had completed a year of pre-med but deciding not to pursue a medical career, she enrolled at Fergusson for her BA. She immediately became friendly with other army brats there: Neera Kapoor, Pippi Jatar and Tazeen Canteenwala. Their set embarked on the kind of social whirl they were already familiar with from army life in Delhi and Gurgaon, where Anna had commanded the Ammunition Depot. There were coffee breaks at Poona Coffee House and films at Rahul Cinema and parties to go to at the club. There was pocket money for rickshaws, treats, books. There was no lack of pleasure or luxury.

Sudhakar, born and raised within a few miles of the college, lived in a simpler, more frugal place, surrounded by people he had known all his life. Most had attended the same elementary school and walked or rode their bikes to Fergusson together every morning. They spoke Marathi almost exclusively and came from professional, middle-class backgrounds with no money for extras. Sudhakar was lucky, he had a merit scholarship, Rs 150 a month, which he used for tuition, books and school supplies so his parents did not have to pay for his education. Meera and her friends considered Sudhakar and his pals old-fashioned and conservative. His circle felt the 'foreigners' were out of their league. So my parents might never have gotten together had it not been for a get-well card.

A love of learning and language runs deep in Dad's family. His great-grandfather, V.A. Modak, studied Marathi and English, picked up other languages like Sindhi easily, and worked tirelessly to have regional Indian languages recognized as college courses under British colonial rule. My grandfather, Shrikrishna Marathe, an engineer, also studied English literature and was a Sanskrit scholar. From his tax collector father, he learned a Marathi shorthand accounting dialect known as Modi, which he used for private journals and in his forties, he taught himself Arabic. He wanted to read the Koran and understand what the text really said rather than how it had been perverted.

Like his father and grandfathers, Dad learned languages easily and enjoyed them. He inherited from the Modaks and Marathes the mind of a scientist and the soul and sensitivity of an artist. Sudhakar was one of those rare human beings who could have done anything and excelled at it. The other important facet of his character and heritage was civic-mindedness. He was raised to believe in good citizenry, in giving back to the community in which one grew up and flourished. He decided to study English and become a teacher, but he embarked on that path circuitously, trying other careers first. As it turned out, he was too thin for the Indian Air Force where he wanted to become a pilot, and although he gave engineering, a profession the Marathes seemed inclined to, a shot, after a year he decided it was not for him.

Like Sudhakar, Meera was the third of four children. In a photograph of her when she was eight, is a snub-nosed, strong-jawed little girl with long, thick, curly black hair. Staring directly at the photographer, her piercing eyes see everything and brook no nonsense. Meera was who she was from birth. Her sarcastic aunts gave her the nickname Miri, meaning black pepper, because of her temper. What they did not understand was that she was stubborn but not spoiled, strong-willed because she believed in justice and integrity, not because she was a brat. Both she and Sudhakar grew up misunderstood.

Meera was independent and clever, compassionate, always fighting for the downtrodden, the sinned against, be it her mother, a maid or a fellow student at school. She was fearless, ready to step in at any moment to protect the underdog, but never spoke a harsh or unkind word to anyone, no matter how much their behaviour might warrant it. All I ever heard her say sternly was, 'Look here!' as she approached a person who was bullying someone, cutting a queue or doing something illegal or unjust. She would point out their mistake and then suggest an option, much to our amusement and chagrin. Then she would proceed to chat with the person she'd just admonished, often inviting them over for lunch or tea. My mother made friends everywhere she went, and people remembered her warmly decades after they had met her.

In December 1965, her boyfriend Dee visited her in Dehu Road. They had met that May and he was so enchanted that he'd asked her to marry him. She was flattered but asked to get to know him before she gave him an answer. This cold December day, she smiled at him when he arrived and said simply, 'Yes.'

Dee was delighted. The two told her mother the news and Vahini beamed.

'Now,' said Meera, always energetic. 'You promised you were going to teach me how to ride a scooter, come on.'

Her family lived in army housing and the streets surrounding their colony were quiet and secluded. Up and down the road Dee and Meera went on her father's heavy Lambretta, stopping and starting as my mother learned to switch gears with one hand, accelerate with the other. She sat upright on the front seat while Dee sat behind her, directing.

'Turn left, Me,' he said, using her nickname, 'Slow down, ease up, brake now…brake, brake…Now! Me!'

The tyre hit a rock and sent the scooter flying onto the verge, throwing Meera up and over the handlebars. She landed in a ditch, unconscious, Dee fell a few feet away from her, his right leg bent at an unnatural angle. Vahini came running out from the house when she heard the screech of tyres and Dee's raised voice. The pair was rushed to the army hospital. My mother was admitted to the ICU and her fiancé was taken to Orthopaedics to have a cast put on his broken leg. For three days Meera lay unconscious in the intensive care unit, her head injury so severe that her family did not know if she would live or die. When her college mates heard that she was in the hospital, they came to visit, bringing flowers and good wishes. The first card she saw when she awoke from her coma and sat up in bed, was from Sudhakar, the earnest boy in her English class. A polite note written in a neat, slanted hand, nevertheless something in it made Meera read and reread it several times.

Then Sudhakar came with her other classmates to visit her at the hospital. The ice was broken and the two became friends. They stayed that way for a whole year until my mother knew for certain that she could not marry the man she was engaged to, and gently broke it off. When my parents began courting, they had embarked on their Masters degrees at Poona University. Meera took the train down from Dehu every morning and, without fail, Sudhakar was waiting for her at Khadki Railway Station, having bicycled all the way there from Prabhat Road. They walked together to the English department in the shade of the banyan trees, talking ceaselessly as young lovers do. Years later, whenever my brother Sameer and I walked with my parents on that road, Mom would put my little brother on her back and I would cling to Dad, my arms tight around his neck, and they would swing us back and forth on the aerial roots of the banyans, while we screamed with delight.

But right now, Sudhakar and Meera were just getting to know each other. They spent all day, every day together. After their classes were over, they sat in the library side by side, studying and writing long letters to each other on foolscap paper. In the evening, Sudhakar walked his love to the railway station to take the train to Dehu. He would hand her a letter to read on the way. Then he raced home to Prabhat Road on his bicycle while she made the half-hour trip to her parents' home. Since there was no phone at his house, Shree Ram Krupa, Sudhakar walked around the building to his cousin's bungalow. His aunt was expecting him. After all, he used the telephone every evening at the same time, dutifully leaving twenty-five paise on the table for his phone call each time.

14. Love & Marriage

Long engagements give people the opportunity of finding out each other's character before marriage, which is never advisable.

—Oscar Wilde, *The Importance of Being Earnest*

My parents never got engaged. They just got married. Thrice. Life with Mom and Dad was one endless celebration. They remembered birthdays, they celebrated all holidays: Hanukkah and Eid, Diwali and Christmas, and they observed all sorts of anniversaries: the day I learned to ride a bike or got into the school choir, the test at which Sam got his karate brown belt. For decades, we marked the day we left Canada to return to India by talking about our friends there and how wonderful our five-year sojourn had been. On my brother's death anniversary, my mother was melancholy but remembered Aditya with love. She and Dad served the students at a school for underprivileged children a special lunch and bought them school supplies.

Our kitchen cupboards were always bursting with homemade treats, but Mom was never too busy or too tired to make special desserts and snacks for festivals. They hosted dinner parties every week, and we often found little gifts from them: thoughtfully handmade cards, quirky notes, books, pressed leaves, a rose by my table setting one morning, an interesting rock from a hike. My parents celebrated life, and showed us in myriad ways the beauty and joy of the world we lived in. So it was not strange to us that they celebrated their three wedding anniversaries every year.

Their first marriage was in a Hindu temple on 16 December 1967. I was made that night. I know because I arrived nine months later. The second marriage was at the registrar's office the following April to make the union official, and since their families wanted a celebration, they tied the knot yet again at the end of that month. By that time my mother was four and a half months' pregnant with me but not showing at all.

When Sudhakar told his family that he wanted to marry Meera, the Marathe elders were perturbed. She was not Konkanastha nor light-skinned. It did not matter that she was lovely, that they liked her cheerful friendliness or that she made Sudhakar happy. It did matter that her people, the Saraswats, ate fish and meat. To the Marathes who did not even touch onion and garlic for religious reasons, this was highly taboo. The Sirsikars seemed dissipated in other ways too—they drank alcohol, entertained lavishly, and did not conform to the Marathes' spare, understated life. Dad's father, Appa, was concerned for another reason. He was not sure that this marriage would be built on a solid foundation. He visited Meera's father to voice his concerns.

'Your daughter wants to marry my son,' said Appa. 'But I'll be frank with you. We are not rich people. Sudhakar will never be more than a poor teacher, he won't be able to support her in the way she is used to living. Please ask her to reconsider.'

To which Anna replied, 'Thank you for thinking of my daughter's well-being. She knows what she is doing. If Meera has made up her mind to be with Sudhakar, she will do what it takes to be happy and for the marriage to succeed.'

Luxurious though her life was before she married, my mother never once regretted her decision, and although money may have been scarce at first, as it is for most young couples embarking on life's journey, both my parents were older and wiser than their twenty-three years. They managed within their means, saved consistently, and made sure their children never felt a want.

One of the secrets to the success of my parents' marriage is that they were friends before they fell in love, shared interests, respected each other, and liked to laugh together. After forty-seven years, Meera and Sudhakar still wake each morning, wanting to be with each other. The other important secret was that Mom quickly realized that if she wanted this relationship to last, she had to check her temper by the door. Both she and Sudhakar had passionate, fiery natures. 'There was only room for one hot-tempered person in our marriage,' she said, smiling.

The last secret, which she grasped neither quickly nor fully, nevertheless made their marriage viable and strong. She was able to be her own person, independent-minded, beholden to no one and nothing but her own sense of commitment and responsibility. Her money and her decisions were her own. Dad never questioned, demanded or interfered. In our home, money was always kept openly for any of us to take and use as needed. My parents shared a bank account and made financial decisions jointly. Mom was always puzzled when she heard her fellow teachers, women, whispering about how they regularly stashed money away from their husbands so they could spend it on 'unapproved' expenses like going to the movies, buying saris or investing in gold, because in my parents' relationship, there was complete trust and respect.

The morning after their wedding, Meera heated some water for Dad's shave, as she had always seen her mother do for Anna. Playing wife, she set out a table mirror, a razor, shaving soap, and a towel and brought Sudhakar a mug of hot water. He took one look at it and said, 'If I wanted a servant, I would have hired one. You're my wife. I can get my own water.' He could also do his own laundry, make his own tea, and cook his own food. All my life, I have seen Dad try to make Mom's life easier, as she has tried to ease his. To his frustration, Mom never quite gave up the fight to do things for him. That is the only subject we saw them argue about when we were children. Though my mother never gave in and let Dad cook once a week or do dishes regularly, he never stopped trying to help. In everything else, my parents presented a united front to us. Annoyingly, they set a standard for marriage and parenting that neither my brother Sam nor I could quite live up to, and they gave us a rare and precious gift: a secure, healthy childhood, singularly lacking in dysfunction.

For their third wedding, Anna planned a formal Hindu wedding ceremony on 30 April 1968. The date was set so Meera, Sudhakar, and their classmates who were to write their MA finals in early April, could be relaxed enough to celebrate. Unfortunately, the exams were postponed at the last minute so my parents were studying till the day of the wedding. When their exam ended at 2 pm on the 30th, they jumped into a car waiting for them outside the exam hall. Anna had also arranged for transportation for all the guests going from Poona to Dehu where the wedding was to be held, and everyone was driven at breakneck speed along the old highway to the Army Officers' Mess to make it in time for the muhurta.

The wedding guests—the Marathe and Sirsikar clans, army friends, colleagues, classmates, Sudhakar's elementary school friends—gathered under canopies on the lush lawn, sipping gin and tonics, chilled Coca-Colas, or chai as they waited for my parents to change into their wedding finery. In the distance, the sun was setting salmon-orange behind the Dehu hills.

Before long, Dad emerged in a thin white muslin kurta-pajama and Kolhapuri slippers on his long, narrow feet. His black glasses framed bright eyes and his Adam's apple bobbed as he stood talking to his younger brother Shrikant and best friend, Manohar Uplenchawar (Bapu), as they waited for the priest to begin the ceremony. The bhatji sat down on a paat and lit the hom.

Flanked by her sister Maya and her sister-in-law Madhavi, came my mother, Meera, draped in cream kosa silk bordered in orange. She was not a blushing bride, eyes downcast, demure. She pushed the end of her sari, embellished with gold thread, firmly onto her strong shoulders and strode out laughing to the man she loved. The embroidery scattered across the sari waved and shook as she walked, her smiling mouth shimmered in a rare wash of 1960s matte pink lipstick.

Meera stood next to Sudhakar and the bhatji began reciting auspicious Sanskrit verses. The guests saw a study in contrasts: a tall, serious man with a pale face and hair, a short woman with dark hair and laughter in her eyes. Then my mother looked up at my father and smiled.

He looked down at her joyful face and returned her smile, the world fell away.

15. Bunny

Swaye Shri Ram Prabhu aikati, Kusha-Lava Ramayana gaati.
Lord Rama listens to the twins, Kusha and Lava, singing of his godly life.

—G.D. Madgulkar, *Geet Ramayana*

'*Tu Sudhakarchi mulgi, na?* Sudhakar Marathe?' ('You're Sudhakar's daughter, aren't you?') asked the old man.

I stopped in my tracks, rather taken aback. 'Uh, yes. That is my father's name.'

I was seventeen and had recently left my parents' home in Hyderabad to do an undergraduate degree in French in my hometown, Poona. I enrolled at Fergusson College where three generations of my family had studied before me. I was only just beginning to get to know this town where I was born and had spent a few summer vacations.

I knew my grandfather Appa's cool stone house, Shree Ram Krupa, like the back of my hand. I knew the location of the best sugarcane juice vendor in his Prabhat Road neighbourhood. My cousins and I crowded into his booth every hot afternoon we could, to gulp down that frothy, refreshing sweetness. I knew that I loved SBDP or sev batata dahi puri, a delectable snack of crunchy flat bread topped with potatoes, onions, yoghurt, sev and tamarind chutney, that was served to eager students strictly after 5 pm at an inexpensive south Indian eatery called Vaishali. Conveniently located across the street from Fergusson College, it had been the town's hang out and meeting place for decades.

What I did not know or understand were Poona's people, their connections, the unspoken etiquette and their social rules. To paraphrase Percy Bysshe Shelley, I was a stranger in my own antique land. So the old man I came across on a rainy August evening as I walked up Bhandarkar Road to visit my cousin Sheetal, was unknown to me. He was walking towards me and stopped me with his question.

'I taught Sudhakar in preschool,' he continued. 'How is he? Tell him I said hello.'

'Um, I will,' I answered, too startled to say more.

The old man continued on his way. I was puzzled. Here was someone who had not seen my father in over thirty years. How could he see a resemblance between that remembered child's face and mine, never seen before? I had not yet grasped what a small community my father belonged to, where clans all knew each other and socialized and intermarried. I did not know that family features were distinct and recognized; a hooked nose, oversized ears, high cheekbones, a certain shade of grey in the eyes. It was unnerving. I had grown up being told by my mother that I looked like Dad and his family, but wasn't that just her way of complimenting the two people she adored?

I knew I had Dad's eyes, his chin, his forehead, his long legs, and his temper. I was, like him, thin as a rail and somewhat narrow-hipped, I adopted his no-nonsense gait easily. By thirteen, I had glasses too and the imitation was complete. Yes, friends often remarked at how much like Sudhakar I was, but I'd never had a stranger say so before. As a child, I really just wanted to look like my ideal woman, Mom. She did not see herself as beautiful but she was. I had fine, straight reddish-brown hair that refused to curl, no matter what I did. I longed for her thick, curly black hair. I had skinny calves that did not develop strongly because I hated to exercise and spent my childhood with my head in a book. She had strong calves from years spent running, climbing trees and playing outside. I yearned for her strength. I gave up easily as a child. I never saw my mother give up on anyone or any task, no matter what the toll on her body. I suffered from dreadful nightmares for years. I knew that Mom who was so calm and unflustered and even-keeled, slept well and soundly. I longed for that kind of peace of mind. I was shy and quiet, tongue-tied often, or embarrassed to speak in public. She was confident, gregarious, friendly to a fault and generous with her time, love, gifts. I wished I could be like her.

They say women become like their mothers as they age. I am glad. The older I get, the more I know I am as much like my mother as my father. My hair turned curly overnight, thanks to puberty, but then I wished that I had *never* wished for curly hair. That I had inherited her Sirsikar nose became apparent when I was a teen. I spent years detesting it but finally came to terms with its shape and even grew to love it.

Whenever I thought about it, I felt fortunate to have inherited Dad's slim build but I knew I would have to work to stay that way. Along the way, I learnt not to give up. If I were given a challenge, I would meet it. If someone dared me to do something, I was no longer scared. In fact, I courted risk the older I got because I began to feel my mortality. I did not want to die without having tried water skiing or parachuting from a plane. I developed courage. And without even knowing it, I had inherited my mother's zest for living, her enthusiasm to try new things, her sense of adventure.

But for now, in Poona, I was not aware of this. And apparently I could not hope for anonymity when I was so obviously a Marathe. People I passed on the street might be related to me or know my family. It happened once that Kalpak, a young man I met at college and with whom I had no obvious familial connection, took me to his grandmother's home to show me her collection of vintage *National Geographic*s. He introduced me to his grandmother, a tall, grey-haired, white-skinned woman I was drawn to right away. She wore a blue cotton sari, faded and softened by frequent washing, but what took me aback was that she was the spitting image of my grandmother, Veerbala. I asked Kalpak about her. Her last name was Golwalkar, he said, which did not explain the resemblance to me and he knew nothing more that was enlightening. Mrs Golwalkar was about my grandmother's age and when I wrote my mother about this curious meeting, she explained that the woman was Veerbala's cousin, her father's brother's daughter.

Alas, the family resemblance was not superficial. Both cousins suffered from Alzheimer's and both had the same experience, years apart. Each woman stepped out of her home one morning, and wandered into the street, not knowing where she was going. My grandmother was walking around her neighbourhood, lost and confused, when my aunt Jyoti spotted her. Jyoti stopped her moped, asked my grandmother to hop on the back, and drove her home. Appa and Tatya kept a closer eye on her after that. Mrs Golwalkar, unfortunately, lived alone. She left her apartment one morning, about a year after I had met her, to go to the market. She was never seen again.

But the old man I met was the last straw. I was not enjoying studying at Fergusson College and I found it difficult to make friends in a place where my peers had known each other all their lives. They found me a new and strange quantity. I was lonely, waiting for each daily mail delivery eagerly, praying for a long letter from my boyfriend, Mathew, and from my friends in Hyderabad. It was evident that I did not fit in to the Poona framework.

I was a Marathe but I was not Marathi enough. For a teen, friends and familiarity are everything. I did not give Poona any more of a chance. I took the easy way out, packed up my things and moved back to Hyderabad, to the comfort of my parents' home, the proximity of friends who seemed to understand me. There I would complete my undergraduate degree. But as lonely and miserable as I had been that year in Poona, I never felt I had wasted my time. Living there gave me a sense of my native self and introduced me to Marathi food, theatre, music and culture in a way I had never experienced before. I was no longer a summer visitor but an inhabitant, observing different aspects of my hometown on a daily basis, noticing a little on one day, having a spark of realization another, meeting relatives over time, beginning to understand how things worked in this world where Dad had grown up.

My grandfather took me to see the old wada where *his* mother had lived as a child. On the façade of the wooden building, now demolished, he pointed out the small window balcony at the very top, with its intricately carved railings and doors. My great-grandmother used to climb into this balcony when she was little and scrunch down and sit there, looking down at the busy road. I smiled to think of that ancient woman as a curious little girl. Appa, Sam and I climbed dark stairs, up and up, to the top floor apartment which our relatives still inhabited. My father's second or third cousins, once removed, welcomed us warmly. I sat on a huge, indoor wooden swing, looking interestedly around as Appa chatted with the family. I wondered about the 'foreign' way in which these people somehow connected to me, lived, and about one young man whose face was uncannily like Dad's.

Another day, Appa took us to his old friend Joshi Kaka's house. We were reluctant to go, fearing we would be bored but couldn't refuse. We sat on stone benches in the small front garden while Appa caught up with his old buddy. Of course, we were bored but then Joshi Kaka's daughter-in-law brought out steaming hot cups of tea and little saucers embellished with pink flowers. There were a few spoonfuls of pale turmeric-yellow pohe in each saucer. The tiny serving puzzled me, especially after I tasted the dish and fell in love with it. I wanted more of that slight sweetness, the crunch of the onions, the pounded rice rehydrated to softness. It had such a different flavour from the pohe my mother served for Sunday brunch: spicy, bright yellow, no hint of sugar. Both were delicious but the Joshi version hinted at my heritage in tantalizing ways.

It is not easy to separate from one's collective unconscious of food. Ever since that day, one of my efforts in the kitchen for three decades has been to deconstruct and reconstruct that dish to my satisfaction. There were other dishes that had an impact on me, which I tasted that year when I boarded with Dad's older sister, Kunda. She was a small, white-haired woman who spoke in the same soft, gentle manner as her father and siblings. Her voice belied the fact that she had strong opinions. She and her husband, Narayan (Nana) Joshi, had what seemed to me a rather strained relationship, which gave me my first insight into the fact that all marriages were not like my parents'.

Nana was a free spirit who lived life as he wanted to, not by the diktats of convention or family. He rode a motorbike well into his eighties; he was a serial foreign language learner; he said exactly what he thought; loved a heated debate; and learned photography and developing at a time when most Indians did not own cameras. His masculinity scared me so I was somewhat nervous around him and tongue-tied because he towered over me, such a vibrant, unabashed presence.

Thirteen years older than Kunda, they met when he taught her German at the Max Mueller Institute. The small, shy young woman was captivated by the unusually handsome, tall young man with the bright blue eyes and direct stare. He was worldly, having studied and travelled abroad and what he knew about she could only yet imagine. Her mother, Veerbala, had worried that Kunda, mousey and bespectacled, would not find a husband easily. I'll show her, thought my aunt.

She and Nana married quickly but their marriage was always uneasy. Kunda had several miscarriages before her oldest child, Ashwini, was born. Older than me by six months, my cousin was an only child for eight years before her younger sister Aditi arrived.

I admired my Atya who travelled to fascinating places like Japan and brought me back books about origami when I was little, and who, it was said, surpassed her husband's knowledge of German, speaking the language like a native. I was amused that when she spoke English, her sentence construction and intonation reflected German. She and Nana often travelled to Germany for work, and at home, they used the language for private communication. I figured my cousins would pick up German easily because they heard it so often, but to them it was just an annoyance.

Despite Kunda Atya's travels, she was quite conventional and cooked traditional Konkanastha food every day. I was not used to such consistency at home, so an opportunity to eat it regularly was delightful. What might have seemed matter of course to my cousins was novelty to me. I never tired of my lunch or dinner served on a large metal plate: fresh polya and bhaat at every meal, with tondli, okra or some greens, sautéed or braised with a hint of jaggery and goda masala—the spice blend of my Konkanastha side; cinnamon, cloves, cumin and other aromatic spices combined with ground up coconut and sesame seed—tart-sweet amti, a chutney on the side, and a small portion of raita or koshimbir. Atya's recipes became familiar staples that I continue to cook like she did. At table, I ate slowly to relish every morsel, mimicking my cousin Ashwini, tearing my poli into edible portions with the fingers of one hand, my index finger raised off the plate delicately like hers, scooping up dal or vegetables deftly in the bread.

I learned other things from Ashwini too. She was busy with college and her friends, and chatted to me about them at home, which helped improve my spoken Marathi. She also introduced me to Marathi-language theatre and music. She had a small role in the college musical and excitedly shared all the gossip from each day's rehearsal with me. When she practised the play's songs religiously, I learned the words too. At the performance, I hummed happily along with the cast.

Pa-us aala, pa-us aala…Ghay-un ashya navya re,
Ye-il Ramacha rajya.
The rain has come at last, bringing fresh hopes of Utopia.

Ashwini listened to other music too on her little boom box, playing everyone from Simon & Garfunkel to a new rising star named Whitney Houston. Across town, my cousins, Rohan and Sheetal, were on another musical journey—Pink Floyd, Journey, Dire Straits—and they took me along too.

The songs I fell in love with forever were the ones I heard over and over with Ashwini; Marathi bhav geet (emotional verses set to music) like 'Sakhi Mand Jhalya Taraka' ('My love, the stars are hidden now, it is dark. At least now, will you come see me?'); abhanga or devotional songs by saints like Dnyaneshwar, Tukaram and Eknath, set to music, and sung by maestros like Bhimsen Joshi and Kumar Gandharva; and film songs like 'Sunya Sunya Maifilit Majhya' ('At this barren concert hall, I sing only songs of you'), the kind that are no longer written today.

Having been away in Canada for years, this music was new to me. Do you recall where you were the first time you heard something musical that moved you beyond understanding? There were two songs I had first heard the summer before and when I think about them, I am transported back to where I first heard them. The first was 'Ghanshyam Sundara', a song composed by Honaji Bala, an eighteenth century Marathi poet. Set to music and used in pioneering filmmaker, V. Shantaram's 1951 classic film *Amar Bhupali*, the song became a huge favourite across Maharashtra and is still sung as a morning song of worship across the state. I had heard Dad humming it occasionally but I really became conscious of the words when Sam and I were at our uncle Padmakar's home.

Seven of us cousins were sleeping in a row on mattresses laid out across the living room floor. There had been a Marathe family get-together the night before and we had gotten to bed late, the party being followed by a ghost story marathon. Except for my father, the Marathes were devout Hindus. Every morning of his life, Padmakar woke early, bathed and straightened the sacred thread that rested on his shoulder. As he cleaned the family altar, lit an oil lamp, placed incense sticks and fresh flowers before his deities, he sang softly in his sweet, melancholy voice. He enjoyed singing but he also used his song as a gentle wake up call for his sons. I was on vacation so I wanted to keep sleeping. Grumbling, I blocked my ears and tried to fall back to sleep but my uncle was relentless. Gradually my hands fell away from my ears and I lay with eyes closed, letting his beautiful voice wash over me.

Ghanashyama sundara
Ghanashyama sundara Sridhara
Arunodaya jhaalaa
Uthi lavakari vanamali, vanamali,
Udayachali mitra aala

Dark cloud-like, beautiful Krishna
The sun has risen.
Krishna, divine gardener, get up quickly.
Morning has come.

Whenever I hear these lines, I am transported to my uncle's house, to my grandfather's bungalow, to all the places of my ancestors. Having grown up with parents who taught English for a living and spoke English to each other and us, I consider it my first language. My familiarity with Marathi is limited but I discovered that I possess a natural and instinctive understanding of its cadence and power, its poetry and mystique. Every time I hear a Marathi song, something tugs at my heart, a feeling of home rises from my soul, from beneath the place where language, upbringing and enculturation live. Even though I cannot understand all the lyrics, their emotion and sensibility are transmitted to me. Every time I hear a Marathi song, I find peace.

*

The other song I heard that summer was the exact antithesis of 'Ghanashyama Sundara'. It spoke to me of North America, my adopted land, sending a message to my Westernized self and appealing to the teenager susceptible to a rock star crush. This too was who I was at seventeen. My cousins and I were lazily whiling away a hot summer afternoon. We were in the cool, second-floor living room at my grandfather's bungalow. The windows were almost completely shaded by mango tree branches and a thick green canopy of leaves sheltered us from the dry heat. The younger children were arguing good-naturedly over a game of Carom. Sheetal and I were listening to her uncle's records on the turntable as she schooled me in the language of rock music.

Her brother Rohan, a year older than me and usually too busy to hang out with us, came in. 'Want to hear something interesting?' he asked, holding up an album with an image of someone's white T-shirt-covered back and faded jeans across a backdrop of the American flag. We nodded, curious. He went on, 'He has some other albums out already. This one is different.'

He slipped the record onto the player and set the needle in the groove. The unfamiliar strains of a guitar, trombone, and raspy vocals filled the small room, folding into the heat of an Indian summer's day. In the USA, the album had come out the previous year, 1984. Since music, movies, books from the West arrived in India rather slowly in the 1980s, our generation began listening to songs long after they had faded off America's Billboard 100 charts and become rock classics. The first side of the album ended and Rohan flipped the disc. I was enjoying the music, pacing back and forth and talking to my cousins at the same time.

And then, towards the end of the album, a song began that

stopped me in my tracks. I looked out through the window and saw the flowers on the bakula tree, the ripening mangoes on the tree next to it, the heat shimmering off the pavement beyond as scooters and rickshaws putt-putted by. I blinked. Time stopped as the music moved. I had never heard anything like this before. I didn't know you could write about feeling this way.

My ears were filled with the rhythm of the song:

I get up in the evening
and I ain't got nothing to say
I come home in the morning
I go to bed feeling the same way.
I ain't nothing but tired,
Man I'm just tired and bored with myself.
Hey there baby, I could use just a little help.
You can't start a fire, you can't start a fire without a spark
This gun's for hire,
Even if we're just dancing in the dark.

The song continued, finished, ebbed away. I barely heard what followed. I wanted Rohan to play 'Dancing in the Dark' again. And again. Over time, I explored Springsteen's other music. It took twenty-five years before I could get to a live concert. In the meantime, as powerfully as 'Ghanshyam Sundara' could calm me, 'Dancing in the Dark' could move me, no matter what my mood, to dance.

When I was working on my second cookbook in 2008, my goal was to finish it by 31 December. Keya and Sanjiv had gone to visit friends in San Luis Obispo. I stayed home that cold winter, a heater at my feet, my eyes on my computer, finishing last minute edits so I could send the manuscript off to my publisher. Whenever I took a break, I played 'Dancing in the Dark' and sang loudly along with Bruce.

I'm just about starving tonight, I'm dying for some action,
I'm sick of sitting 'round here trying to write this book,
I need a love reaction
Come on now baby, gimme just one look.

Springsteen's energy gave me the strength to keep going, but I learned that it was the energy and endurance I inherited from my parents that taught me how to finish what I had started.

I was definitely Sudhakar *and* Meera's daughter.

16. Sunday's Child

When he shall die,
Take him and cut him out in little stars,
And he will make the face of heaven so fine
That all the world will be in love with night
And pay no worship to the garish sun.

—William Shakespeare, *Romeo & Juliet*

What did Antoine Marfan and Etienne-Louis Arthur Fallot have in common with Aditya Marathe?

They were doctors whose names were given to illnesses my baby brother, Aditya was born with; Marfan's Syndrome and a Fallot's Heart. This meant that he was out of luck in the game of life. When Aditya was ill in hospital, our grandfather, Anna, had his horoscope made, as if that would somehow help. The astrologer said my brother was a path bhrasta yogi, a saint who had fallen from his place. 'He will either have a very long life and become a saint again, or he is just here to repent for sins he committed in another life. When his penitence is complete, he will be able to depart in peace.'

Whether one is dogmatic and superstitious and believes what astrologers say, or a sceptic who does not, the prophecy turned out to be true: Aditya was born just after I turned two and gone before my third birthday.

His death haunted me. Some children have an imaginary friend growing up. I had a real brother I had lost. For years, I talked to Aditya, keeping him abreast of what was happening in our lives or complaining when I was angry with my parents, because he was the only other person who knew them as I did. '*You* understand,' I mumbled whenever I was scolded. I knew he did.

I had arrived in the world in less than six hours and my life echoed my birth in the ease with which I continued to receive its gifts. The same was not true for Aditya. It had taken sixteen hours for my mother to give birth because he was unusually long, with spidery arms and legs that had trouble making their way out of her body. He was born on my paternal grandfather Shrikrishna's birthday and the first sign that he was not healthy was that he was as blue as Lord Krishna. The second was his length, twenty-four inches. Doctors examined him and told my parents that their little boy had a congenital heart condition called Tetralogy of Fallot and a genetic illness known as Marfan's Syndrome.

Not many people had heard of Marfan's in 1970. It is a disorder that affects the body's connective tissues. A long jaw and prominent chin, Arachnodactyly, a high palate, heart conditions like Fallot's, which affects normal blood flow, scoliosis, flat feet, macro-opthalmia (shifting corneas), and weak joints are all signs of the Marfan's patient. The brain is unaffected. At the time my parents were told that one in a million people have the syndrome. Now we know it is much more common; about one in five thousand children are born with Marfan's. Most inherit the gene but no one in our families was known to have it nor were there tests in India at the time which could have determined this before my brother, or even I, was born.

Marfan's Syndrome was named in 1896 after the French paediatrician, Antoine Marfan, who had observed its symptoms in the facial features of a little girl and described the condition. Abraham Lincoln and his sister Nancy are said to have had it, as is the famous composer, Sergei Rachmaninoff, whose unusually large hands and delicate, spindly fingers with their wide span, were renowned. Most recently, numerous pro basketball players and Olympic swimmer Michael Phelps are well-known personalities with the syndrome.

To my parents, naturally, their newborn was perfect and the doctors at the teaching hospital in Poona where Aditya was first diagnosed, agreed. They thought he was a perfect example of the illness, displaying every significant symptom. When the senior doctor first saw my baby brother, he got very excited because he had never seen an actual Marfan's patient before.

'Ma'am,' he asked my mother, after giving her the bad news, 'Your son is a classic case. Could we use him to teach medical students about Marfan's?'

Meera was taken aback, even slightly offended. But having once wanted to be a doctor, she understood the man's eagerness. In her characteristically generous way, she thought, we are at the hospital after all. If we can contribute in some way to the education of doctors treating Marfan's Syndrome, we should. She nodded her head in agreement. Over the next few months, as she watched her baby closely, she also shared her observations with his doctors. 'The lenses in his eyes shift sometimes,' she said. 'He is often short of breath. He cannot open his legs wide because he has adductor spasms.'

'Mrs Marathe,' said a doctor, admiring her acuteness. 'You have told us about more signs of a Marfan's patient than we had known before.'

In his short life, my brother spent many days at a time in hospital, first being operated on for a hernia five weeks after he was born, and then over the next few months, treated for pneumonia, a bronchial infection, and ultimately, cardiac trouble. Groups of medical students gathered by his bed on those occasions and he was exhibited from head to toe by the teaching doctor. When Aditya was not an educational model, he was poked and prodded for medical tests.

'He had to be given so many shots,' Mom told us when we asked for a bedtime story about our brother years later, 'that he was really scared of needles. When he saw a white coat coming toward his bed, he would moan, "Mama, Mama," and hide his face in my side. Poor little fellow. He really suffered. His little thighs were like sieves, they were so marked with puncture wounds from the shots.'

Initially his prognosis wasn't bleak. Our paediatrician was out of town when Mom took Aditya in for his two-month checkup. Ajeya Joshi, the locum, was a tall, gangly man who examined my brother and then said, 'I understand your son's health issues.' He held out his long arms. 'See, I have Marfan's too.'

My mother had been living in knowledge isolation, as it were, so she was pleasantly surprised and a big smile emerged on her face. 'So...' she asked hopefully, 'People with Marfan's can live normal lives?'

'Oh yes,' replied Dr Joshi, 'As you can see, I have, and many others do too. Often, people with Marfan's are just very tall, with long limbs and fingers.' He went on to explain that some patients exhibited other signs ranging from heart or lung trouble to glaucoma. 'Since your son has so many and such severe symptoms, life will be very difficult for him. Still, if we can get his heart condition taken care of, he may have a chance.'

This gave Mom something to hold on to. She was a young mother, living with Aditya and me in Poona while Dad worked in Dhule, a six-hour drive by bus. My father taught all week and made the trip south each Friday, to spend the weekend with us and help Mom out. Anna and Vahini, my maushi Maya and my father's younger brother Shrikant and his wife, Mangal, helped too. I stayed with my grandparents when Mom was at the hospital with my brother, and when she came home, my aunt and uncle kept Aditya company. He loved being with them and bounced up and down excitedly in my mother's lap whenever they visited.

Unfortunately, he could only show excitement in that way. He never learned to sit on his own, stand on his own two feet, or walk. 'He was all skin and bones,' Mom said. 'I bottlefed him my milk because his lungs were so weak he could not nurse at my breast. And when he was a bit bigger, he ate dal and rice and other food, but he did not put on any muscle and his spine was so weak, he could not hold himself up. But he smiled, he listened, he spoke a few words like Mama and Baba, and expressed pleasure when he saw loved ones. He was so intelligent, you could see it in his eyes. They were wise. But he never cried, even though he was in so much pain all his life.'

If Aditya's heart had been healthy, he might have lived. Today, surgeries for Fallot's heart are commonplace but not then. On 5 July 1971, my brother went into cardiac failure and was admitted to the army hospital at Southern Command in Wanowari, where cardiologists revived him and put him on oxygen. He never left the hospital again.

Five months after Aditya's birth, Mom's brother Nishu and his wife, Manisha, had had twin girls. Neena was brown-eyed and black-haired like her father; her sister Leena was blonde and blue-eyed like her mother. My uncle Nishu who adored babies, said to Mom, 'Meera, look how lovely our children are. Maybe Leena and Aditya will marry each other one day.'

Mom smiled a bittersweet smile. 'Let's see,' she said, looking down at the ill baby she held in her arms.

My uncle's twins were healthy and happy for the first four months of their lives. Then on 7 July, Leena had a bad case of diarrhoea. Her mother Manisha was a doctor's daughter. She knew what to watch for. When her baby's loose motions did not stop, she took her to the National Defence Academy hospital close to thier home. An inexperienced young subaltern doctor examined the baby.

My aunt told him, 'She needs glucose. Her electrolytes need to be replenished.'

The young doctor looked at her contemptuously and laughed.

'Who's the doctor here?' He turned to the nurse. 'Keep an eye on the child before we decide how to proceed.' He advised that she not be given any liquids.

Leena was put in the children's ward and Manisha and the nurse watched over her, but the baby quickly became further dehydrated and lost consciousness. Within a few hours, my once healthy little cousin was dead. When the doctor arrived again for rounds, my aunt was rocking her baby's lifeless body back and forth in her arms and crying softly, my uncle kneeling by her side. The young medic's face drained of blood. After officially pronouncing the baby dead, he asked to speak to my uncle privately.

'Please sir, I am so sorry,' he mumbled. 'Please sir… Don't report me, it'll be the end of my career.'

Nishu looked at him with dying eyes. 'Yes…' he said thoughtfully. 'My daughter is already gone. There is no point complaining. You don't have to worry, doctor. I won't say anything. But please…don't ever be so callous with a life again.' He stepped away and turned back to his wife and daughter.

In the Hindu tradition, children under five years old are not cremated. Leena's body was wrapped in white muslin and she was laid to rest in a little grave in nearby Uttam Nagar on a windswept hillside. My uncle Nishu never recovered from her death. He found comfort in a bottle of rum and began his downward spiral into alcoholism. The Sirsikar family was plunged into sorrow by the death of one baby and the imminent death of another. Nishu regretted ever having planned for the children's futures, feeling he had somehow jinxed them.

My brother suffered for more than three weeks after Leena's death. 'His happiest day in hospital was 25 July,' Mom remembers. 'That was the day Shrikant and Mangal came to visit. He was so happy to see them, he bounced up and down. He did not have his mask on but that was the only time he did not need it. And he ate a bowl of soup. He really relished that meal.'

My aunt and uncle held Aditya, smiled at him, and spoke soft, sweet words to him as they rocked him back and forth. Thankfully, Aditya did not suffer too much longer and he left this world more swiftly than he had arrived in it. Just after midnight, between 30 and 31 July, he was gone. But for my mother, it was the longest night of her life after the longest year.

That evening, holding her baby close in the paediatric intensive care unit, Mom looked around at the other mothers. All of them were hugging their very ill children, staring longingly into their faces, hoping for a miracle. In the dark night, a sudden and eerie sound tore the silence apart. A dog began to howl, starting low and winding up to a sharp *woo* as the frightened women listened. A dog's howl is a bad omen, signifying an impending death. Each mother hugged her baby a little tighter and prayed that her child would live. My mother looked down at her little boy with his saucer-like brown eyes and wispy hair. Helplessly she had watched him suffer for months. He looked up at her and smiled, stroking her arm softly. His breathing was laboured.

She prayed, 'God, if any of these children are to be taken tonight, please take my son. I don't want him to suffer any more.' Pulling Aditya's frail little body closer, Mom kissed him all over his face, whispering words of love. He heaved a sigh. Then his body expelled one last bowel movement. His breathing slowed, his eyes lost focus and then regained it again to look at his mother. He smiled his sweet smile at her and stopped breathing forever. She sat and looked at him for a long time until a passing nurse saw that he was dead and called in a doctor.

Then it was a blur. Mom called Anna to the hospital. Dad was now working in Ahmedabad and would not know about his son's death for an entire day. After my mother had dealt with hospital bureaucracy and been handed a death certificate, she carried Aditya's body to a waiting car. 'Let's take him to Shree Ram Krupa, please,' she requested her father. 'He's a Marathe and should go to their house.'

When Anna's car pulled up in front of the bungalow in the Eighth Lane, Appa came rushing out to the gate. He had been given the news of Aditya's death though it was two in the morning.

'I've brought your grandson to you,' said the strongest woman I know, holding the inert body in her arms and walking towards the front door.

Appa nodded but put up his hand to stop her. 'We can't take him into the house,' he said.

My mother stopped. 'Why not?' she asked, puzzled.

'My mother wouldn't like it,' said the dutiful son, my sixty-one year old grandfather. 'The idea of a dead body scares her…'

'I see,' said Mom. 'But he is *your* grandson.'

Appa, who shared a birthday with Aditya, looked down at the body and was silent. After a long pause, my mother silently turned on her heel and got back into the car. She and her father drove to the Khadakvasla house where Anna-Vahini were living with Nishu. Every so often, Anna looked over at his daughter. She sat completely still staring down at her son. She said nothing. She did not cry.

I had spent the week with my grandparents. That morning when I awoke, Anna was not home. He had received Mom's phone call from the hospital and driven out to her. My grandmother played with me and fed me breakfast, making little mouthfuls of chapati mushed into milk and sprinkled with sugar, and singing me a Marathi feeding song:

Ithe Ithe bas ga cheou
Bunny ghale jey-ou.
Daana khaa, paani piy,
Bhurrh, udun ja!

Come and sit here, little sparrow
Bunny is going to feed you now.
Eat your grain, drink your water,
And—bhurrh—fly away home!

'When is my mummy coming home?' I asked.

Vahini wiped her eyes and sniffled, 'Soon, babi, very soon.' She hugged me close.

That morning was cool and rainy, the weather reflected the gloom that blanketed the house when Anna and Mom walked in. My grandfather sat down heavily in his favourite armchair. I immediately climbed into his lap and hugged him. I could hear my mother whispering to her mother in the corridor. Then she came into the living room.

'Come here, Bunny,' she said softly. She put her arms around me and picked me up. Sitting down on the divan, Mom set me gently on her lap. I looked at her face with its soft skin and brown, smiling eyes. They looked sad but they were still smiling as she hugged me close. 'Bunny, Aditya's gone. He died this morning.'

'Where's he gone, Mom?' I asked, thinking of the little boy I adored and whom I loved to hold in my arms, even though he was almost as tall as me, and I swayed as I struggled to manage him.

She looked out of the window at the cloudy sky. 'Up there, dear,' she said. 'He's gone up to heaven.'

I looked out of the window and then back at my mother. 'Oh, then he'll have the stars for a mosquito net,' I said, putting my hand on her soft, dry cheek. I caressed her forearm as I always did, drawing as much comfort from it as I gave.

It did not seem odd that Mom was not crying. It was years later that she told me she did not shed a tear until three days after her son's death. Only when Dad reached Poona and held her in his arms did she break down, the tears falling quietly till her sorrow spent itself.

Aditya was buried in an unmarked grave with no fanfare, right next to his cousin Leena. 'At least they can be together now,' said Nishu, holding my mother in his arms as earth was thrown into the grave.

And there the cousins lie sleeping peacefully together under the shining stars.

17. Made in Wales

I wonder if home becomes more important when you spend so much of your life travelling.

—Jan Morris, travel writer

After Aditya's death, it was Providence that my parents could travel far from home, away from reminders of him.

Dad applied to the University of Bangor in North Wales to study for a Masters in Linguistics. He received a full scholarship and was able to go. He left India that September and we followed a few months later, arriving at Heathrow Airport on Dad's twenty-seventh birthday—27 November 1971. I was only three, so my memories of Bangor are very vague, but when I look through the photo album of that year, I know that, a year in a foreign land did my parents good. Happiness resurfaced.

Even in the early 1970s, the tiny village of Bangor, with its narrow, steep-sloped, winding streets and cobblestoned sidewalks, was a melting pot. My father had Lebanese, Indian, Pakistani and Israeli classmates, as well as English and Welsh. My parents are still in touch with these friends with whom we walked through the woods, picked bluebells, sat in meadows where I got bitten by red ants, and made miniature castles in the sand on a cold, grey day near Caernarfon Castle.

I look at photographs of potlucks, picnics, English teas, sing-alongs but I remember none. There is only one clear image in my mind's eye from that time. As Paul Theroux wrote in *Picture Palace*, 'Art should require no instrument but memory.' In my recollection, we are in a Eugene Boudin painting of sailboats on a bright blue sea. Our friends take us out on the water. It is a sunny Welsh morning but I sniff the salty air and watch the sky quickly turn dark. The water gets frothy with whitecaps, and I have to pull my cardigan closer to my chest. My father is wearing a faded blue cable knit sweater and his long brown hair flaps about his forehead in the strengthening wind. Before he knows what is happening, a gust knocks his thick black glasses, without which he is blind, off his face and sends them flying into the water. I remember nothing more.

Other stories Mom has told me over the years, like about how I once got my way. It is memorable because of its rarity as I was neither spoiled nor willful. In our little house at 17 Albert Street, my parents and I shared an attic bedroom. It extended the length of the house and had a sloping roof and skylights. There was a double bed and, against the far wall, my crib. After a few months, I complained to my mother about the sleeping arrangements.

'Why does Dad get to sleep in the big bed with you every night but I have to be in the crib? That's not fair.'

My mother laughed. Dad nodded seriously. 'Fair is fair,' he said. That night, he squeezed his gangly six-foot self into my crib and folded his limbs in. To my delight, I could luxuriate on the bed with my mother. Dad got a crick in the neck for his troubles but he also gained my undying respect.

As he worked on getting his degree, I was just embarking on my educational career. My preschool was apparently a happy, nurturing place because, unlike most of my experiences of Indian schooling, I have no unhappy memories of Cae Top. My class took afternoon naps on little mats and I do remember being unable to fall asleep and staring at the ceiling for the requisite twenty minutes, turned on my side, observing the sleeping children. I preferred snack time. The British government provided free milk to schoolchildren so we drank cow's milk—I was used to water buffalo milk in India and disliked it—out of little glass bottles every day. It was a novelty to me and peeling off the blue aluminum foil cover was fun because there was rich yellow cream stuck to its underside. I licked that off and slurped the milk through a straw.

Mom, never idle, got a job at a telephone factory where she assembled machines every morning after walking me up a hilly street to school. She was so quick that she assembled more phones than some of the other experienced workers who became disgruntled. Luckily for her, mom was also pleasant and friendly, so won them over and made her case to the management.

'If I can make more telephones in the time I have, isn't that better for you?' she asked. 'I don't mind what the others do, I just want to be productive.' So, she was allowed to make more telephones than the other workers. It is a sign of how lovable Mom was that her co-workers ended up not only *not* minding her high productivity but becoming friends with her. In the bargain, she inspired them to assemble more phones and earn more.

In 1982, a decade after our time there, we went back to visit Bangor. When we stopped to see our old house, my mother knocked on the neighbour's door. Mrs Evans had been very old in 1972 but to my mother's delight, she was still alive and she remembered exactly who Mom was.

'Hello, Meera, how are you, luv?' she asked, as if we still lived next door and Mom had just dropped in to borrow some sugar.

'Oh, Mrs Evans, hello. I am so happy to see you,' replied Mom, hugging the frail, white-haired, old lady before disappearing into her house to chat for a few moments. Dad, Sam and I waited outside. I rolled my eyes because I was thirteen and intolerant of my mother's excessively friendly ways. Mothers! my eyes scoffed while Sam, my youngest brother and nine-year-old henchman, giggled understandingly.

It was his first visit to Wales, but he had been here before.

My brother's full name explains a lot about him. Sameer Abhiram Jesus Emrys Marathe is quite a mouthful. Sameer means breeze in Sanskrit and an entertaining or delightful companion in Arabic, but he was given the name because my parents thought of it as a union of theirs, Sudhakar and Meera = Su+Meer. He was named Abhiram because his Hindu birthday was on the anniversary of Rama's birth, Rama Navami, but I recently discovered that Abhiram is not a variant of the name Rama, as my parents had thought. Serendipitously, it means delight or delightful, rather like the Arabic meaning of Sameer. As for the middle name Jesus? That was my doing. My year at Cae Top had given me a foundation in Christianity and I admired the stories about Jesus I heard there. I insisted on naming my brother too and though the name didn't stick, it delighted me to name him. And then there is Emrys, possibly the most puzzling part of his name for those who do not know his history. It is a Welsh name given to Sam in honour of our dear friends from Bangor, Emrys and Gwyn Edwards. It reminded my parents of our happy year abroad.

Sameer Abhiram Emrys was born in India in 1973, but he was made in Wales.

18. The Fenugreek of Parents

You can know the name of a bird in all the languages of the world, but when you're finished, you'll know absolutely nothing whatever about the bird...So let's look at the bird and see what it's doing—that's what counts. I learned very early the difference between knowing the name of something and knowing something.

—Richard Feynman, *The Physics Teacher, Vol. 7, Issue 6*

Bitter fenugreek leaves are an acquired taste.

I detested them when I was seven. My preferred foods were potatoes, rice, Coca-Cola, ketchup, gingersnaps, cream horns, plums and bulls' eyes—little stripy mints with smooth, shiny, glazed surfaces. The only vegetables I liked eating occasionally were green beans that Mom sliced really fine, sautéed with cumin seed and topped with minced coriander and freshly grated coconut.

We lived at the University of Poona from 1973 to 1977, and went up to my grandparents' at Dehu Road most weekends. One Saturday before we were to head there on the commuter train and I was excitedly hopping about from one foot to another, impatient to get to Anna's, Mom called me to lunch. 'Come on, Bunny, let's eat quickly so we don't miss that train!' she warned me, setting chapatis, rice and dal out on the table.

I rushed to it, pulled out my chair to sit down, and then I saw the methichi bhaji, sautéed fenugreek greens. I made a face and dawdled. I didn't mind the other food but swallow the methi I could not. Thinking about it now brings back the nausea I felt that day, how the bites of bhaji rose back up into my throat. I was skilled at bringing food back up if I didn't like it and I tried this tactic several times that afternoon, looking to see if there was any sympathy forthcoming from my mother. Nope. The rule was that you had to eat what was served to you. You did not have to have seconds but tasting was essential.

'You're so unfair,' I sniffed softly, big tears forming in my eyes and dripping forlornly onto my plate and down my cheeks, where I licked their saltiness up. I had sat down to lunch excitedly, hoping the meal would pass quickly and we could be off on our way to Dehu. Now here I was, unable to leave, stuck at the table with the rest of my family waiting patiently for me. I tried a few more bites.

Mom said, 'Why don't you mix the methi with rice and yoghurt? Mmm, that will be delicious.' She helped me stir it all together. Ordinarily, I loved dahi bhat but today it didn't help. After rearranging the food desultorily, feeling my father's sharp blue eyes boring into me, I thought of another way.

With the innocent wiliness of a child, I tried hiding the greens under my bowl of lentils and my plate. Both tilted alarmingly and obviously, over the mounds of vegetable. It was no use. Finally, Dad said, 'If you don't finish up, we will miss the last train. Then we won't be able to visit Anna this week.' It was not a threat but a statement of fact.

My parents were not going to bend. I took great gulps of all the food on my plate, not caring if I chewed, simply swallowing it down to remove it from my sight. It was a long two minutes of 'spoon, pretend-chew, swallow,' hoping each mouthful would slip down my gullet. Nausea was replaced by the fear that I wouldn't go to Dehu. Get on that last train I would.

On such occasions, I veritably hated my parents for their strictness and discipline. Why didn't other children suffer like I did? I listed all their flaws to Aditya silently. No Bournvita in my milk—everyone added Bournvita to theirs but I couldn't even have sugar; no soda, except on very special occasions; no inappropriate TV or movie viewing—read 95 percent of Bollywood films—and no late nights. I had to eat what I was served at meals—sometimes yuck; I had to eat vegetables—always yuck; and, I had to exercise—double yuck. Worst of all, I had to use my brain. I was, shall we say, in the manner of many children, lethargic. I didn't want to think. I wanted answers fed to me but rarely ever did I get a simple answer to a question I asked, particularly from my father.

'Why can't you just tell me?' I would wail, not wanting to really think about the etymology of the word *centrifuge* or the concept of *inertia*. Minutes would turn into hours as he essayed with me to unravel the mysteries of a word or a scientific idea, trying to help me learn how to ask the right questions and solve the problems myself. His eyes seemed to bore into mine coldly, I always lost what, in my mind, was a staring match. Tears pooled in my eyes and slid down my cheeks. A weaker person would have caved in at the sight of me. Not my father.

Luckily for me, my parents' personalities complemented each other's. My mother has always been my biggest fan, full of praise, Bunny can do no wrong, while Dad has always pushed me to try harder, to see more sharply and differently, to think more precisely. Naturally, I grew up thinking he was very tough, but my mother? I knew my mother was love itself. She was full of giggles and laughter, and like her father, I never saw a frown on her face.

One of the things I loved most about her was that she never held a grudge or minded saying sorry. When she and I argued or she scolded me, I would go off in high dudgeon. Before long and certainly before bed that night, whether I'd repented or not, whether it was her fault or not, Mom would come to me, pull me close and generously apologize. She taught us never to go to bed angry. 'You never know what will happen tomorrow,' she said. 'Don't waste time being upset with the people you love.'

Mom was also the person who taught me to pray, not for things I wanted, but in gratitude for all that I had been given. After our bedtime story, she listened as we recited 'Shubham Karoti'. Then she sang in her high-pitched, sweet voice the songs she learned as a teenager or had heard her mother hum as she cooked. We fell asleep peacefully, knowing we were loved.

*

The year of fenugreek was 1975 and my father was a junior lecturer at the University of Poona's English Department. In my short life, I had already moved six times so it was thrilling to live in a house on the university campus and settle at last into the kind of life I always envied other children for: one house, one street, one school, one best friend. Yet, despite the semblance of normalcy, my life was not really like the other girls'.

When I was chasing butterflies in the meadow in front of the university's beautiful Victorian main building, perched in a tree with my head in a book, or visiting my grandparents, life was perfect. When I was at St Joseph's Secondary School, I felt sad, ostracized, lonely. I constantly asked my Maker why I was different, why I could not just be 'normal'. My classmates' lives seemed to accentuate this gulf. It was not only that I was smaller than them because I was a year or two younger or that I always came fourth in a class of forty, missing the top three spots recognized for academic excellence. Nor that the girl who always came first was consistently mean to me (though Numbers 2 and 3 were always kind and are still friends). It was not that my mother wouldn't buy me the expensive black Mary Jane shoes that my peers wore and that I coveted, nor that my father was not a doctor or engineer like the other dads but taught English for a living. It was none of those things alone. It was all those things and more.

My parents were odd, compared to the other girls'. I mean, who was in love and happy with each other after years of marriage?

Other mothers and fathers did not act like mine did, laughing, talking endlessly to each other, having fun. Our house was strange too, full of books and visitors, my mother cooking up a storm without any servants to help her. She did not seem to need naps. She never sat down, with an exhausted sigh, to rest. Dad lacked the squishy potbelly that designated a father in my eyes. He walked to work, ran easily, and scrambled deftly up our giant mango tree to pluck raw mangoes that Mom would turn into sticky jam and mustardy pickles.

My working mother did not cook Indian food every day and I frequently took sandwiches for school lunch while the other girls brought tiffin boxes filled with complete Marathi meals: chapatis, cooked vegetables, lentils, rice, and mango pickle. My classmates looked at me funny, but envied me my Western lunch. I looked at their neatly packed tiffins and longed for both their lunches and their conventional, stay-at-home moms. I wished my mother looked like Every Mom; middle-aged, fading into the background, plump body wrapped in a sari, hair pulled back into a bun. Aggravatingly, my mother had an enviable figure and wore jeans and dresses. Her hair was short and, horror of horrors, she was often mistaken for my sister.

'Kaumudi, your sister's come to pick you up,' a senior girl said one afternoon.

'That's not my sister,' I mumbled grumpily, slouching off to get my satchel. On the way home, I asked Mom petulantly, 'Why can't you dress like the other mothers?' and sulked because she laughed in amusement.

'Don't pout,' she smiled, looking down at me. 'You're such a pretty thing, you don't want your face to get stuck that way.'

I pushed my lip out further because I knew I was not pretty at all. I didn't have black hair or eyes or lashes. I pouted when the older girls at school stroked my silky brown hair. They exclaimed at my big eyes—how green!—and my soft skin. They squeezed my cheeks till tears came to my eyes and I felt even more alien and other.

Worst of all was the PE teacher. To her, for some unfathomable reason, I was both threatening and to be threatened. Miss D'Costa abhorred me. I was the perfect victim; shy, small, quiet and scared. With her burly, athletic body and cropped, coal-black hair, she looked like a body-builder and stalked around St Joseph's terrorizing us, while I made myself as invisible as possible, hoping she would not spot me.

During mandatory inspection in gym class, I could not hide. We stood in rows—Red House, Blue House, Yellow House, Green House—and she inspected our uniforms, bloomers, nails and shoes. One day she scolded me about the sloppy state of the red sash at the waist of my cream uniform. That did not seem enough to merit ten laps on a sunbaked field. I sighed. I seemed to spend much of my class time running laps. Like when I held up my hands for Miss D'Costa to see and realized I had forgotten to take nail polish off after the weekend. I shivered when she admonished me. Nail polish was not allowed and I must scrape it off immediately.

We all carried razor blades, broken in two parts, in our pencil boxes. We used them to sharpen our pencils to a very fine point and, when we needed, to scrape off varnish. Only, my little hands had not developed control with sharp things and I sometimes ended up cutting too deep in, removing layers of nail and stopping just short of drawing blood. Then I ran ten laps, scrunching my jagged looking nails into my fists so no one could see.

And of course, there were my shoes. On PE days we wore white canvas shoes at St Joesph's. This was in the days before brand name running shoes with colourful swishes and stripes. Our shoes were white, ugly, flat-soled and lacking support. When they got dirty, we washed them by hand. You could buy white polish in a liquid or cake form, which worked well on canvas. Mom bought the less expensive cake that you dampened with a wet cloth and rubbed onto your shoes. It did a spotty job, I thought, and Miss D'Costa definitely agreed. She announced often that we all needed to use liquid shoe polish, the Cherry Blossom brand. My mother refused, saying it was too expensive.

'Didn't I tell you to tell your mother to buy Cherry Blossom?' Miss D'Costa demanded one morning. 'Do ten laps, on the double.'

I joined a small group of delinquents being castigated for various infractions. As a child, I hated to run and I was slow so I trudged my way reluctantly down the track while the other girls whizzed past me. I stared at the dust they kicked up and looked at how far I had to go. The sun beat down overhead, the boys from Loyola's on the hill were looking down at us and laughing or whistling, and I knew I was never going to make it. Until…a funny thing happened. I was running so slowly that the others soon caught up with me on their second turn around, and I thought, I'll just join them and start my 'second' lap too. I looked at Miss D'Costa, busy at the other end of the field. She was not looking at us. I grew bolder, doing my slow-fast routine every other lap, trying to look nonchalant. I ended up 'finishing' the run with the other girls. In reality, I had maybe completed only six or seven laps. Guilt? For the first time, I felt none for this was my little payback to a teacher I hated with all my heart.

It was around Cherry Blossom time that I started having nightmares and was reluctant to go to school. And then, Canada saved me. Soon after I started fifth grade in June, my parents told me we were moving that September. Dad was going to do his PhD at a university in Ontario. I was now a student-in-waiting. And this time I was happy to say goodbye.

I only understood how severely I had been terrorized when we returned to Poona five years later. Mom and I were shopping when I saw a familiar figure. That short black hair, stocky, muscular body and determined walk? It was Miss D'Costa. My stomach dropped. She had her back to us so I grabbed my mother's arm and dragged her quickly across the street. 'Come on,' I whispered, 'Come *on*, Mom.'

'What's going on, Bunny?' she asked after we were safely across.

'It was Miss D'Costa,' I whispered. My mother smiled and drew me close as we watched the bobbing black head disappear into the crowd.

Sometimes parents see the fruits of their labours immediately, sometimes they must wait a long time for the lessons they've taught to be understood. I didn't know why my parents insisted I eat my greens, work hard on whatever I was learning and not buy Cherry Blossom just because everyone else was. I was an adult before I figured out that though they had occasionally seemed harsh, they were teaching me important lessons I was not likely to learn in any school. They helped me to become myself: independent, strong-minded, healthy, hard-working, principled. They taught me to look beneath the surface and see things and people not for what they seemed to be superficially, but for what they really meant. They guided me to question, to reason, to persist, to deconstruct and reconstruct, to make connections, to trust my instinct and to also use my logic—skills that have stood me in good stead in my work as a writer and chef.

19. Beth & Jerry

He who respects the Infant's faith
Triumphs over Hell & Death.
The Child's Toys & the Old Man's Reasons
Are the Fruits of the Two seasons.
— William Blake, *Auguries of Innocence*

'Do you know the meaning of "bird" in American slang, Bunny?' Jerry asked.

I sat humming in the hammock. He handed me a chilled gin and tonic and sank onto his grandmother's green wicker rocking chair so we could enjoy our aperitif together. We were on the porch of his wood-shingled summer cottage overlooking Lake Michigan. Dutch Boys Landing is on the eastern shore of the great lake, somewhat diagonally across, in a northeasterly direction, from Chicago. The water was placid and the day was finally cooling off. A breeze had begun to blow and we were enjoying the beginnings of a glorious sunset, as the meat sauce for dinner bubbled on the stove. Sunlight drenched the wood floor of the porch and filled the space with pleasant yellow light.

'Yes,' I nodded. 'A girl, a woman.'

'That's right,' he replied. 'And *you?* You are a *certain* kind of bird.'

I raised my eyebrows questioningly.

'A hummingbird,' Jerry elucidated, smiling at me.

I grinned and started humming again and we both stared out at the lake he so loved, where eighty-four years of his memories swam.

Professor Gerald Eades Bentley Junior, one of the foremost William Blake scholars in the world, was born on the other side of Lake Michigan in Chicago in 1930, around the time my paternal grandparents were meeting and falling in love. Better known as Jerry, to differentiate him from his father whose name he bore, he was thirty-eight when I was born and forty-five when we met. For me, our meeting was the start of a lifelong love affair. Next to my parents, Jerry is the person I can turn to for anything. The foundation for our relationship was laid on trust and respect between child and man and a love of literature and good food!

Now I am about the age he was when we first met in 1975. That August, Jerry came as a Fullbright Fellow to Poona University where Dad taught. I was a tiny, shy little girl with big eyes, Jerry a tall American with a booming voice, flowing white hair and beard that made local people think he was older. He filled up a room in a way that made other men seem meagre. When he hugged Mom, she was tiny in his arms and when he hugged Sam or me, he gathered us up, arms wrapped completely around our bodies, enfolding us in love.

Jerry, a gentleman and a scholar, is happiest when immersed in his Blake research. For pleasure, especially during the relaxed summer months at the cottage, he reads Kipling, C.S. Forester, Mary Renault or Wodehouse. He sits in his favourite armchair, to the right of the fireplace, so he can turn his head and look out at the ever-changing lake water. He sips cognac by a warm fire and loses himself in his book, but he's never annoyed when interrupted by a grandchild, daughter or friend who has a question, or wants to chat as they pass through the living room. He simply puts a finger on the line where he stopped and looks up with a smile. In all the years I've known him, I've never seen him lose his temper. The most frustration he expressed was a deep sigh when he was ill pleased or a slight alteration of tone when he called his wife, 'Elizabeth,' dipping the second syllable in his deep voice, instead of his usual Beth.

Jerry was an avid traveller who taught abroad every third or fourth year. China, India, Algeria, England, France were some of his favourite destinations, but he lived in the Australian outback, visited Tahiti and Fiji, and set foot on every continent but South America and Antarctica. He has studied, researched and taught at some of the finest universities in the world, but he never talks about his accomplishments, focusing instead on the people he's with, asking them about their work and preoccupations, genuinely interested and always graciously offering help should they need it. Countless students and friends have benefited from his generosity but one would never know it from a conversation with Jerry.

He has the rare quality of being able to engage as easily with children as with the adults in his life, be they his friend, a Western Michigan woodsman and deer hunter or the great academic, Northrup Frye, whom he and Beth entertained in Oxford. The erudite scholar is easily shrugged off. He is comfortable swimming out to second bar in Lake Michigan, narrow boating on the Thames, bicycling through the mountains of France, doing handstands in five-foot deep lake water for my brother and me, showing us how to eat corn in rows as if he were a typewriter, making a *tring* sound at the end of every row, chopping wood for a fire, or singing silly songs or limericks to amuse us.

Jerry has the canny ability to serendipitously pull forth from his memory a quote, poem, story or song for any occasion. One of the songs he sang for us frequently and which we recorded in the 1980s and I learned to sing, was an American folk piece that we knew simply as 'The Logger Song' ('The Frozen Logger' by James Stevens and Ivar Haglund, 1949). This is how it began:

> *As I walked out one evening, t'was in a small café,*
> *A seven foot, ten inch waitress to me these words did say,*
> *'I see you are a logger, and not just a common bum,*
> *For nobody but a logger stirs his coffee with his thumb.'*

It went on to tell the sad tale of the strong logger who nevertheless froze to death at 1,000 degrees below zero. We clamoured for it and Jerry's deep, sonorous voice gave pathos and humour to the clever lyrics.

A self-proclaimed Luddite, Jerry resists technology, using computers rather grudgingly for work, and avoiding the telephone. His wife, Elizabeth Budd Bentley, was just the opposite. Beth had her finger on the pulse of the zeitgeist, embracing change as fervently as he denounced it. Dynamic and energetic, she had succeeded in life against all odds, by sheer dint of will. Beth was highly intelligent but also street smart, wise but oddly childlike, calm and collected but sensitive enough to feel a child's pain and cry in compassion. The reasons for this lay in her Minnesota childhood.

While Jerry was raised upper middle class, the child of academics who lived a cosmopolitan and urbane life, Beth was born in the Midwest, in the small town of Montevideo, Minnesota. Her father, Raymond Budd, was a banker, kind and caring, who lost his money and job in the Great Depression and turned to farming for his livelihood. His daughter Beth was born in May 1930 and her mother died a few days later, leaving her baby to be raised by father and grandmother. Beth had to take life by the horns. When she was thirteen, she began running the house, looking after her father and older brother David, managing the finances, cooking, cleaning and keeping the family together.

She made sure to excel at school because she had figured out that if she wanted a successful future, she would have to make it herself. Having to struggle so early, I think that Beth decided early on her approach to life, challenges, and hardship. Her attitude is characterized by a song I heard her sing when she was older and suffering from Parkinson's. We watched her go from the active fifty-five year old woman who lithely ran up the hill to the top of Golconda Fort when the Bentleys visited us in 1985, to a woman whose body Parkinson's often brought quite literally to a standstill. As the disease progressed, Beth found that her legs frequently betrayed her, freezing her in place for moments at a time or her hand trembled so much, she couldn't pick up a pen or reach for her coffee. Whenever this happened, she paused, looked down at the floor and then up at us. Smiling, she sang:

> *You've got to accentuate the positive*
> *Eliminate the negative*
> *Latch on to the affirmative*
> *Don't mess with Mister In-Between.*

She determined at a very young age to spend her life being happy. There was something else she knew early on, her daughter Sarah said. As a child, she decided there were certain men she did not like. 'I could never marry anyone with red hair,' she once told a classmate, shuddering. 'Nor anyone named Jerry.'

*

When Beth graduated from high school, she received a prestigious scholarship to Grinnell College in Iowa, which she refused because she did not wish to be tied down for four years. Instead, apart from doing a full course load, she worked on campus and juggled two jobs to pay her way, scrimping and saving to get by, sewing her own clothes and living frugally. Unlike Beth, one of her college mates, Alida Tolman, had grown up in Chicago, one of three daughters of a wealthy industrialist named Bronson Tolman. Alida and her sisters went to elementary school with a clever, red-headed boy named Jerry. Their parents were friends and the families bought lakefront property together on the private beach known as Dutch

Boys Landing. Alida, Martha B and Ruth spent summers with Jerry, swimming, hiking, climbing the sand dunes, canoeing and camping.

Alida and Beth became close and travelled to Europe together the summer they were twenty. It was 1950. They headed across the Atlantic, their first stop, a camp in Wales. Alida knew her childhood friend Jerry was travelling in Europe at the same time with his best friend, Jim Williston. Jerry and Jim started their summer as strawberry pickers in Wales so Jerry's mother Esther suggested her son look Alida up and make sure she was enjoying her trip. So the two handsome young men showed up at the Welsh camp one cool evening and invited the girls for a drink. As they were getting ready, Alida confided to Beth that she thought Jim Williston cute.

'Don't you worry then,' said Beth. 'I'll take care of Jerry for you.' She purposely slipped onto the bench next to him at the pub so Alida and Jim could sit together. The evening flew by and Beth was surprised by how much she enjoyed Jerry's company, though he was a redhead.

Beth and Jerry were destined to meet twice more that summer. They bumped into each other on a bridge in Venice. A few weeks later, they found themselves in Paris at the same time, ran into each other at the theatre and decided to have dinner afterwards on the Champs Elysées. Later the four wandered the city, ending up by the famous cathedral on the île St-Louis. Jerry sat down on a bench with Alida next to him. Jim and Beth made themselves comfortable on the neighbouring bench. They joked and laughed late into the night. Finally, Alida stretched out, resting her head on Jerry's lap. Jim soon followed suit, putting his head on Beth's lap and letting sleep overtake him. Jerry looked over his friends' sleeping bodies and smiled at Beth. They sat in the little park in the shadow of the Notre Dame all night long, talking in low tones while their friends slumbered. By the next morning, each knew they had met the person they wanted to spend the rest of their lives with.

Vaman Abaji Modak's son, my great-grandfather Ramchandra Vaman Modak (right) and his wife Anandi (Gangu) (left)

Marathe Family Portrait
L to R (standing): Purshottam, Vishnu, Lili, Indu, my grandfather Shreekrishna, Ram
L to R (seated): Lakshmi holding her daughter Vijaya, Yamuna, my great-grandfather Chintamin Gangadhar Marathe, my great-grandmother, my grandmother, Padmavati (nee Veerbala) holding her daughter Kunda, and Sanjeevani with Dada Kaka's son, Madhukar

Veerbala Modak, aged 18 (my paternal grandmother)

Shreekrishna Chintaman Marathe (my paternal grandfather)

Veerbala and her older sister, Manu in their home at Sadashivpeth

Lt. Col. SM Sirsikar, my maternal grandfather

My maternal grandmother Surekha (nee Shakuntala) holding
her first-born, Ramesh, my grandfather Sadanand (Anna),
family friends, the Kinares

L to R standing: Meera, Nishikant and Maya Sirsikar
Seated: their mother Shakuntala, also known as Vahini, Garden City, Dehu Road cantonment, circa 1965

L to R, back row: Sudhakar Marathe holding Sameer, Shrikant holding baby Mukund, Padmakar holding baby Sudarshan
L to R, front row: Kunda's daughter Ashwini, Bunny (Kaumudi), Madhuri, Pramodan behind Niranjan (photo credit: Narayan (Nana) Joshi)

Sudhakar and Meera with one-year-old Bunny, Poona 1969

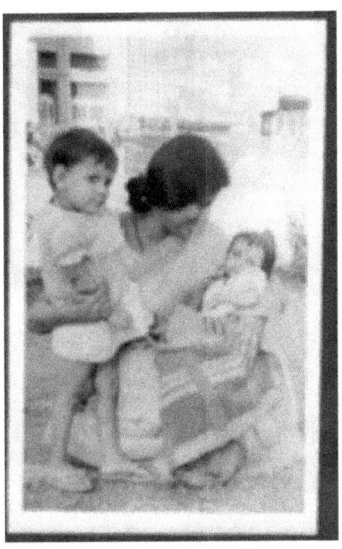
Meera holding Aditya and Bunny, 1971

Aditya and Meera (photo credit: Anju Van Wersch)

Appa holding Kaumudi & Ai Aji holding Pramodan, the two oldest Marathe grandkids

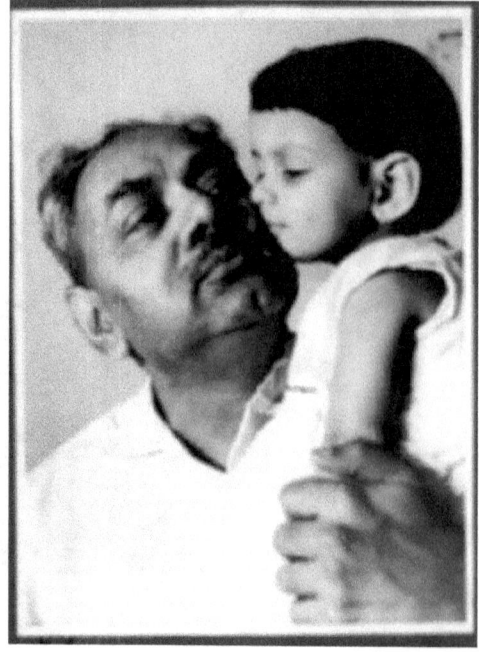

Anna with his eldest granddaughter, Kaumudi whom he called Banna, circa 1971

Bunny on Dehu gate, circa 1975 (photo credit: Sudhakar Marathe)

Jerry & Beth Bentley on their honeymoon, circa 1952

Bunny, aged 9, Lord Roberts School photo, London, Ontario, 1977

Bentleys & Marathes with friend Ravi Deshpande at the Bentley home in Toronto, Halloween 1979

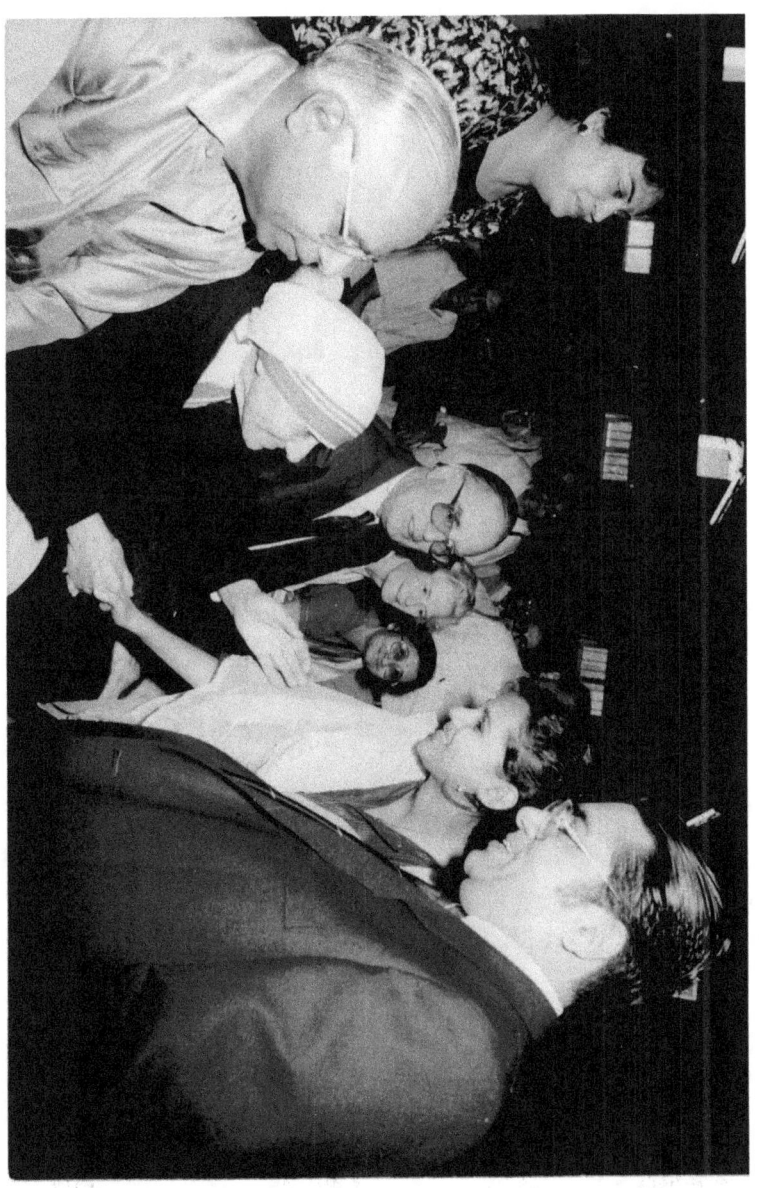

Mother Teresa and Kaumudi shake hands, Irfan Khan in the foreground

Kaumudi, Keya and Sanjiv in the snow at Mount Wilson, California, circa 2006 (photo credit: Lancy/Mavis Quadros)

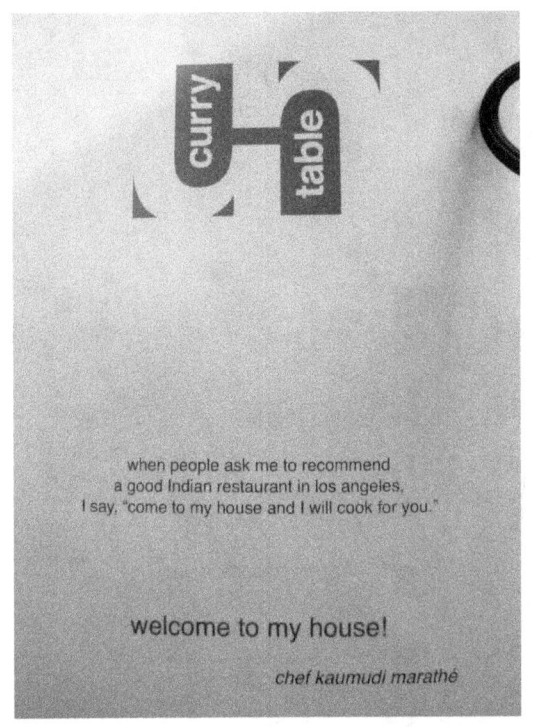

The Un-Curry Table pop up restaurant menu (photo: Vanessa McGrady)

Kaumudi teaching an Un-Curry class, cutting jaggery, circa 2007-2008 (photo credit: Sanjiv Bajaj)

Kaumudi enjoys some pani puri and falooda on a visit to Bombay to film home cooks, 2010 (photo: Sameera Khan)

A Marathi plate—Santosh, beet raita, peas with lemon and ginger—shot for the Un-Curry website, 2007 (photo: Uta Briesewitz)

Shrikhand surrounded by fresh raspberries and dessert bowls, Un-Curry catering gig, 2010 (photo: Kaumudi Marathé)

Kaumudi, Sanjiv and friend prepping for the first Un-Curry pop up dinner, Surfas, Culver City, California, November 2010 (photo: Vanessa McGrady)

Keya, Kaumudi and Ever spend the day in Santa Barbara, CA, December 2013
(photo: Keya Marathé-Bajaj)

Kaumudi peeps out from behind Jerry at the cottage on Lake Michigan, 2015 (photo: Lorraine Johnson)

Kaumudi and Dean Douglas at home in Glendale, California, 2013 (photo: Jagruti Gala)

Friends seen through the window at Viet Noodle Bar, Kaumudi's 40th birthday party celebration, September 6, 2008 (photo: Sanjiv Bajaj)

That autumn, Jerry invited Beth to his college, Princeton, for the big football game on Thanksgiving weekend. There he proposed and two years later, both having completed their degrees, they were married. In characteristic fashion, Beth took charge of her husband's life, managing it as adeptly and cleverly as she had her father's. She organized their children's schedules, the family's travel arrangements and social life, their investments and banking. Jerry focused on his education at Oxford, his teaching at the University of Chicago and at the University of Toronto, publishing academic papers and books, and lecturing around the world.

In looks they could not have been less similar. Jerry went from red to blonde early and as long as I've known him, he's had long white hair and a beard. Beth had golden-brown hair. He had hazel-brown eyes, hers were bright blue. There was more than a foot height difference between them and when I was a child, I was always embarrassed and ducked my head when she stood on tiptoe to kiss him. Beth was plump and comfortable when I met her, but in 1940s and '50s photographs, she looked like a Hollywood movie star with her stunning face and poise, her shining hair worn in a bun, and her fashionable silk frocks. Her piercing eyes missed nothing and she kept her hair longer than waist length for her husband. He brushed it lovingly each night before bed, and each morning she braided and wrapped it into a bun. To the romantic seven-year-old for whom white people were still rare and unknowable, Beth and her two then-teenaged daughters, Sarah and Julia, seemed like the beautiful princesses in my book of fairy tales. I'd never seen hair so long and golden on anyone except for my Russian doll an uncle had brought home from one of his sea voyages.

In Poona, our families became lifelong friends. In the forty years since, we've experienced the joy of a friendship that's spanned years and continents, and because I moved to America, I was able to see the Bentleys every year and visit the cottage I remembered from my childhood. Jerry's and my friendship grew thanks to a shared love of books and poetry, a similar quirky sense of humour, and that rare ability to communicate without words I also had with my grandfather.

*

During that first year together in Poona, the Bentleys and Marathes shared so many lovely moments like a trip to the circus and fair up the hill at Chatushringi or the time we climbed Singhagad, Shivaji's hill fort on the outskirts of the city. I ran and skipped ahead because though I disliked walking, I loved to climb. Near the top, we went through a stone tunnel where the temperature was lower than in the open, breathing sighs of relief when we emerged into the sunlight again. Jerry gave me a ride on his shoulders and I clutched the top of his head gingerly to keep my balance. I was excited because I knew what was on the other side. Navwari-clad women sat in a row, with terracotta pots of salted buttermilk to sell. What a treat to sip that taak in little railway tea glasses. Spiked with chillies and mustard seed, it was tangy and naturally cooled by the earthenware container, refreshing us completely.

That December Jerry and Beth decided to host a traditional English Christmas dinner. Their friend, beekeeper Pascal Leclercq, flew in from France. He came from a tiny village in the Jura Mountains close to the Swiss border, the home of Comte cheese and Vin jaune, and was red-cheeked and jolly, the classic bon vivant. Beth scoured the Poona markets for just the right ingredients and somehow found what she was looking for. I am not sure she would be able to in twenty-first century India, but forty years ago, consumer choices might have been fewer but accessibility to out-of-the-norm products was less fraught with political angst.

The Bentleys' colonial university bungalow sparkled on Chrismas Eve. There were twinkling lights, decorations and English-style crackers for the dinner table, set up in the central room of the house. Guests gathered around the table, which glittered in the candlelight and groaned under the delights on the white lace tablecloth. This was a party unlike any I'd known before but what I recall with extreme clarity is the pièce de résistance. After we were seated, Sam and I barely able to see over the top of the board, Beth made a dramatic entrance with a heavy platter and set it down in the middle. I put my hands onto the table and pulled myself up for a better look. Glistening brown and golden on the silver platter, in all his roasted glory, was a wee little pig. My mouth fell open and I stared slack-jawed at the critter, only ever imagined live in fairy tales. I stared at his face, eyes, and snout, then gasped at his mouth, which was stuffed with an apple. The Westerners oohed and aahed at this delectable Christmas roast. The Indians at the table were stunned into horrified silence. I know the consternation I felt as I watched Jerry carve up the animal.

Memory can be faulty though. Years later, Sarah and Julia told me it was probably in Toronto that Beth roasted suckling pig. Funny, I only remember roast goose there and that too was a first for me. But wherever the suckling pig was served, it was one of many strange culinary introductions I would receive from the Bentleys during my childhood. Whether I welcomed them or not, these experiences broadened my horizons and stretched my palate. In the NO column was the beef tongue, large, pink and quivering, that appeared on the table at the cottage one evening. We worked our way through the dense, chewy meat patiently but I vowed never to try it again. Then there was a rare roast beef, which oozed blood as it was carved. It took many years of living in the West before I could appreciate meat served so rare. And once Beth served split pea soup that other guests exclaimed over but which to our Indian family seemed like dal. The idea of eating only thick dal for dinner, dal sans cumin, turmeric or red chillie powder, was baffling.

When I was twelve, we spent Christmas with the Bentleys in Toronto. One day Dad, Jerry and I were out shopping for stocking stuffers and stopped in at a gourmet food shop. While Jerry ordered some French cheeses, I stared curiously at the canned goods lining an entire wall. Soon Jerry joined us and after taking a look at my curious eyes, pulled two tins off the shelf. Was I surprised to find them in my stocking on Christmas morning? Indeed. I'd have preferred chocolate or candy. Octopus? Mussels in olive oil? No, I wasn't ready to explore them yet but it struck me that Jerry was taking me under his gastronomic wing. He put new tastes before me, as my father was wont to do with books, to see what caught my fancy.

I also had a long YES column. It was with the Bentleys that I fell in love with lobster, dipped in hot butter sauce, and sipped a Shirley Temple at the age of ten. It was with them that I first tasted champagne, ate a fruit called avocado, scrunched up my face at grapefruit, and tried Mexican food in 1979, when the cuisine was about as exotic in North America as Indian food. And it was because of them that I tasted dim sum long before the concept of small plates became widely popular, then trendy, and finally commonplace.

On my first solo trip away from home in London, Ontario, I took the train to Toronto to spend a weekend with Jerry and Beth. On Saturday, Beth took me out for a girls' afternoon in China Town. We stopped for lunch at a Hong Kong dim sum restaurant. It was the age of innocence in the West about food beyond meat and potatoes, and such places were exotic and rare. The Chinese lanterns, deep green bamboo in pots, the smell of incense and soft-footed women in embroidered red satin blouses pushing metal carts, fascinated me.

After we were seated, the lovely women moving softly through the room stopped at our table and lifted lids patiently. There were baskets filled with strange delights that Beth or I pointed to. The woman would lift one onto our table and stamp a piece of paper with a symbol to indicate what we had requested. That afternoon, I learned how to use chopsticks but more significantly, I learned how to hold my own at a restaurant and how to make choices about what to eat. As I devoured this lunch of intricately and meticulously shaped shu mai and baozi, delicately cooked shrimp and scallops, crisp, bright green baby broccoli with oyster sauce, and fried rice with lotus root, the words dim sum—touch the heart—did exactly that.

I fell in love forever with the exquisite beauty that was food.

20. 246

*They say the moment that you're born is when you start to die
And the first time that we said Hello, began our last Goodbye.*

—Roger Whittaker song,
words & music by Johnny Burke

One year, I had three birthdays on three continents.
That was when I turned nine and on that birthday, I came alive. On 6 September 1977, my parents, my four-and-a-half-year old brother Sam and I boarded a Singapore Airlines 747 from Bombay's Santa Cruz airport, bound for Toronto. We made a stop in London, where, thanks to the time difference, it was still 6 September and when we reached Canada, it was excitingly, still my birthday for a few minutes. After over twenty-four hours of travel, I was too tired to care.

Travelling to Canada on a plane was the most exciting thing I'd ever done. I stayed awake long after we got off at Toronto airport and said hello and goodbye to the Bentleys who were headed to England for a year. They were the reason we were here. Jerry had suggested Dad apply to some Canadian universities to do a PhD. Being accepted by all, he decided on the University of Western Ontario for more than its academic calibre. It was close to Toronto where the Bentleys lived. So it was ironic that just as we arrived, they were leaving. Jerry hugged us and Beth kneeled down to squeeze Sam and me, planting kisses on our cheeks. In the days before 9/11, meeting at an airport terminal was possible. I admired the feat of planning to do so via airmail letters. After a few moments of rushed conversation, we parted, taking a Greyhound bus to London—not the British capital but a small town 120 miles southwest of Toronto, on the 401 highway. I peered out into the darkness, trying to see this strange new world.

Ever since I'd heard we were moving to Canada, one thought had consumed me: a colour TV. There were none in India at the time and I longed to watch television on a colour set. I prayed fervently that we'd have one in our rental, thinking about it to the exclusion of almost everything else. So when we reached 246 Hyman Street, a weathered yellow Victorian house, I was wide awake, exhaustion left behind halfway around the world. Were my prayers about to be answered? We walked into the hallway that led to our new home. My parents hefted suitcases up the stairs and piled them at the top. I followed them curiously. A landing ran almost the entire length of the apartment, from the L-shaped kitchen at the back end and what would become my parents' bedroom at the front. Stepping off the stairs, I could see right into the living room and glimpsed the edge of a television. I held my breath and moved forward. Yes, I thought, there it is. Was the telltale red, blue, green colour band there?

'Oh yes, oh, thank you, thank you,' I whispered. 'It is colour!'

My parents were busy moving luggage around and looking over what would be our home for the next five years. I knelt down reverentially in front of the television that dwarfed me, and released my breath. I turned the knob and colourful zigzag lines appeared as the set warmed up. I stared in awe as the squiggles morphed into the body of a clown in a yellow suit topped with flaming red hair. I watched him gesticulating for a few seconds. Then the image flickered, pixelated again, and sucked itself into a small white dot, disappearing from the screen. I stared at the blackness, horrified.

Over the next week, I turned the set on hopefully from time

to time, praying for it to work. It never did and my parents put it on the curb on garbage day. The only TV we could afford after that was a small portable black-and-white, with antennae. For the duration of our Canadian sojourn, I watched colour television only when we visited friends. And I learned an important lesson. Praying is good, but you have to be very careful what you ask for and how specifically you request it! For instance, there is no point saying, 'Please let there be a colour TV.' You need to request something like: 'Dear God, please let there be a colour TV at the apartment we are moving to and please let it work well and let me be able to watch this colour TV for the whole time we are in Canada!'

Our new home was a mystery, to me and my young parents. The USA was a nation hailed and celebrated in India in the 1970s but not many people knew much about the country to its north. That September, our family began a love affair, which in my case never ended. When I say home, I usually mean many places, but I rarely ever mean Poona, the town where I was born or Bombay, my adult home for seven years. To me, the word home conjures up images of my family's five happy Ontario years. London, Ontario, is where I first consciously learned about food, dance, music, history and literature. It was my epiphany, my awakening.

Canada was a British colony and the small town we moved to bore the name of England's capital. Every major street in London, Ont., as the town is often called to differentiate it from its namesake, reflects its heritage—Richmond, Oxford, Wellington, Pall Mall, Adelaide, Dundas—as do the names of parks and schools and the river that flows through it, the Thames. In the late nineteenth century, London, Ont. was slated to be the capital of what was called 'Upper Canada'. According to legend, however, the powers that be realized that London's proximity to the American border could be a security issue and settled on the more distant city of Ottawa instead. So when we arrived in London a century later, it was the Middlesex County seat in name and a university town in reality. The glory days of its downtown were over and its population of 150,000 was a blend of working-class folk on the south end and academics and professionals in the north.

It was autumn when we arrived. The city was dotted with tall maple trees, their leaves turning golden, yellow, maroon, and orange. Playful black squirrels ran about everywhere, and the streets were empty. When I realized how far I was from all things familiar, homesickness set in. Where was Anna when I needed his hugs? Who was my cousin Ashish playing with now that I was gone? And had my best friend Radha found someone to replace me? Luckily, I had my younger brother as a playmate and since the school year had just started, we could go to Lord Roberts and make friends, which took my mind off home.

Enrolling us was so painless that my mother was amazed. 'They can start right away?' she asked the adminstrator incredulously, thinking of Indian school waitlists.

'Yes, of course. Why ever not?'

And what were the fees, Mom wanted to know, crossing her fingers and hoping she could afford them.

'Fees?' the woman looked puzzled. 'Ma'am, this is public school. It's free.'

*

School was like nothing I'd ever known before. Suddenly there was no heavy satchel to carry, books stayed at school, imagine that, and after being accustomed to hours of nightly homework, I now had none. Instead there were field trips and music lessons, projects and choir. It was a dream.

Though I had started fifth grade in Poona, because I was only nine, I was put into the third grade at Lord Roberts. I later realized I was the only non-white person in my class but it didn't matter. The term 'person of colour' had not been coined and I wasn't aware of colour prejudices until much later in our time in Canada. Once, years later, I was called Paki but I didn't even know its meaning till Mom explained it was a derogatory reference to Pakistanis. She also told me that the word Pak meant pure. 'Let it go,' she murmured generously, 'they don't know any better.'

My parents made friends with my teacher, Mary Southcott. She was a single mom and we went on picnics and hikes with her and her son, Dallas, that first year. The most memorable was a trip to Lake Huron in the dead of winter, one of the coldest on record in Ontario. When we got to the lake, we saw waves of water that had frozen as they crested. We walked over giant hills and valleys of frozen water that stretched as far as the eye could see and I pretended I was a mountain climber, scaling the Himalaya.

Soon after I started school, I was taken out of my third grade classroom for speech therapy. Apparently, I pronounced thirty, forty, and other words with R in them, wrongly. I was not to say, 'Thuhty, fouhty, thuhty-three, fouhty-three' in an English accent anymore. I was to roll my Rs and say, 'Thurrty, fourrrty, thurrty-three, fourrty-three,' much to my parents' amused annoyance. In the classroom, Miss Southcott discovered that though I was young, I knew way too much math to be kept in third grade.

She moved me to the other side of the room with the fourth graders, where I fell madly in love for the first time in my life with a husky, strawberry blonde kid named Paul Dayton who never knew I existed. A hundred miles to the northeast, in a small town named Oshawa there was another blue-eyed, strawberry blonde kid a little younger than me, named Dean Douglas. We did not know the other existed till we met in California twenty-two years later. One day, we would find we had a lot in common, having grown up in Ontario at the same time. I love how when I break into the national anthem for fun, belting out, 'Oh Canada, our home and native land,' there is one other person who knows the words and can enthusiastically join in.

I made friends with a sweet boy named Jon Wilmot, who

developed a crush on me. Jon, Kenneth Vigeant and I walked home together after school, meandering through the streets, exploring abandoned houses in our neighbourhood and playing in the autumn leaves. A third grader named Anouk Bikkers invited me over to her house to play after school and our families became friends. And there was a girl named Wendy, who was kind enough to invite me to her birthday party that year.

Birthdays were celebrated rather simply back then in that milieu. You went to someone's home with a small gift like Laurentian colour pencils, ran around in the backyard, ate burgers and potato chips, cake and ice cream, then went home. Decorations were minimal and the terms 'party favour' and 'goody bag' didn't exist. We didn't have a car so Mom walked me the mile or so to Wendy's house in a working-class neighbourhood south of Hyman Street. I was very shy and became tongue-tied when faced with Wendy's family, which dwarfed me. I was maybe four feet eight inches tall at nine. Wendy at the age of ten was five feet three inches and 130 pounds, the youngest and smallest in her family. Her brother and mother thought I was exotic. They asked me to sit down so I perched at one end of the couch. They sat down too, tilting it alarmingly with their weight so I began to slide down towards them and had to brace myself with my feet. There was stilted conversation for a few moments when they asked me about India and smiled at my 'accent.'

When we went to the table for dinner, I pulled out a heavy chair and sat down, my heart sinking. In front of me was a plate piled high with spaghetti and meatballs the size of tennis balls. That's a lot of food, I sighed to myself, how will I finish it? Wendy's teenage brother who was sitting across from me started laughing because my face was hidden from view behind the mound of spaghetti. The family kept remarking about how tiny I was, giggling amongst themselves. Embarrassed, Wendy did her best to make me comfortable and distract me with conversation. I wove spaghetti around my fork, cut into one meatball and ate a few morsels, trying to make headway in my dinner. Soon, everyone else's plates were empty while I had barely managed to eat a quarter of my food. I left Wendy's that evening feeling awkward and out of place, small and insignificant. Fortunately for me, I soon realized that her family was the exception, not the norm, in size and behaviour. I also realized something else that evening. Despite my parents' teaching, I didn't actually have to finish my food if I didn't feel like it. Liberation.

*

At the other end of the food spectrum was Anouk's family. Her family had migrated from Holland; her father Rudolf was an artist and lithographer and her mother, Thera, a stay-at-home mom who also helped her husband with his printing work in their garden studio. The first time I went to their home, I was enchanted by rooms that seemed straight out of a Vermeer painting. Spare, well-lit, and European in sensibility, the house was filled with Rudolf's colourful abstracts and the sound of music, for it seemed as if Anouk, her brother Tibor or their father were always practicing the cello.

'Hello, Mrs Bikkers,' I said when Anouk introduced me to her mother. She had invited me to come eat lunch at her house, round the corner from Lord Roberts, because mine was too far away to get to and from during break.

'Bunny, hello. Please call me Thera,' smiled Anouk's mom.

'OK, Mrs Bikkers,' I replied, unfailingly polite. I was unable to say Thera easily for at least another six months. She smiled and led me into the dining room. I will never forget my first look at the work of art that was the Bikkers' lunch spread. At the far end of the room, near two windows, was a long harvest table flanked by wooden benches. Platters of charcuterie nestled against a board on which French cheeses—Brie and Camembert—sat in harmony with Dutch Edam and Gouda. On a wooden board were arranged sliced breads I had never seen before—pumpernickel, rye, and other dark, whole-grain loaves. Slices of bright red tomatoes, apples and pears beckoned. This was what lunch should look like, I thought.

I sat down with eyes as big as plates and unpacked my Kraft cheese sandwiches. We'd been in London for a month and my parents were still grocery store novices. After a lifetime of shopping at Indian markets where you selected your own fruits and vegetables after looking, sniffing and pressing; had whole-grain ground at a flour mill; and ordered meat cut fresh at the butcher's, Western supermarkets were a mystery. Mom found it tough to judge the readiness of tomatoes wrapped in cellophane and sold on a Styrofoam tray or the quality of frozen chicken in a bag. Margarine was the popular butter alternative in the 1970s and my mother was trying it out after years of making butter by hand at home. She also bought the standard, soft white loaf bread that was available in grocery stores not knowing of healthier options yet, while Kraft processed cheese was her choice of sandwich filling because European cheeses were not widely available and Kraft was a brand she recognized. Anouk and Tibor looked at my food and then at each other, a glint in their eyes.

Thera put a plate down in front of me, saying, 'Bunny, please help yourself to some of our lunch too.'

I was delighted and Anouk couldn't wait to jump up and say excitedly, much to her mother's embarrassment, 'Oh, then could we have your sandwiches, please?' She and her brother never got to eat white bread or processed cheese, and you know what they say about the grass being greener? I gladly handed over my bag and filled my plate with Thera's bountiful offerings. Every mouthful of my thinly sliced dark bread topped with flavourful cheese and mustard was eye-opening. I washed it down with chilled milk and ended my lunch with another treat I discovered that day—schokoladenstreusel, Dutch chocolate sprinkles.

Before I knew it, two months had flown by and it was time

for Halloween. I'd never heard of the holiday and the thought of collecting candy from the neighbours was very strange, carving a face on a pumpkin even stranger. 'Wouldn't they rather cook it?' I asked Mom.

She smiled, but in our house that year and every year after that, on 1 November, jack-o-lanterns were transformed into sweet pumpkin fried bread, pumpkin-mustard seed raita, or even chunks of pumpkin sautéed with cumin seed and salt. The seeds were toasted in the oven with oil and salt for a tasty little snack. And then, the winter came.

Ontario's snow belt, in which London lay, saw the worst winter in a long time. My family took it as the Canadian norm, having nothing to compare it with. Dad looked out of the window one afternoon, smiled and gestured to us to come look. Tiny whiteness was falling from a grey sky. We stared awestruck, then squealed gleefully. Mom pulled matching parkas, that someone had kindly given us, over our heads. My brother looked like a cute little Eskimo with the furry hood around his face which had inexplicable East Asian features and straight black hair cut in a fringe. The four of us ran downstairs and onto the street. Sam jumped around, sticking his tongue out to catch the falling flakes. I saw and touched and tasted snow, after having read about it for years.

It was cold but also sparklingly fresh on my cheeks and tongue. Watching it fall from the sky gently and silently was miraculous. It made me feel very small and very large at the same time. The silence in my ears was immense. Utterly consumed by the snowfall, I raised my face up and let tiny flakes drift onto it and melt on my skin. As its warmth dissolved them, my eyelashes were laden and then shut by the snow's cold weight. I laughed. My brother and I skipped down the sidewalk, raising mittened hands to the sky.

We must have played in the snow for hours before heading inside, wet and weary. All through the night it snowed and when we woke up and peered out of our bedroom windows the next morning, the city was gone, only a dove-grey sky lingered. A white blanket of bumps hinted at houses and towers and cars and even the trees were weighted down by their icy cargo. Now I knew what Laura Ingalls Wilder meant when she wrote about snow and Jack Frost making pretty patterns on the windowpanes. Walking to school through snowdrifts was less pleasurable. What I came to love that wicked winter were blizzard days. You stayed home from school, snug and warm, drank hot chocolate with marshmallows and sat at the kitchen window, feet on the heat vent, reading a good book and occasionally looking out at the snow floating down and piling up on the already white city.

When Mom and Dad were contemplating going abroad to study and wondering how to support a family of four on a student income, various relatives had suggested they leave us behind in India. 'It'll be more affordable for you. Put them in boarding school and we'll look after them during the holidays and make sure they're taken care of.'

Dad's bursary was really enough only for one person, perhaps two, so financially that would have been the most sensible thing to do. Luckily for us, my parents put family, love and friendship before money. 'This will be an adventure for them and us,' they said. 'We'll manage but we won't leave them behind.'

So they lived carefully in Canada, eking out Dad's scholarship and stipend, and supplementing it with jobs that Mom took on. She must've been exhausted but we never felt the burden. We didn't eat out but who did back then? They didn't buy a car but anytime we had to go somewhere, kind friends picked us up or we walked or rode our bikes. They did not spend on new clothes often, but again, friends kept us supplied with useful hand-me-downs or bought us clothes and shoes for birthdays and Christmas.

One of our parents was always home when we were, the kitchen bursting at the seams with delicious home-cooked food and snacks, and the house filled with books and music. Mom and Dad took us to the library regularly, enrolled us in swimming lessons every summer, rode bikes with us on the weekend. Dad made our Halloween costumes—a Jack of Hearts playing card for Sam one year and the 246 Hyman Street door for me—and helped me with homework and science projects. Mom taught me how to cook and Sam how to bake. And they volunteered at our school. But the most wonderful thing about them was that they ensured we spent time together as a family. We had Family Game Night and Movie Night years before they became media concepts. Dad introduced us to Canasta and we waited eagerly for weekends so we could have a long card session. We played Scrabble and Monopoly together regularly. Saturday nights were a treat because we got to watch a double feature on the public TV station. TVO's *Saturday Night at the Movies* with Elwy Yost jump-started my film education with classics like *It Happened One Night*, *The Bridge on the River Kwai* and *The Man in the Grey Flannel Suit*.

The longer I live in the USA and the longer I live—period—the more dysfunctionality I see in families and in relationships between parents and their adult children. I can only wonder at it, for I don't know what it feels like first-hand. When my American friends hear that my parents are coming to visit, they always ask two questions. 'How long are they coming for? Where are they staying?'

'They're coming for a few months. They're staying with me.' As unfashionable as it might be to say so, I like my parents as well as love them. Perhaps because they were so young when they had me or because they are young at heart or because they so are avant garde, they were fun and exciting. I admire the thoughtful, liberal way they raised us, never lying, always taking the time to explain situations to us and listening to our thoughts, presenting a united front and not hesitating to say no when no was needed, and treating us with respect and kindness from the time we were babies. Sure, I frequently disliked them or detested their rules or ways of doing things, but I never lost sight of how fortunate I was to be surrounded by their love, generosity and thoughtfulness.

The other rare quality Mom and Dad possess was sacrifice. It was inherent to their natures though they never talked about what they did for us, nor what they gave up so that we could have something. I don't know how many extra hours Mom had to work so I could go on school trips and French exchanges in Quebec, but go I did. If there were only two chocolate candies left in a box and we had already eaten our share, Mom would still insist on our having them. 'We've had enough treats to last a lifetime. You two eat them,' she'd say. 'It gives me joy to see you eat.' She made sure we enjoyed our childhood to the utmost. 'Don't be in a hurry to grow up. Make the most of this time you have.'

Dad was quiet but we felt his caring in his actions. When I was ten, he got me a ticket to a Roger Whittaker concert, walked me there, saw me to my seat and was waiting outside the theatre for me when it ended. The ticket was ten dollars but my parents could only afford one so they decided I would go, knowing how much I loved the singer's voice. Another time, Dad got student tickets for a concert by the Academy of St Martin in the Fields Ensemble, founded and conducted by Sir Neville Mariner. He took me because I was studying music and he thought that I'd appreciate the opportunity the most. True, but I was thirteen! The lovely music literally put me to sleep. I rested my head on Dad's shoulder and the sounds of violins and cellos carried me away to dreamland. But I never forgot that outing. Twenty-seven years later, I took my daughter, with great excitement, to hear the same ensemble perform at UCLA's Royce Hall. Excitingly, Sir Neville was conducting not only the orchestra but also some music students we knew from the Colburn School where Keya studies ballet.

Probably the biggest gift my father gave me in Canada was one that I didn't realize for many years was a gift. I was fascinated by ballet, despite having two left feet and abhorring physical exercise. I read about it constantly and longed to take classes, pestering my mother to send me to a school near our house. Finally Dad said,

'All right. I'll make a deal with you. Get up at five in the morning and go for a run. Do it for a month and I will happily register you for ballet classes.' I pouted and was silent.

Dad was being unfair and unreasonable as usual, I thought. I didn't run. I wish I had. But I didn't. The only lessons I got were outside the ballet studio. Not getting to take ballet, the lesson was to work hard for what I wanted, to sacrifice for what I wished to achieve. Nothing would come easy, no matter how fortunate or naturally gifted I was. I thought Dad was being really hard on me but because of him, I learned to never give up, to always give my best to a task.

Other than my parents and the Bentleys, Grant Boland, my seventh- and eighth-grade teacher, and a woman named Janie McLeod had the most impact on my Canadian childhood. Mr Boland was a no-nonsense man who managed a mixed grade classroom successfully, brooking no nonsense from students and making math and history and art interesting. He was the first person who complimented my writing, saying that my words were very evocative. When I visited Canada for the first time after having left at the age of thirteen, I looked his number up and called.

'Mr Boland?' I asked when I heard his familiar voice on the line.

'Bunny! Hello,' he replied, recognizing me though I was twenty-four years older. 'Did you ever write a book?'

'Yes, Mr Boland, I did,' I said, telling him about my recently published *Maharastrian Cuisine: A Family Treasury*.

His characteristically understated Canadian observation, 'I always knew you would!' kept me smiling for a week.

The other person who made me want to write a book was Janie. When I was ten, Sameer and I were riding our bikes down Hyman Street. It was a breezy autumn day and the sun made the fire-coloured maple leaves on the ground glow. We set out from 246 and a few yards down, on the steps of one of the newly refurbished brick townhouses, we saw an old woman. She was younger than

I am now, but to a ten- and five-year-old, that's old. Also, she was having trouble stepping down each riser, so she looked older. I dropped my blue bicycle on the sidewalk and ran up to her.

'May I help you?'

She smiled, surprised, and gave me her hand. We slowly made our way down the few steps together. We introduced ourselves and our new friend said her name was Jane. She had severe arthritis. I knew all about it because Anna had it too.

'Do you live here?' I asked.

'Yes, my husband and I just moved here from Toronto.'

'You have to come over and have tea then,' I invited. 'Mom would love to meet you.'

We must have exchanged numbers because she called my mother the same evening and told her how friendly and helpful her children had been. Next thing I knew, Jane—she asked us to call her Janie—and her husband Jock were having tea at our house and we were invited to theirs for afternoon snacks and fun.

'I miss being in Toronto and Jock is often away on business,' she told Mom. 'I don't know anyone here and I like talking to your children. Please send them over to spend time with me.'

We liked her too. Thoughtful and kind, Janie became a friend to each of us. Sometimes I was invited over on my own, on other days it was Sam's turn. At the time, my mother washed our clothes in the bathtub and hung them out to dry on a clothesline because we had no washer and dryer. When Janie heard this, she was horrified. She told Mom we should do our laundry at her house. Before Mom knew what was happening, Sam and I had taken over her job. Janie and Jock had a colour TV in their bedroom and they had told us we could watch it while the clothes were being washed. We would carry the laundry basket over in my wagon after school, race down to the basement and get the clothes started, dash up two flights to the bedroom, leap on Janie's bed and lunge for the remote control. I was older and bigger so I generally won the race and got to choose what I wanted to watch. Sam just went along. The delight of watching sitcoms in colour, the luxury of being able to switch from channel to channel, nothing could compare to this joy. But when Janie heard that we sometimes squabbled over what to watch, she did something that made us love her even more.

She bought another TV. This was a smaller, colour set for the kitchen. Now we could each watch what we wanted. Our once-a-week treat satisfied us both and saved my mother's hands. Naturally we thought of Janie as our fairy godmother. The washing machine and television were only part of the story. Janie showed us interesting books and puzzles, she posed intriguing questions and waited patiently for our answers, she took us out to eat, gave us birthday presents we had our hearts set on, told us fascinating stories of her childhood in Colorado and anecdotes about her three children.

But what I loved most about Janie was that she was not judgmental, loved me unconditionally and acknowledged the value of my dreams. I told her I wanted to be a writer and she believed that I would be. She began sharing snippets and vignettes from her family story she was writing. I later realized that there were many Americans who did this because, as descendants of European immigrants, they didn't have the documented lineage Indians take for granted. Reading Janies's book, I thought, how cool! Maybe someday I will write a book about my family too.

For my thirteenth birthday, Janie took me out to dinner on my own. I was excited about my first restaurant outing as an 'adult' and dressed in the white eyelet dress and heels I'd worn for eighth grade graduation. We drove to Sorrenti's, a stylish Italian restaurant downtown where the wooden fans revolved slowly and the waiters seemed to glide noiselessly through the room. To be handed my own menu, to peruse it and order whatever I wanted for a change, without my mother worrying about the cost and suggesting I share something with my brother to save my host money, to converse like an adult, this was a real thrill. I savoured every moment.

My parents made many other friends during our sojourn, sometimes much to my dismay. I wished Mom wouldn't talk to people everywhere we went. She talked to them at the library and the bus stop and the park. Warm and loving, she drew people to her and our house was always full of friends and food and laughter. One afternoon, she met a pregnant woman named Renee at a park near St Joseph's Hospital. Renee was a New Yorker who'd moved to London with her husband Dick who taught physics at UWO. Dick and Renee were the first Jewish people I ever met, with accents I later recognized as East Coast Jewish, and a big-city cosmopolitan attitude. The couple often brought back high-tech kitchen appliances and other gadgets from New York. They also brought a bohemian lifestyle and attitude, which I found eccentric but came to appreciate in hindsight. Dinners at the Holts were always interesting and superb. They had a long, rambling garden with a rose arbour where we ate in the summer. Eating al fresco in the sunshine with flowers bending over us was strangely intoxicating and romantic. The food tasted so much more fresh and sumptuous in that picturesque setting.

Dick made his own pasta, kneading the dough and running it through a newfangled pasta machine as I watched, open-mouthed. He also did something else I'd never heard of. Dad, and most other people I knew, drank instant coffee, Nescafé. Dick ground his own coffee beans in an electric mill. I watched as the dark chocolate-coloured beans pulsed and hopped through the machine, and breathed in the rich aroma when he opened the lid to pour the ground coffee into an Italian espresso maker.

No matter how wonderful dinner was though, Sam and I tolerated it impatiently, waiting for what was coming after. Dick had grown up in 1950s America and his parents documented his childhood in home movies. He had once made the mistake of playing them for us and we begged for them every time after that. If he had the energy to dig up the film reels from the basement and set up the projector, we got to see them again. We giggled at his *The Little Rascals*-esque antics, because we couldn't reconcile the adorable, plump little boy on the screen with the large, goateed man we knew.

*

We soon settled into a routine. Our lives were busy and Sam and I were preoccupied with school. At some point, my mother started me on a weekend paper route. She wanted me to have the experience and I managed to save enough for my airfare back to India a few years later. Every Saturday and Sunday morning, I got up early, piled newspapers in my red wagon and delivered them in our neighbourhood, my younger brother in tow.

While Dad did coursework, research and then started writing his dissertation, Mom worked several jobs, sometimes simultaneously. She helped an old man write his memoir, cleaned houses, babysat and even tried her hand at catering. Indian ingredients were hard to come by in the 1970s but she made really delicious food with what was available. When I was ten, I wanted only to read, not learn how to cook but I couldn't sit idly by while my mother was working. One day, I asked if she needed help. She was rolling out fresh puris and said I could learn to fry them.

I was short so Mom put two thick phone books down on the floor for me to stand on. When I was at the right height, she taught me how to handle the slotted spoon, to not be afraid of the oil but safely slide a puri into it, to manage the heat so the puris fried at the right temperature, puffing up immediately, and to drain them well to prevent them getting oily. For the longest time that was all the cooking I did but it was a memorable start. We had so much fun together that frying puris became our mother-daughter time. We talked and giggled and the puris were ready in no time. When I got married, I asked Mom for one utensil from her kitchen to take to mine. That was the slotted spoon with which I had learned to fry puris in London.

Apart from time with family and friends, much of the beauty of my Canadian life came from the Central Library where you'd find me ensconced in an armchair, reading book after book after book and filling my orange backpack with fifteen or twenty more when I heard the dreaded announcement that the library was about to close.

The other place I loved to go was the Bentley cottage at Dutch Boys Landing. We drove with Jerry and Beth on our first summer, our family in the back seat of the old navy-blue Renault, divided into pairs by a large Kashmiri carpet that rested down the car's length. It could have been a long, uncomfortable, seven-hour drive from London, crossing the border into America and traversing the breadth of central Michigan to reach the lake. But to us, everything was new and exciting and the hours passed quickly. I had books to read and I had my imaginings. Small towns and villages, a prosperous land, the America of bygone days—town squares, stately city halls, Art Deco bank buildings, wide main streets, shingled houses and gardens springing to life in the early summer heat—captivated me.

And Dutch Boys turned out to be so much more than I'd dreamed. Turning off the paved road, unlocking a gate that closed the property off from the rest of the world, driving down the dirt path between hills on the east and sand dunes on the west, sloping down to the water, we peered out through birch, beech, ash and maples for glimpses of the lake we'd heard so much about and then, after Sam and I had nearly burst with anticipation, there it was. The third in a row of five cottages, shingled, green-roofed, on a rise, closed in by trees, a screened in porch with two hammocks swinging gently in the breeze. There was a tree house in the beech by the steps leading to the lake fifty feet below, and the Think House, Jerry's study on the hillside behind the cottage.

We had the back bedroom where Jerry and later his daughters had once slept. I nabbed the top bunk. We had Jerry's old Asterix and Tintin comics to read, and he showed us a trapdoor that looked into the kitchen below. Wooden walls, wooden floors, the smell of wood in our nostrils and sand between our toes the whole time we were there. We became shiny brown from hours spent in the sand and jumping off the jetty into the cold water. We screamed when algae wrapped around our legs like mischievous mermaids and shrieked with pleasure when Jerry picked us up and threw us into the lake with a resounding splash. On rainy mornings when we had to eat indoors, we devoured cinnamon toast or a very special treat, Long Johns—long, custard-filled donuts. We waited in the cold evenings for Jerry to light a fire in the living room, and snuggled into my mother's armpit on the couch, listening to the grown-ups talking as the sun went down or Jerry reading a story out loud.

School-summer-school-eighth grade graduation-ninth grade. Five years flew by in a flash. Before we knew it, I had finished my first year of high school, Dad had his PhD in hand, and he and Mom were winding up our life in London and planning the only real vacation my family ever took together—two weeks in the British Isles en route to India. Sam and I had begged our parents to find a way for us to stay on in Canada. Sticklers for the rules—we were there on Dad's student and family visas—and determined to return to their home and work as teachers, they did not attempt to talk to immigration attorneys or research a way to stay on. Instead our last month was filled with farewell parties and trips around Ontario to see some of this magnificent land we had grown to love.

After tearful goodbyes to our London friends, we spent a week with the Bentleys in Toronto. Jerry, knowing my love of Harry Belafonte, took Mom and me to his concert where we sang joyfully along to 'Day-O', 'Scarlet Ribbons' and 'Jamaican Farewell'. Janie came to Toronto for our visit. She had heard me talk about ballet for years and understood my adoration of the National Ballet of Canada's principal dancers, Karen Kain and Frank Augustyn. Jock, who was on the board of NBC, took us to the opening night of

Giselle. Sitting in front row seats, able to see Karen Kain's pointe shoes right in front of me, was sheer ecstasy.

Giselle and Harry Belafonte were distractions that briefly staved off the pain of the inevitable. We had arrived in Canada on my birthday and it was on my mother's, May 29, that we left the place where I had come alive.

Goodbyes are never easy but this one suspended me forever in the no-man's land between East and West.

21. The Kingdom of the Seven Hills

Walking in sunlight, all of my journey
over the mountain, through the deep vale.
Jesus has said, 'I'll never forsake thee.'
Promise divine that never shall fail.
Heavenly sunlight, heavenly sunlight,
flooding my soul with glory divine.

—Baptist English School hymn,
Kohima, Nagaland

The soft cloud slid in through the door, hiding the sunlight and shrouding us in moist greyness. Kohima's seven hills were hidden from view. I took a sip of the hot tea my parents had let me start drinking because it was winter and we had no central heating. Charcoal braziers at our feet warmed us a little and the tea heated us up from within.

Sam and I laughed, amused by the casual liberty the clouds took with our hospitality. It was commonplace to see them travelling through buildings in Nagaland's capital, situated on a mountain ridge in the lower Himalaya 4,000 feet above sea level. But we had only been there a few weeks and the sight was still freshly exciting to us, especially when it was our house that was visited.

Just as quickly, our guest had passed through the windows and sunlight suffused the space again. We finished our drinks and got up to help Mom with breakfast. Cooking took a little longer here because she used a kerosene stove. We had applied for a gas cylinder for her countertop range but service took a while to kick in anywhere in India. Mom had travelled back several centuries in the kitchen over the course of a few months in 1982. We had left Canada that May. A brightly lit kitchen with an electric range, large refrigerator, ample counter space and hot and cold running water had been hers for five years. Now in November, we were living in northeastern India on the Indo-Burmese border, and Mom's kitchen was barebones.

Dark, smoky and makeshift, it had a three-foot-deep barrel for water which the city supplied briefly twice a day. Instead of a sink, there was a floor level area for washing dishes or clothes. Mom did not have the convenience of built-in cupboards either, just a few open cement shelves where she stored supplies, and no refrigerator but a small metal cupboard with screen doors that held the day's freshly boiled milk and the yoghurt and cream Mom collected to make butter each week. Plastic gallon jugs contained kerosene to fill the two small brass stoves that sat on a short concrete counter and needed frequent replenishing. Some of our family's most delightful and cozy meals were cooked in that kitchen and I happily spent time there, helping my mother because everything was foreign and exciting. I had the luxury of relishing this old-world experience when I chose, unlike Mom who had no choice but to cook there on a daily basis.

It had taken us five days, a hundred and seven hours to be exact, four trains and an army jeep to reach Kohima across the trunk of the nation from Dehu Road. Returning from our Canadian sojourn in June, we stayed with my grandparents while Dad applied for teaching jobs. A position at a new central university in Nagaland sounded promising. Not many people travelled to the Northeast in those days but we made the arduous journey, which required even Indian nationals to get a special permit to enter the mountain state. We packed up our belongings and got on a train, despite people's warnings about the ferocity of the tribal Naga people and the frequent skirmishes between them and the Indian army battalions stationed there.

Anna had written letters in advance of our trip, arranging for his younger brother to meet us at Nagpur railway station with tiffins full of home-cooked food—batatyachi bhaji, puri and Nagpur's famous thick, green-skinned oranges—and a junior officer to check on us and bring us more home-cooked food during our eight-hour wait at Calcutta's Howrah station.

I was very familiar with Indian local trains but an overnight journey across the country was a new adventure. Mom and Dad did their best to keep us entertained over the long days trapped in a train compartment, pointing out temples, birds, crops in the fields. Whenever the train stopped, Dad hopped out to stretch his legs and smoke. He'd take us for a walk to look at our train or the others at the station and to marvel over the workings of coal or steam engines. He talked of sidings, sleepers, and gauges—broad, standard and narrow—and explained how trains were scheduled, how they changed tracks, how engineers understood signals and communicated with each other.

Often I only paid cursory attention. All I wanted was to go home to Canada, not be carted off to the ends of the earth. I missed my friends, I wanted to finish high school in London and I longed for the comforts of home and travel in the West. I detested the dirt and heat all around me here and I was frightened by the thought of contracting strange diseases like elephantiasis and leprosy that I read about in the newspapers. Staying in touch with my Canadian friends was challenging when letters took weeks to reach. They were moving on with their lives and I was just moving, moving, all the time moving. Our peripatetic life was probably one of the biggest frustrations of my teenage years.

When I pulled myself out of my funk, there was so much to take in of this 'homeland' that was so foreign. Sensory overload made my head spin. Heat, colour, crowds, smells. I looked at the people everywhere, the colonial railway stations, the picturesque villages nestled under tall, wide-canopied banyan, peepal, neem and tamarind trees, beyond which cropland stretched. Farmers were ploughing their fields with white oxen, breaking at midday to eat lunch in the shade. Boys splashed after water buffalos in sludgy ponds.

In retrospect, thanks to train journeys like this and the years I spent in India from the ages of thirteen to twenty-eight, I developed a grounded understanding of my country, which I would never have had if we'd stayed abroad. As painful as my transition from West to East was, it allowed me to learn about and experience the real India. My eyes fill with tears when I hear my national anthem but India is not a mythical place, some romanticized wonderland, to me. It is a living, breathing, evolving reality; often frightening, always inspiring, an endlessly perplexing mystery.

On that trip though, as many hours as I spent looking out of the train window, I spent in the filthy hole that was the compartment bathroom, alternately vomiting and suffering from hideous bouts of diarrhoea. Something had made my body, unused to Indian germs, very, very sick. In Nagaland, I learned with horror that I had contracted amoebic dysentery and worms. Over the year it took to get rid of them, I was constantly hungry, eating like a horse to feed my teenage body and all its illegal residents.

I was feeling a little better by the time we reached Dimapur on the Assam-Nagaland border. From there it was a road trip up to Kohima, and before we knew it, we were in the hills. The weather was cooler than in the plains and we stared curiously out of the jeep. Amidst thick foliage were wooden, two-storey houses that reminded me of the lodges of the Canadian Iroquois. Mountain folk walked on sturdy legs in traditional tribal sarongs. They carried produce or grain in woven grass baskets on their backs, supported by head straps. Dad, avid birdwatcher, noticed that there were none in the sky. A colleague later explained what has since become a cliché, 'There is a saying here that Nagas eat everything that flies except airplanes and everything with four legs except tables.' Birds had been hunted so aggressively that most were extinct.

*

The new university turned out to be a corrupt, inefficient place that did not really want Dad's enthusiasm or energy, so he was frustrated at every turn. In his positive way, he tried to make the English department a pleasant learning place, but getting things done on a day-to-day basis was challenging. Teaching was not much more satisfying because, though students wanted to get degrees, they lacked a solid undergraduate foundation for an MA in English literature. Sam and I, however, had the time of our lives in Nagaland. The weather suited our bodies which were used to Canadian temperatures, the air was clean and clear, and Kohima felt like the perfect bridge between our life in Canada and the life to come in South Asia. Ethnically related to the Chinese, Thai and Mongolians, the Nagas referred to their mainland countrymen as 'Indian,' not identifying as part of that group. Many had converted from their tribal religions to Christianity in colonial times and were devout, God-fearing people who attended church regularly. Gentle, unlike what we'd been led to believe, the Nagas loved their children, raised their animals lovingly and lived at one with the world around them. They were also more Westernized in the 1980s than people in other parts of India, watching pirated Hollywood films on their VCRs, listening to radio stations that played Western pop music and reading English-language books, while maintaining strong connections with their tribal cultures.

The Indian army's presence had fostered a dislike and suspicion of 'Indians' but we never saw the ferocity mainlanders mythologized. And as always, my parents knew how to fit in. They wanted to learn about local culture and food; they used traditional forms of greeting;

and learned words and expressions in several Naga languages. They had no desire and did not attempt to colonize or condescend to Nagas the way the government had done for decades. So we made local friends and were welcomed into their homes, much to the surprise of the 'Indians' we knew there.

To get anywhere from our little apartment on a hillock on Burma Road, we had to climb up and down hills of varying sizes. We became stronger and more active than we had ever been, hefting knapsacks full of groceries for miles with Mom and Dad. University students played table tennis near our place every night. Lacking other entertainment, we joined them, making friends and learning a skill or two. Thanks to those few months, both Sam and I are hard to beat at Ping Pong!

When school started, we climbed steps cut into several hillsides to reach Baptist English School, better known as BE School. Attending chapel was an important aspect of school life and involved a lot of singing, which I loved. So I learned Bible verses as hymns and singing them still brings great comfort. I also liked school because I made good friends. Adela and Temsunaro welcomed me into their group which included fraternal twins Lhousibinho and Kepeloubinho, and Kevilozhonuo (also called Kevi), a tomboy full of fun. We read the romantic graphic novels popular in Nagaland, trading them amongst ourselves, bought tangy fruit candy from the corner shack near BES, and walked around the schoolyard in twos and fours, gossiping and giggling. After school, we often strolled to Kevi's to hang out. Her family had a bakery, so she would go into the shop below the house and gather a plate of slightly sweet buns hot from the oven, and fresh elephant ears, buttery and rich. Sitting in her living room, we'd munch our treats as we watched soap operas on colour television, which had finally arrived in India just in time for the 1982 Asian Games in New Delhi! A young woman named Anita Sood, whom I would become friends with decades later in California, was making waves there, establishing herself as India's one and only star swimmer and showing Indian girls that competitive sport was not only for men.

My Naga friends were from different tribes so I learned a little about the Ao and Angami, the Lotha and Rengma, and how their languages, names, food and textiles varied. I often ate at Adela's house and the food—chunks of meat; beef and pork mostly, simple but flavourful yellow lentils over rice and spicy, steamed, garlicky greens—was satisfying and delicious, resembling Chinese food more than Indian. The expression about airplanes and tables was not far from the truth. An army friend of ours talked about keeping his German shepherd puppy close, out of fear that local folk might steal him one night, to make a Naga wedding delicacy, rice-stuffed dog. While we never experienced this particular delight, we frequently saw meats, herbs and spices that were not part of our diet. At the bazaar one morning, I spotted a freshly cut buffalo head for sale on a vendor's mat. The woman also had what looked like button mushrooms displayed on the ground. Sam and I looked at each other. We missed button mushrooms and asked Mom to buy some. She talked to the woman and and came back, saying with a smile, 'Those aren't mushrooms. They are slugs.'

Another day, some boys knocked on our door and asked if they could take down the wasp's nest on our porch. 'Sure, if you want to,' said my mother. 'But isn't it dangerous? Won't you get stung?'

They told her not to worry and formed a human ladder onto which the littlest boy scrambled. He brought down the nest and handed it gently to a friend so the wasps were undisturbed. The boys gathered around and pulled the insects out with their hands, deftly plucking off their wings and excitedly popping them into their mouths; a crunchy, protein snack.

But the most startling culinary adventure we had was on a picnic at the property of a politician named Thenucho. 'Let's take rest,' said Thenucho to my parents when we reached his property outside Kohima, using the translation of a Naga greeting, which made sense when you considered how far guests typically walked for a visit. When they had 'rested' and drunk some tea, the adults went on a tour. Then, sitting down outside a rough shack that housed rudimentary utensils and pots and pans, which the family used on visits, Dad admired the landscape and our host's plans for a house. A brood of hens walked by, a large, black rooster strutting amidst them, showing off his bright red coxcomb.

'Now that is a handsome rooster,' said my father.

'Oh, you like it?' asked the politician.

'He is magnificent, isn't he?' nodded Dad, praising the bird's size and proud walk.

In the blink of an eye, before my father knew what was happening, Thenucho had grabbed the rooster by the neck and bashed his head against a rock. Handing the bird to a servant, he proudly said, 'Now you will enjoy him for lunch.' He was honouring his guests by offering them his pride and joy, the cock of the walk.

My parents were shaken, rendered speechless. Luckily Sam and I missed the killing because we were paddling in the stream that ran through the property. At lunch, however, I was taken aback when the delectably flavoured chicken stew proved a bit too rustic. I saw a beak on my plate and looked up aghast at my mother. We picked out feet, feathers, and even the cockscomb as we ate and our appetites dwindled to nothing. Sam and I set our plates aside but my parents had to eat everything on their plates to acknowledge their host's kind gesture.

We left Nagaland that June because Dad got a job at the University of Hyderabad. This time we headed to the heart of India, where I would spend the rest of my teenage years and Sam would finish his education. Although my parents did not know it, they would put down roots in the land of rocks, living there for three decades.

For me, it was another story.

22. Land of Rocks

*Flanked by hot cold
crack-witnessed rock
stands the tamarind
borne in accord with*
                    sprung from
unknown all-knowing
                    plans.
*Its ancestors had language
before ours acquired*
                    voice.

—Sudhakar Marathe, *Thalamium*

Once I left Hyderabad in 1989, I knew I would never live there again.

It was a town drowning in its ancient ocean bed, though the water had disappeared millennia ago. Hyderabad's mammoth rocks, still lakes, avenues of majestic shade trees, Indo-Persian architecture and gracious culture enchanted me. Ruled by the Qutb Shahi kings from the sixteenth century onwards, this ancient city and modern state capital blended Islamic architecture, traditions and cuisine with the Hindu and Christian customs of the native Telugu-speaking people. I was there for the critical years of my adolescence, the last years of my childhood. But the city felt hung over, literally and figuratively, from the Nizam's era, an aristocratic existence lived in a leisurely and gracious manner on the backs of hardworking labourers. That languid attitude continued in the upper-middle-class families I got to know during my college years. Among the men, there seemed to be little aspiration towards a responsible adult life and though the young women I knew wanted careers, many of them were slotted for marriage soon after getting their degrees. The lack of ambition was enervating and I felt myself being sucked into its drifting nature. I had more energy and drive than that. If I wanted to be a writer, I had to leave. And yet, as heartbreaking and contradictory as those teen years were, I have no regrets because I lived them to the utmost, on the dance floor and in the library, looking out of dusty windows in rickety city buses, or exploring the exquisitely wild campus we were lucky enough to call home.

At Stanley Junior College, I was for the first time in my life, unwittingly absorbed in the group of popular girls—Sunitha Muthyala, Anupama Reddy, Elahe Hiptoola, Lubaina Tyebji, Dureshahwar Siddiqui—who were intrigued by my accent. 'Where are you from?' Elahe asked one day as we ate lunch under a giant peepal tree.

'Uh, Poona,' I replied.

I was somewhat distracted by Duresh who was scratching the back of my arm and asking at the same time, 'Do you wax?' I had no idea what she meant but whatever it was, I didn't do it.

'But your accent?' Elahe probed.

'Oh, I lived in Canada,' I replied. Turning to Duresh, I said, 'No. What do you mean wax?'

'How do you get the hair off your arms?' Duresh asked.

'I don't,' I answered, looking at the fine, scant golden hair on my arms, still unsure of what she meant. 'Uh…I just don't have much?'

'Wow.' She raised her eyebrows. 'For how long?'

'For how long was I in Canada? Five years.'

'Oh, where?' said someone else.

'London,' I replied.

'Oh, London. How long were you there?' they asked, puzzled.

'Five years,' I repeated.

'So five years in Canada, and five years in London,' one of them did the math. 'You lived abroad for ten years.'

'No, five,' I insisted.

'OK,' they said, rolling their eyes. It was only a year later that I understood they'd thought I'd lived in London, England, and somewhere in Canada too.

*

I learned quickly to keep my family's literary lifestyle and my interest in books away from most of the people I met at college or through my friends. Conversations with them or at parties revolved around relationships, jokes, movies, sports or gossip. Learning how to make small talk took me a long time and didn't come naturally so I was often silent, and though I had a quirky, silly sense of humour, my peers found me very serious. Only my close friends saw the ham that I am. I was used to evenings spent with my parents and their friends who talked about physics and art, literature, economics, and politics for hours on end. I kept an ear on their conversation while I did homework at the dining table, and often joined in once it was done. But I left this side of me at home when I took the hour-long bus ride into town for college.

Although my friends and I were high achievers and did well in college, we were bored by uninspiring teachers. So we'd often skip class and go on adventures—to the old city, Charminar, where we admired Hyderabadi lac ki chudiyan and devoured mouth-wateringly spicy mirchi bhajis and ragda pattice from street vendors, or to see a film in Secunderabad and follow it up with éclairs at Paradise bakery.

Sometimes Duresh and I took a bus to her house on Lakdi ka Pul and watched videotaped American TV shows and talked about clothes and boyfriends. Her family lived in an old haveli with no apparent architectural merit. As with many other old homes in the central city, it had been subdivided again and again so I could not tell what the original design was like, or who else lived there and why. We crossed the dusty front yard covered in red earth and entered the living room through an enclosed verandah. Duresh's room was created by sectioning off part of the living room with a plywood partition. We sat on her bed until we felt nibbly and headed to the kitchen. I rarely ever saw her mother but when I did, I admired the kaajal in her eyes, and her lips and teeth stained orange from years of eating paan, the heavy gold bangles on her wrists, and a large nose-ring that made me want to get a piercing too. She was always smiling and generous. I devoured her cooking in those years and loved her for the exciting glimpse into a world of gracious leisure.

I've always been fascinated by how and where people cook and Mrs Siddiqui's kitchen was no exception—a makeshift room at the end of a long, inner verandah. I didn't understand how anyone managed to cook in that small space, from which emerged delicacies like Shikampuri kebabs, khatti dal and biryani. I followed Duresh into the dimly lit space and she slipped the lids off huge pans resting on the stove. She filled bowls with hot rice and the tangy tamarind and curry leaf-flavoured, sour khatti dal that Hyderabadis love. We ate at the round marble-topped table in the cool dining room, under a slowly revolving ceiling fan. When there were Shikampuri kebabs on the side, I was in heaven.

My favourite kebab of all time was a shammi, a mix of meat and Bengal gram, cooked with spices, ground into a paste and shaped into flat patties that were pan-fried. Mom had started a tradition of making them on my birthday. Shikampuris upped the ante by adding a little surprise. When I first I bit into one, I thought it tasted like Mom's shammis but inside *this* patty was a filling of finely minced raw onions, green chillies and tender coriander. That fresh, crunchy bite in the midst of soft meatiness made my eyes widen.

Then it was just a few short steps to discovering biryani—layered Basmati rice and mutton with rich spices; mirchi ka salan—large chillie peppers in a sesame seed sauce; bagara baingan—aubergines stuffed with a spicy coconut, peanut and tamarind mixture; sutar pheni—a local shredded wheat, available in spiral forms, sugared and plain, and my favourite, qubbani ka meetha—apricot pudding with cream.

The other cuisine I discovered in Hyderabad was, oddly enough, Gujarati Muslim. My friend Elahe belongs to the Bohri Muslim community and though her family had come to Hyderabad years ago from Bombay, they maintained their traditions, including the communal style of eating on a shared plate. For me, eating this way took some getting used to because I worried about hygiene and my food space being invaded. Once I saw the thal, I was more sanguine because the platter was so large that a family of six had enough space to serve themselves a portion and eat without their food mixing with anyone else's.

My family lived in Gachi Bowli, fifteen miles out of the city, so I often stayed at Elahe's if we were going to a party. She also invited me to stay in March when we wrote our exams because studying for, and writing, three-hour-long tests was exhausting enough without having to travel long distances in the burning Indian summer. In the late 1980s, Ramzan, the month of fasting, coincided with exams, making life extra difficult for Muslim students. At Elahe's, we broke the day's fast together after sundown and woke up around four for the family prayer and first meal before starting the next fast. The thal was set on a little stand on the carpet. After the family had prayed and put away their prayer mats, we gathered around the platter for a sumptuous meal designed to tantalize the taste buds and fill the belly to take on a day's abstinence.

I didn't mind getting up early because of the treats in store. I could always go back to sleep for a few hours after eating. Of all the delicacies that the cook, Krishna, made, what I remember best are the tiny meat samosas with crisp pastry wrappers, and haleem, a ground meat and pounded-wheat porridge that was a Hyderabad Ramzan speciality.

But it was not just food I fell in love with. It was also Rajeev. When I first heard about him, I had a boyfriend. Mathew and I met at my grandfather's house and I was captivated by his good looks, love of literature, clever way with words, and wry sense of humour. But he lived in Kerala and we had no real way of meeting in the foreseeable future so ours was an epistolary relationship. Still, when Elahe kept telling me about this other boy she wanted me to meet, someone she thought of as the male version of me, I refused.

It took a year for Rajeev and me to finally meet and it was at the bottom of an Olympic-size swimming pool. My friends and I were going to a dance at the Secunderabad Club. I wore an ivory silk top with narrow black pants and Roman sandals, and dangling hoop earrings that glinted through my red-brown hair. The night was magically dark. Someone had had the clever idea of using the pool as a dance floor so all the water had been drained out. Peering in, we saw a DJ mixing music ten feet below and climbed down the steps. Dancing in a big group as teens often do, we felt no particular desire to pair off. Laughter flew up into the air around us. I had rarely spent much time with people my own age because we moved so much and I'd never had a chance to settle down anywhere. So I was enjoying the camaraderie, the feeling of belonging. I liked these people, they seemed to like me and I was content to be in the moment. Suddenly, I noticed a man with curly black hair, in a light pink shirt and khakis, rush across the pool after a girl who seemed agitated. I raised my eyebrows.

'That's Rajeev,' Elahe whispered. 'And *that* was his girlfriend.'

'Oh.' I'd heard about their tempestuous relationship.

Elahe called, 'Rajeev, come meet Bunny, remember I've been telling you about her?'

The girl had disappeared and Rajeev stopped in his tracks and walked over reluctantly to us. After all the buildup our friends had given us, it was inevitable we wouldn't like each other. I could tell he was disgruntled and distracted by the way he said hello. He must have thought I was a shy stick-in-the-mud because of how tersely I responded. He quickly continued on his way, in pursuit of the girl. Nope, not for me, I thought.

The next time we met was a year later at Nampally railway station. My friends dragged me there en route to dinner to say bon voyage to Rajeev who was catching the night train to Bombay. He was headed to flying school in Texas. 'He's studying to be a commercial airline pilot like his father,' Elahe said.

I stayed behind while his friends surrounded him, wishing him all the best and hugging him enthusiastically. He was the life of the party even though he raised my hackles. We both nodded desultorily at each other when reintroduced. Then the whistle blew, he hopped onto the train and headed west. I couldn't understand what Elahe saw in him or why she thought we were anything alike and I didn't give him another thought.

The next year, I moved to Poona while my friends enrolled at St Francis Degree College. As soon as I could head home over summer break, I did. The night I arrived, Elahe insisted I go to a party with the group. 'I can't wait to hang out with you.'

In the car, she introduced me to a new friend. The girl looked me up and down, saying, 'You're right, Elahe. She has the face of an angel,' and dismissed me with that backhanded compliment. The conversation moved on to what was happening in college and suddenly I felt as if my life had moved on without me because I had moved without it. My old friends had new friends, events had taken place that I had no part in, we had no common memories to reminisce over. Yet again, I found that I belonged neither where I was living nor where I'd lived.

Despite the summer heat, it was pleasant on the rooftop of our host's house, with a cool breeze and stars bright in a dark sky. 'OK,' I whispered, shaking myself. 'Come on. Cheer up. You're with your friends, you're at a party, this'll be fun.' Then I turned around and saw my friends disappearing down the stairs to the bathroom. I stayed on the terrace but I didn't know a soul, so I looked lost and helpless. There was music on the stereo but no one was dancing and I hoped my friends would return soon. Ram was sitting on the other side of the terrace. He gave me a broad, friendly smile, we knew each other slightly, but said nothing. I smiled back and wondered what to do. Suddenly, out of nowhere, someone was sauntering towards me. He had watched me struggle with my lack of company. It was Rajeev. I had not known he was in town. I looked at him as if for the first time.

'Hello,' he said in a dark chocolate voice. 'Bunny, right? So? You're all alone. Would you like to dance?'

I could have kissed him for his compassion. Instead, I smiled, tongue-tied, and we stepped onto the dance floor, moving to the rhythm till the beat slowed to a love song. I liked the way he moved. Then he brought me a vodka and lemonade on ice, and we walked over to the roof's edge, leaning against the railing and looking out into the starry night. As we talked, something electric emerged and crackled between us. I took a shy look at his large brown eyes and listened to his low-pitched laugh and wondered why I had ever disliked him. Mysteriously and miraculously, Rajeev seemed to understand me and to know what I was thinking, even when I did not speak. Cheekily, he made fun of me good-naturedly and I didn't mind. And he made me laugh. He was kind and chivalrous, and most importantly, I felt I'd found the person to whom I could say anything. Elahe had been right.

Rajeev and I spent the entire party together. We took a long walk, we talked endlessly, unconsciously ignoring everyone else. I watched him throw his head back and laugh from his throat uninhibitedly when I said something amusing. I could not keep the smile off my face and I knew for certain that I had never before smiled so much in such a short span of time. What had not happened ten feet below the ground in the swimming pool, happened two years later thirty feet above it. By the time the party was over, we were hopelessly in love. I was nearly nineteen, he was 363 days older.

We spent a crazy year infatuated with each other. I got to know his extended family, we discovered we both loved cricket and tennis, our hands fit together beautifully, he liked that I balanced on culverts whenever I could, and I liked the way his teeth caught in his lip when he smiled. But none of that was enough. We were young, immature and unprepared for the influence our friends would have on our decisions. At its most simple, our timing was all wrong.

In 1987, Rajeev was one of the youngest commercial pilots in India. He had a job with the nation's only domestic airline and was literally living in the jet set. Having a serious girlfriend would have cramped his style. As for me, my plans did not revolve around waiting for him to propose. I had things I wanted to do. We made many mistakes in our short-lived relationship, Rajeev and I. The one thing we got right, however, was realizing our importance to each other. Though my other Hyderabad friends fell away, he and I stayed connected. He came to my wedding, and decades later we are still good friends, sharing landmarks and milestones. We have met on three continents and watched each other grow from callow teens to ambitious twenty-year-olds, calmer thirty-somethings and somewhat wiser people in our forties.

One year, we met in San Francisco. Rajeev tried to plan a birthday picnic for me because, though he is not a planner, he knows that I am. The packing of a basket with some ripe cheese, a baguette, fruit, wine and olives; the ritual of finding the perfect spot to sit; the spreading of the blanket and the meticulous laying out of the food; the liberating sensation of eating al fresco, is joyful.

The weather had other ideas. Rain made the picnic impossible but the pleasant dream of it was like clear summer light. The company was delightful, the rosé refreshingly cool, the baguette crusty, the Époisse soft as butter and pungent on my tongue. The picnic 'un-had', like our relationship unexplored, keeps its allure. And the knowledge of being understood, the thought of an outing intended for my enjoyment, is my gift to cherish. To paraphrase my favourite line from Paul Theroux's *The Picture Palace*, the best meals are the ones not eaten, they're the ones in my mind's belly.

In Hyderabad, I found love and friendship, established my sense of self, worked on my craft and cemented the desire to become a writer. Over six years, I saw the city's natural beauty and gracious culture eroding. Unplanned development was changing the old kingdom irrevocably and to my way of thinking, not for the better. It was painful to watch.

Hyderabad was dying. Teenage was over. It was time to move on.

23. The Year of Magical Thinking

Life changes fast.
Life changes in the instant.

—Joan Didion, author of
The Year of Magical Thinking

Life changed for me the moment I reached Bombay. Suddenly I felt free. To dress the way I wanted, go where I wanted and do what I wanted. What London had done for my childhood, the Bombay of 1989, pre-Babri Masjid riots, would do for my nascent adulthood. I was almost twenty-one and raring to get on with life. The city welcomed me into its muggy, gritty, expansive arms. I had been in no hurry to leave my parents but I needed a bigger dance floor to twirl on.

Life, for me, had always been a series of happy accidents. But moving to Bombay, starting media school, meeting writers and filmmakers and political activists, understanding that the world I had always dreamed of was really at my doorstep, was exhilarating. From 1989 to 1990, I set off down the path towards the writing I wanted to do, and the friendships I had always yearned for became a reality at last. Best of all, the year came to a close with my falling in love again, which I had found it hard to believe I would.

I had travelled to Bombay that June to write the entrance test for the Social Communications Media (SCM) course at Sophia BK Somani Polytechnic and was delighted when I passed. I stayed for the next stage of the process selecting forty women students from hundreds of applicants. There was an interview with a panel led by Jeroo Mulla who headed the department and taught film and photography. What if I had not gotten in? I have no idea. But I did get in, and in retrospect, I think Ingmar Bergman and Alexander Dovshenko had a lot to do with it.

When I was five, my parents took me to a screening of Bergman's *Wild Strawberries* on the Poona University campus. Sven Nykvist's cinematography moved me and my imagination filled in colours on the exquisitely lit, black-and-white filmscape. It's possible that *Wild Strawberries* started my love affair with cinema and though I revelled in its happy, childish summer scenes, what stayed with me was the disturbing, powerful dream sequence, with its images of a mortality confronted. Fifteen years later when asked in the SCM exam to describe two film scenes that had moved me, I wrote about the clock without hands in the Bergman dream scene, and the terror the old man must have felt seeing his own death before him. I didn't know that Jeroo loved Bergman and taught his films in the course. Nor did I know when I wrote my description of the second scene that Jeroo taught Dovshenko's pioneering 1930 film, *Earth*, with its exquisite shots of stalks of wheat blowing in a field. I knew nothing about the film but I'd recently seen a movie called *Witness*, a mystery set in Amish country, starring Harrison Ford. One of the most memorable images to me was of an expanse of golden wheat rippling in the breeze.

I learned more about film, photography, art, writing and the media that year than I could ever have dreamed or hoped to. I could research and write, discuss and debate, in ways I'd wanted to for years and I got practical, hands-on training in radio and television reportage and filmmaking. Jeroo had professional journalists, filmmakers and ad men on faculty, giving the students the chance to interact with professionals like P. Sainath, Ravi Hazare and Sidharth Bhatia with whom they might later train. Jeroo also brought in stellar guest speakers: Mark Tully of the BBC and filmmakers Javed Akthar, Arun Khopkar, Anand Patwardhan and Rinki Bhattacharya.

At Sophia's, I also met three women who became my closest friends. Leena Pandit, Jagruti Kapasi, Sameera Khan and I were twenty. In the years since, we have seen each other through disastrous jobs, failed love affairs and challenging child-rearing moments. We have attended each other's weddings and stood by each other during painful separations and messy divorces. Between us, we have seven children; four girls and three boys, ranging in age from twenty-one to seven. Two of us married early, two of us married late. Two of us studied abroad after our journalism degrees, another two ended up living outside India. We might meet annually or after a space of several years. No matter how long it is between meetings, when we see each other it is as if there was no gap, no pause in conversation.

The last significant event of my first year in Bombay was meeting a young architecture student named Sanjiv Bajaj. I was the photographer, he the model. I'd been at the Polytechnic for eight months and never seen him, though he lived right next door. One lazy Sunday afternoon in late January, my roommate, a textile design student, asked me, 'You're studying photography, could you take some good pictures of my fabrics?'

She loaded me, another dorm mate who was modelling for her, and her props into a car. Her male model had ditched her so she parked outside college and ran into a compound. 'I'll be right back. Family friends of ours live here,' she explained. 'Maybe their son will help me out.'

A few moments later, she emerged with a tall, young man who walked over to the car and looked in the window to say a friendly hello. I looked up from under a pile of fabrics into the face of an angel. Translucent brown eyes gleamed down at me and a slim hand reached up to brush thick black hair off his forehead. Red lips broke into a wide smile on the face of the boy whose name was Sanjiv.

'Hi. Your car's pretty full. I'll meet you up there. I can walk.' He headed up the hill while we drove, my head in a whirl because (a) he had chosen to walk (big points in my book) and (b) I had just seen my future.

Over the next few months, Sanjiv and I got to know each other better and dated almost exclusively. By the time the SCM course ended in May, I had a job at the *Free Press Journal* and a serious romantic relationship. Bombay gave me an exquisite opening of doors.

It was my *happy* year of magical thinking and I couldn't wait to see what the next few years would bring.

24. Getting the Story

Persons appear to us according to the light we throw upon them from our own minds.

—Laura Ingalls Wilder, *The First Four Years*

Anyone can write. I'm a case in point. I have been writing for more than three-quarters of my life but I didn't start off that way.

Unlike other arts, painting, music, ballet, which require specialized training and often a certain inherent skill, talent or body type, writing is democratic. Any writer will tell you that anyone can be a writer. All they need is the discipline to hone their skills every day. For the first decade of my life, I hated to write. Then in Canada, Mom made me keep a diary. When I was eleven, Mom sent a poem of mine to the local broadsheet. *The London Free Press* published it. By then I was hooked. I told my journals everything and having no close friends because we moved so much, my notebooks became my confidantes.

When I was fifteen, Dad's friend, the well-known Oriya poet, Jayanta Mahapatra, came to lecture at the English department in Hyderabad. During the visit, Dad casually said, 'Bunny, you might like to show Jayanta some of your poems.'

Ugh, how embarrassing, I thought, wishing that Dad would not ask me to perform for guests. But I fetched my book. The poet read many poems slowly and thoughtfully. To me, seeing my work with his eyes, it was melodramatic teenage drivel; hyperbolic, overly sentimental, tortured, mostly about unrequited love. I felt sorry for him. Yet, I knew there were strengths. My subject matter may have been personal or mundane but my secret weapon was my ear. The sounds of the English language were so comforting and familiar that I could easily detect a false note in the spoken and written word and I worked to achieve a natural and rhythmic cadence in whatever I wrote.

The poet looked up. 'These are very good. Don't give up, you have talent,' he said. 'Make sure you write every day. Even if you don't feel like it. One day I will see your work in a book.'

Despite his kindness, it soon became evident that I was no poet, but what I learned from Jayanta Mahapatra was a lesson I would learn over and over. Practice makes perfect. From that day I started carrying my notebook everywhere. The more regularly I wrote, the easier it got.

The other component to my growth as a writer was the time I spent telling stories. As quiet and shy as I was in public, my mother was fond of telling people, 'She is quiet only till you get to know her.' I chatted to Mom incessantly. I discovered I was funny and learned to recount an amusing incident so that the punch line really had an impact on listeners. Oral storytelling solidifies memories but they are still viscous like jelly. The teller can shift, jiggle, tweak, alter, embellish the tale each time, based on his audience and the frequency of telling. Writing a story down on paper cements the memory, making it permanent. As James Salter wrote in his novel, *All That Is*, 'There comes a time when you realize that everything is a dream, and only those things preserved in writing have any possibility of being real.'

*

In June 1990, my best friend Sameera and I started our first jobs as reporters at the *Free Press Journal* in Bombay. We got to know a cast of characters there who made us laugh, think, argue, and become better reporters. There was the gentle Sonal Patel; our soft-spoken assistant editor, Arun Sinha; and the noisy genius who stomped into the newsroom one day and has stayed with me ever since. Jerry Pinto.

Jerry freelanced for the *FPJ* and came in to submit work to our managing editor, the great Janardhan Thakur. Jerry towered over everyone and when he walked into the newly added, air-conditioned computer room, his head nearly touched the low ceiling. We were working at clunky desktop computers, F1 and F2-ing our way to modern reportage. When Jerry threw open the door, he said something characteristically off-colour and made all the male reporters blush, except Stanislaus D'Souza who just chuckled. Me, demure, proper and only twenty-two, was astonished by the man's obnoxiousness. I stared at him coldly and turned back to my article. Emerging from the cool room some time later, I saw Sameera happily sipping chai with Jerry and talking excitedly about her next story. She introduced us and I reluctantly said hello. Jerry loves to tell the rest of the story.

'Nice nail polish,' he said, looking at my long nails. 'Nice orange colour.'

I looked at him, then at my nails and said haughtily, 'That's not orange. That's tangerine.'

I was acutely aware that while Sameera had a nose for news, I did not much care about it at all, particularly political news. My interest in getting the story was a literary one. Sameera is the daughter of Irfan Khan, a journalist who had been working in the early 1970s and who, during Prime Minister Indira Gandhi's ruthless Emergency roundups of press people, was assistant editor at *The Indian Express*, New Delhi. He faced police harassment and though never actually arrested, was regularly interrogated at Red Fort. Then he was sent to be editor of the *Express*' Vijayawada edition, away from the political hub of things. He also edited

JP Narayan's *Everyman's Weekly*. So his daughter had grown up around news and politics. For me, it was not essential to wait for the newspaper each morning the way Sameera did, to open it with excitement, pore over the headlines and then debate the news stories, the reporting, and the issues. I did not have a favourite page I turned to with bated breath.

And yet become a journalist I did, developing a genuine interest in news. I grew the nose and learned to know when a good story was lurking beneath the surface of a casual comment or a mundane event, but inevitably I was really driven by the need to craft an excellent piece of prose. For fifteen years or so after becoming friends, we secretly admired in each other what we felt we each lacked. I was in awe of the way she could take a news story and put it into historical and political context, analyzing it and providing perspective as it unfolded. For her part, she confided in me one day, 'I wish I could write like you, Bunny.'

There are two main threads I've pursued as a journalist and writer. The first is the desire I developed to know, the curiosity to ask questions of whomsoever I was with and most certainly of people who seemed as if they were doing interesting and unusual things with their lives. Everywhere are stories waiting to be heard, stories needing to be told. The other is my desire to document vanishing aspects of society: food, traditions, mores, buildings, neighbourhoods, history being lost to time and change.

Luckily, I did not yet have much freedom to write what I wanted. There was news and I had to cover it. Not having a choice about what stories I would be assigned on a day-to-day basis, I learned to write on demand and quickly.

That's why I say anyone can be a writer…if they work at it.

25. To Tell the Truth

Newly lit lamps
in the houses across the street
make me look out at the wet August evening
that holds up the vast unknown
in such small delicate hands.

—Jayanta Mahapatra, *Twilight*

'There's a fire! Stop!'

When I was an intern at the *FPJ* in Nariman Point, Sanjiv and Leena worked nearby. One evening, they picked me up after work. Leena was driving us home, past Mantralaya, the state government buildings, towards the Oberoi Hotel so we could turn onto Marine Drive and head north. As we passed the Oberoi, a flicker of light caught my eye.

'Stop, stop, Leena, please,' I exclaimed. 'I see flames.' I have to admit now that, fresh out of J-school, I was more excited about getting to cover this news story than anything else. We parked and I ran across the street. Sure enough, smoke was billowing out of the ground floor windows of the building, near one of its restaurants. I asked a hotel staff member what had happened and was told that a blaze had broken out in the basement. Guests were being evacuated and fire engines were beginning to whine their way to the site. I called my editor Janardhan Thakur to ask if he wanted to me to cover the fire. He did. No other reporters were on the scene but I was inwardly hopping up and down with excitement because this was front-page news.

'Come back and file the story when you've talked to the management and bystanders,' Mr Thakur told me. 'I'm sending Shashikant (Bajpai, a staff photographer) to you.'

As I interviewed hotel guests and staff, I saw Shashikant loping toward me. Once he had the photographs he needed, we headed back to the office. It was quiet, only the reporters on night shift were arriving and sipping glasses of chai to ease into their workday. I waved to Stanley and his buddies at the sports desk, sat down at my computer and wrote excitedly. Thankfully no one was injured in the fire, probably caused by a short circuit, and it was put out by the next day. Still, a fire in a hotel of that stature was big news. Mr Thakur hovered, bird-like, eager, as he always was when there was a good story in the offing. When I was done, he sent it off to the print room to be typeset. 'Good work,' he patted my shoulder, as I prepared to head home. 'That's a front-page byline.'

Seeing my name on that story, under the masthead, the next morning was the pinnacle of excitement for a twenty-two-year-old cub reporter. There were other thrilling moments in 1990: the time Mr Thakur gave me the opportunity to write an editorial and on another day, an op-ed. There were the stories I filed about the housing scandal that was raging in Bombay's northern suburb of Vasai. And there were assignments that went beyond thrilling to frightening. I went to Mantralaya to interview a recently elected senior Legislative Assembly member who belonged to the sectarian Shiv Sena party. When I was shown into his office, he stood up and stretched his arm out in what I considered a Hitleresque salute.

'*Jai Maharashtra*,' he said. '*Jai Bala Saheb*' (long live Maharashtra, long live Bal Thackeray, the leader of the Shiv Sena).

I responded politely, folding my hand together. 'Namaskar.'

He looked disgruntled but we sat down and started the interview. One of my questions was about Thackeray and I referred to him as Mr Thackeray.

'*Bala Saheb mahna*,' he commanded. 'Refer to him as Bala Saheb.'

I tried to move on, asking my next question. He stopped me, putting out his hand. 'Your name is Marathe,' he said in Marathi. 'You should be asking me these questions in your mother tongue.'

Noam Chomsky once said, 'The duty of journalists is to tell the truth. Journalism means you go back to the actual facts, you look at the documents, you discover what the record is, and you report it that way.' I did not tell the politician I did not believe in his party's record. I did not say that I believed Thackeraywas a tyrant with a political party whose manifesto was predicated on sectarianism. I also did not say my loyalty was first and foremost to my country.

I simply explained that I wrote for an English language paper, that English was my first language and that my Marathi was not good enough to allow me to ask him the questions I needed to. He did not like my response. I was asked to leave and as I stood up, so did the politician. He stuck his arm out in the typical Shiv Sena salute and gave me a stern look, saying by way of farewell, '*Jai Maharashtra. Jai Bala Saheb*.' His eyes dared me not to echo his words and as I looked at him, I quaked inside.

'Thank you,' I replied firmly, folding my hands together again. '*Jai Bharat*.' Then I turned on my heel and walked out of the room.

*

I was innocent back then, outspoken and fearless. I also think that I was more than a little lucky on several occasions to come away unscathed. I did not, however, feel very fortunate the morning I got to work before the rest of the reporting staff, and was given the assignment of covering a suicide near my office. It had happened just a few moments earlier. As a child, I had been easily frightened, suffering from nightmares, unable to watch horror or suspense films without shivers and screams, and dreaming about them afterwards. I was also notoriously squeamish about dirt, vomit and blood. On that morning, I got my first adult lesson in detachment. There was no way out, I had a job to do, no matter how horrible I found the circumstance. I steeled myself to be brave as I walked to the office building where the young man had jumped. As I entered the compound and strode towards the body which lay face down on the pavement, I felt my self move out of my head and float in space above my body. My emotions were hung up dry and safely out of reach of the sticky wetness of blood.

The man was tall, late-twenties, working class. He had climbed to the top of the twelve-storey building on that bright summer's day and jumped because nothing made sense anymore, because a love affair had gone wrong, his demons were haunting him too often or he just had no one to talk to. He lay in a widening pool of blood and as I talked to bystanders, I was struck by how darkly crimson it was. I walked around the body, the face not visible and likely shattered. I can still see the checked shirt and dark blue pants, the shape of the young man's skull. He looked as if he were just sleeping. I hoped he was at peace.

As I filed my story, I expected nausea and fright to set in. Much to my surprise, they did not nor did I ever have a nightmare about the young man. My fear of ghosts vanished and I took a few more steps towards growing up, only feeling a deep sadness for the dead man's wasted opportunities and his family's ignorance of his passing.

*

The essence of why I became a writer was to hear, understand and make sense of the story and its reward has been the variety of work I've done and the people I have met. There is no time to stagnate or be bored and I know now that this is the secret to keeping my interest in writing alive. How can one get bored interviewing Renzo Piano and Charles Correa, B.D. Garga and Nisha Ganatra, Madhur Jaffrey, Nissim Ezekiel and Imtiaz Dharker? I am compelled to learn their histories, understand their narratives, their unique reasons for being and their motivation for choosing the work they do.

Every meeting has been memorable but if I had to choose from twenty-five years of such interviews, four are etched deeply in my mind, because each person was fascinating and because each resulted in an unexpected souvenir of the encounter. I once interviewed Bombay-based painter Mehli Gobai in anticipation of one of his upcoming exhibitions. We met at his home where he showed me some of his work. I was fascinated by the person and the art, and excitedly mentioned Mehli to Jerry, who is one of those people who knows everyone. Of course, he and the artist were friends and of course they had already talked about me. He smiled. 'Mehli told me he met you.' He paused dramatically, 'He said you were one of the five most beautiful women he has *ever* seen.'

'Really?' I was astonished and flattered.

Sanjiv and I had gotten married just a few months before and I told him this story, rather amused. A few weeks later, we went together to Mehli's exhibition at a gallery in the Fort. The artist was hanging paintings and I introduced him to my husband. I couldn't stop laughing when Jerry reported the next day, 'Kaumudi, Mehli says that you are lovely and all, but your husband? Now *he* is really something else!'

Soon after that, I moved to the USA where Sanjiv was to study at the University of Texas. One evening, Jerry stopped by with a bon voyage gift, flat and long and carefully wrapped. 'What is it?' I wondered, tearing off layers of newspaper to see.

'Something for you to remember Bombay by,' he replied as I uncovered a framed pen-and-ink nude and gasped.

'It's one of Mehli's. I asked him if I could have it for you.'

*

After a lifetime of having smiled over Mario Miranda's cartoons, especially the iconic beaten-down Every Indian Man with the Nagging Wife who appeared in *The Illustrated Weekly of India* when I was a child, I was honoured to interview him one day. I visited his

Colaba apartment filled with art and plants, a dog and a tortoise or two strolling the cool tile floor. Still a shy twenty-something awed in the presence of greatness, I asked my questions hesitantly but Mario was so kind and unassuming that he put me at ease.

Sameera and I were working at the *FPJ* then, one of the many publications for which Mario drew. We were horrified to learn that those cartoons, and the press photographs our colleagues shot, were simply tossed aside the day after publication, giving new meaning to the truism, 'Today's news is tomorrow's history.' They lay in a stack in the newsroom before being condemned to the trash bin. One day, I stood staring at a large sketch by Mario in that pile. He had drawn it to commemorate a now forgotten cricket series. A montage of images celebrated India's cricket madness. In one frame was his famous, endearing, Bollywood actress, Miss Nimbupani. She appeared distracted on the set of a love scene, asking the crew, 'What's the cricket score, yaar?'

Her director begged for more realism in her acting, asking that she visualize doing the scene with a famous cricketer. 'Imagine Imran Khan is making love to you,' he pleaded.

In just a few quick strokes, curves and words, Mario captured, with tender gentleness and humour, the national mania. I laughed out loud before putting down the picture. Two days later there it still was. 'Mr Thakur, may I take this home?' I asked. 'No one seems to want it.'

'Yes, yes, of course,' he answered walking by, head filled with the day's editorial. 'Give it a good home.'

The second time I interviewed Mario was even more special. I was now freelancing for *The Times of India*, *The Indian Express* and *The Pioneer*. I had created a niche for myself, writing about local history, architecture and conservation. However, I was often asked to write other features and human-interest stories. My editor at *The Pioneer* once suggested a weekly column about friendships between prominent Bombay personalities, accompanied by a black-

and-white portrait. Bal Mundkur and Sharada Dwivedi or Mario Miranda and ad man and theatre personality, Gerson Da Cunha.

After interviewing Gerson who was rehearsing for a play, I headed over to Mario's. Earlier that day, I had asked the editor, 'What if we don't use a photograph? I could ask Mr Miranda to draw a sketch instead?' The editor liked the idea and Mario acquiesced graciously, asking me to wait just a few minutes. I watched as he sketched deftly and quickly, and the image of Gerson performing in Shakespeare's *Richard III* with Mario cheering him on from the audience, took shape. The column and illustration were published that weekend and I got to take the original home.

*

My souvenir from Amitabh Bachchan was what *he* is most known for, his voice, and what every Indian girl of a certain generation wanted from the Angry Young Man of Bollywood, his autograph. In my wildest dreams, I couldn't imagine I'd ever meet this larger-than-life man who had filled my daydreams when I was seven and whom, along with a besotted nation, I had watched transform Indian cinema, admiring his humour and his tall, dark lankiness in *Sholay*, *Kabhi Kabhie*, and *Amar Akbar Anthony*. But by the time I was twelve, I had outgrown the crush and mainstream Hindi movies.

Fashion photographer, Gautam Rajadhyaksha, asked one day if I'd do some work for him. He was collating his photos for a book and Amitabh had agreed to write the introduction. Now the actor was busy shooting a music video for *Ek Rahen Beer* so he was willing to have a writer ghostwrite a few paragraphs. Gautam liked my style so he requested me to meet with Mr Bachchan, record an interview and try writing something in his voice. My introduction was never used.

But I had shown up at the Jesuit school in Bandra where Amitabh was shooting with a bevy of dancers. He was as tall as he appeared on screen, I thought, glad of the opportunity to watch him perform before our talk.

'That voice really is something else,' I muttered, setting up my mini voice recorder. Having reviewed my questions, I tussled with another problem that had plagued me for days. I was here in my professional capacity and as much as I would have liked to, I didn't think I could ask Amitabh for his autograph.

Yes? No? No, Bunny, you should not! said my inner voice and I nodded in agreement as I watched him walking towards me. He greeted me warmly, shaking my hand. We sat down towards the back of the theatre and I asked if I could turn my recorder on.

'Of course,' he replied. Then he asked me my name again.

'Kaumudi,' I repeated as my tape recorder rolled.

'That is beautiful,' he said, looking at me curiously. 'What does it mean?'

And the son of a poet was delighted when I answered, 'Moonlight.'

I asked him what he thought of Gautam and his photography and how he would like to introduce him. He answered my questions in his deep, sonorous voice. And as we wrapped up our conversation, he smiled widely at me. At me! The professional, calm journalist flew out the window, replaced by a seven-year-old sitting in front of her Hero.

'May I have your autograph, please?' she asked and was met with a brilliant smile and a flash of pen across paper.

*

Of all the fascinating people I've had the good fortune to meet, be it India's first woman photojournalist, Homai Vyarawalla, or Australian cricketer Allan Border, none has been more tangibly moving or well remembered as the brief meeting which I was unprepared for and did not know I would ever have a souvenir of. In 1990, when I was still a *Free Press* reporter, Janardhan

Thakur sent me on a routine assignment to cover a press event at Asha Daan. Hindustan Levers was organizing the Missionaries of Charities programme and Sameera's father, Irfan Khan, their head of corporate communications, asked that I cover it. More than two decades later, my memory of the event is vague at best. After the speeches and show, a line formed of people eager to meet the chief guest, Mother Teresa.

She sat modestly, smiling and shaking people's hands, her small frame flanked by the larger figure of the Dutch CEO of Levers and another bigwig. I admired her and had a Canadian high school friend whose dream it was to work with her one day. I would love to tell Veronika I had met her hero, but I shied away from lining up to see famous personalities, subscribing to the notion that nothing much was to be gained from a thirty-second meeting with illustriousness. So I would have quietly slipped out if I could. Uncle Irfan, however, had other ideas.

He found me edging for the door and called me over. 'You've got to meet Mother Teresa.' Being thus summoned, I waited and when it was time, Uncle Irfan introduce me to the wonderful lady. 'This is my daughter's friend, Kaumudi,' he explained. 'She is a reporter at the *Free Press*.'

'Oh yes,' said Mother Teresa, looking up at me, smiling sweetly and taking my hand in her soft one. As it surrounded mine, holding it firmly, I looked down at the wrinkled pink skin and felt a warmth radiate from her to me. It was a rare and positive energy. A quarter of a century later, I still remember exactly how her hand felt and how she gave me her precious chi. Several months later, Sameera handed me an envelope at work. 'Here,' she said casually. 'Papa sent these for you.'

I opened the envelope curiously. Inside were two copies of a photograph I didn't know anyone had taken, a black-and-white, and a colour copy of the moment when Mother Teresa held my hand in hers. My breath caught in my throat. I was transported back to that day when she was smiling up at me and I was returning her smile wholeheartedly. From her eyes and her touch, I knew I was in the presence of greatness, far beyond anything I could comprehend.

And small, delicate hands were holding up to me the vast unknown.

26. I Want to Write a Book

I hold a beast, an angel, and a madman in me, and my enquiry is as to their working, and my problem is their subjugation and victory, downthrow and upheaval, and my effort is their self-expression.

—Dylan Thomas, poet

One afternoon in Bombay, I woke up from an intense dream in which I longed to write a book.

After a year at the *Free Press Journal* and two years teaching video and radio journalism at my alma mater, I'd decided I wanted the flexibility of being a freelancer. I knew I could make a good living that way and I was developing my own writing niche. Sanjiv had gotten a job with Rahul Mehrotra, who was opening an architectural practice in the city after finishing his Masters at Harvard University's Graduate School of Design and was about to change the way urban Indians looked at architecture. Sanjiv was ecstatic to find work with this thoughtful and talented young architect.

My husband's interest in preserving the city's local and colonial architecture coincided with my love of history. I began writing about architecture and interior design for *Inside Outside* magazine whose editor Sheila Shahani and I developed a warm relationship. I also wrote for a number of broadsheets, including a local history column that was born out of Sunday morning walks that Sanjiv and I took with our engineer friend Sualeh Fatehi, and anyone else who wanted to go. We explored parts of the city beyond the main two thoroughfares that most people seemed to stick to. We discovered interesting bits of local history, folklore, food and culture in a rainbow city packed with people of every ethnicity and religion. There were Armenians, Goans, East Indian Christians, Gujarati and North Indian Muslims, Parsis, Anglo Indians, Koli fisherfolk, Baghdadi Jews and Marathi communities from other parts of the state, who were either new migrants or had a long tradition of residence, life, work, and worship in the colonial city. We explored parts of town I might otherwise never have known and ate at local eateries and I got the opportunity to settle in and really know the city where I thought I was going to spend the rest of my life. The weekly article for *The Times of India* was very popular, illustrated in pen-and-ink by Sanjiv. It led to other assignments I was delighted to accept.

*

One night, I worked till 4 am completing an article for *The Times of India*. I was young, energetic and not having children yet, I had the freedom to work late into the night and catch up on sleep the next day. That is why I was napping that afternoon, on the diwan that converted into our bed at night. The endless honking of cars outside the window of our small, one-room apartment at Sukh Sagar no longer bothered me. The heat did not bother me either. I was so tired I slept deeply and dreamt.

I had always had intense dreams that I could remember clearly after waking up. In this one, I was champing at the bit to write a book. I was twenty-six and it seemed like the time was right. I felt restless like I needed to get started on a new project.

I woke with a start, thinking, it's time, Bunny. As I lay there pondering my dream, the grey telephone rang. I picked up the receiver and said hello.

'Kaumudi?' enquired a gruff, cigarette-roughened voice. It was Sharada Dwivedi, renowned local Bombay historian whom I had interviewed for several stories.

'Hi, Sharada.'

Without further ado, she enquired, 'How would you like to write a book?'

'What?' I exclaimed, my mind doing a doubletake. Once it had stopped whirling like a dervish, I continued. 'Yes, of course, I would…love to.'

'Well, good. Come down to BPI (Business Publications India) in a couple of days and I'll introduce you to the editor, Chandralekha Maitra. She can tell you more about it. We are looking at publishing an introduction to India's temple architecture.'

I hung up, my breath caught in my throat. Oh my God, I thought. This cannot be happening. This cannot be happening… Oh God, it is!

The smile stayed on my face as I waited on tenterhooks for my appointment with Chandralekha and Sharada at the BPI office. Meanwhile, my mind travelled all across the nation, I jotted down ideas of what a book on temples would look like, and I went to the Bombay Local History Library at St Xavier's College and dipped into the work of Stella Kramrisch, leading authority and documentarian of Hindu architecture. In my mind, this was a project that would take years of travel across India, and if possible, Pakistan and Bangladesh. The possibility of photographing the little-known temples of Kashmir, Sindh and Bengal was intoxicating. I saw myself in a study, surrounded by books, photographs, maps, putting together a comprehensive history of India's Hindu architecture. A writer's dream come true.

As with many of my dreams and prayers, there was an important caveat. Soft-spoken and kind, Chandralekha Maitra expressed pleasure in meeting me and explained her vision. 'We want this book to be part of a series on India, for Indians and foreign tourists. Short, affordable, an easy to read introduction to Hindu temples.'

This meant several things:

1. There was no budget for photography so the plan was to use stock photos that I could source.
2. There was no budget for travel so all my research would be secondary.
3. There was a very short turnaround time so I would not be spending years researching this subject.

'We need the book in three months,' she finished and I blinked in shock. 'Do you think you could do it? And does that interest you?'

I was dumbfounded. Three months to research and write a book about this abundance of ancient architecture? Then again, why not? I could do it. If someone asked me to write a book in this way today, I would stop and have a very long think, but the wonderful beauty of youth is that it permits you to take crazy risks. I recovered my composure, took a deep breath, and jumped off that cliff.

'Yes, I'd love to,' I smiled. 'I'll do it.'

Figuring out how was something I didn't consider until I was in a cab headed home. But figure it out I did. I gave myself two months and three weeks to research my material. I made copious notes, pored over photographs and plans, framed a structure and began writing paragraphs as they came to me. That left the last week of my time for a fullscale writing session. We had bought a desktop with a colour screen using the money I received as an advance from the publisher. We set it up on my walnut desk that had held the Brother typewriter, my twenty-first birthday gift from Mom and Dad.

I started writing in earnest on a Monday that first week of December, and worked twenty hours straight, pausing only to eat, use the bathroom and sleep for a few hours. My brother was staying with us. He and Sanjiv kept me supplied with cups of tea and food. Jerry Pinto stopped by to offer encouragement. Seven days, twenty hours a day, five thousand words each day, and I was done. I took a cab to Chandralekha's and handed her a floppy disc containing an edited, pristine 35,000-word manuscript.

*

Temples of India: Circles of Stone was published in 1998 before my thirtieth birthday by which time I had already pitched another book to Chandralekha. 'No one has written a cookbook in English about Marathi food,' I told her. 'I would love to document recipes from my grandmothers, aunts and friends.' She loved the idea so I started work on *Maharashtrian Cuisine: A Family Treasury*. We moved to the USA in 1996 so I did a lot of my research long-distance and also travelled to Maharashtra to interview relatives and friends. While Sanjiv was getting his Masters at the University of Texas at Austin, I was collating the recipes for my first cookbook.

It appeared in 1999 and when I saw the author copies, I was horrified to realize that the typesetters had missed the i on my first name on the cover, printing it as Kaumud Marathé instead of Kaumudi Marathé. I asked my publisher to redo the cover and, of course, he replied that he could not. I called my parents, upset and frustrated.

'Did you know that when Toni Morrison's first book was published, her name was printed on the cover as TONY?' asked Dad. 'You're in good company, you see?'

His question gave me a great idea. I went out and bought black Sharpies and used them when I signed copies of the book, filling in the i at the end of my name.

Each copy of my book became a special first edition!

27. Tie & Knot

You have to love. You have to feel. It is the reason you are here on earth. You are here to risk your heart. You are here to be swallowed up. And when it happens that you are broken, or betrayed, or left, or hurt, or death brushes near, let yourself sit by an apple tree and listen to the apples falling all around you in heaps, wasting their sweetness. Tell yourself you tasted as many as you could.

—Louise Erdrich, *The Painted Drum*

Ganesha, the elephant god, remover of obstacles; baby Krishna, symbol of fertility; Annapurna, the goddess of food and plenty.

My mother put three little silver idols down on the table. I'd grown up with them. Though my parents were not religious, the idols were cleaned regularly and a lamp lit for them on festival days.

'Which would you like, Bunny?' Mom asked.

I looked at the little figurines. In Maharashtra, a mother gives her daughter these deities when she gets married. Mom had already given me a silver Ganesha but she wanted me to also have one of her statuettes. 'They've brought me good luck. Choose one and I will keep the other for when Sameer gets married.'

I think she secretly hoped that I would have a child soon. I was born within a year of their marriage and she would have relished being a grandmother. So, I considered Annapurna and Krishna. I loved children but knew I did not want to have a child until Sanjiv and I felt our marriage was truly stable. I also wanted to accomplish certain career goals so that I would never grudge my child the time I gave him or her. Subconsciously too, I knew that having a child then was absolutely the wrong thing to do. And the feminist in me was not a big admirer of Krishna who played fast and loose with the women in his life.

So I chose Annapurna. She would bring me good fortune, I hoped. We would always have plenty. And since she was the goddess of food and I loved food, she seemed like a good omen. Perhaps thanks to her, food began to play a large role in my life. For my first cookbook, I suggested a picture of her for the cover and the publisher liked the idea. So Krishna languished.

I took a long time to understand the term tying the knot. On 12 December 1991, we were dressed in our wedding finery, I with my great-grandmother's fig-coloured silk and gold shela around the traditional yellow silk sari in which I was given away by my honourary uncles, Sanjiv in a beige silk kurta with thin green stripes. Wide-eyed and innocent, we looked like babes in the woods, much younger than our twenty-three years. We stood in my parents' garden by my prajakta tree. When we had to make our seven ritual circumambulations around the sacred fire, the priest tied the end of my shawl to the end of Sanjiv's. Thus attached, we made our cautious way around the flames while the priest recited Sanskrit verses about our vows, the meaning of marriage and the prospect of our lives together. When the seven trips were completed, the knot between us had been tied 'forever'.

*

On my wedding day, there was a pout on my lips, anger, resentment and probably a premonition of doom in my heart. My fiancé's family had not accepted me and I was hurt and confused. Sanjiv's father boycotted our wedding and his mother came reluctantly. We were a very young couple by any nation's late twentieth-century standards. And we looked about fifteen, which is what had brought us to this day in the first place. We had tried just living together. This was fine in 1990s America or Europe, but Bombay? I was a rookie journalist living in a working women's hostel, Sanjiv was finishing architecture school, living at home as most Indians do, even after they get married. We were young, in love, and just wanted to be together. Since his family did not approve, we had nowhere to go, like every other dating couple in that city, to be alone. We spent our paltry incomes eating out every evening, wearing ourselves ragged just to be with each other after work and school, with no private space for intimacy. When we finally decided to get an apartment together, finding one became our second job. Due to some very tough housing laws, no one wanted to rent out their apartments in Bombay. The few we found were either exorbitant or dismal, offering shared entrances and common use of the kitchen. As soon as landlords saw us, however, even those places became unavailable. 'We need to see a marriage certificate,' they said, virtually in unison.

Then there was the fact that Sanjiv's family was not pleased about our relationship. My parents, as modern and liberated as they were, had an old-fashioned suggestion that made sense. 'Why don't you get married? If that is what you plan to do in a few years, consider it now. It would make Sanjiv's parents happy and will enable you to rent an apartment.'

I found it ironic that once we decided we would get married and informed Sanjiv's family, they asked, 'Why bother? Just live together.'

In the face of conflict, however, we were spurred to do what felt right. Get married we would. Being pushed in this way, perhaps we were doomed from the start. And yet we made things work for a long, long time. We shared a love of architecture and travel, we loved talking politics. Over time, I won Sanjiv's family over and learned all about his Sindhi community and culture. Bada mummy, his grandmother, had taken to me instantly and was unfailingly kind and warm, which helped me ease into the Bajajs' life and patterns. She talked to me in Sindhi so I learned the language enough to understand what relatives were talking about. And she taught me about Sindhi food. I asked her questions about life in Shikarpur (in the Sindh, now in Pakistan) where she grew up. Her stories of the Bajaj haveli and the food cooked there in an era of luxury and leisure were astounding. Giant handis were filled with chunks of lamb, tomatoes, onions and spices, sealed with dough, and lowered into pits in the garden. They were cooked slowly overnight over an open flame for a succulent, flavourful dish you could scoop up in chapatis.

'Ooh,' I said, 'Bada mummy, that sounds so good. Can we try making it here?'

So she directed Asha, our family cook, who was from Bengal but adept at cooking our family's specialities, through the cooking process and proudly served me the dish when it was done.

'*Khao, beta,*' she said. '*Bahut accha banaa hai.*'

And was it ever, the meat falling apart in my hand, aromatic with cinnamon and cardamom, redolent with nostalgia. As I ate, I was amused and intrigued that Bada mummy could insist so confidently that the dish was delicious even though she was a strict vegetarian who had never tasted meat of any kind. How could she know? I wondered. Was she just trying to make me eat more, as she often did?

But no, there was a really important lesson in her comment. I pondered this for years and the more I cooked, the more I began to understand how she had known. She didn't need to taste. There is a smell to raw meat that alters as it cooks. The meat takes on the flavours of the spices, yoghurt, oil, salt, and develops a composite aroma and taste. An experienced cook understands whether the meat is ready, what it lacks and if it tastes right.

Though I didn't do it consciously, I also connected with my mother-in-law through food. After all, she was most often to be found in the kitchen. Hers was a large family that entertained lavishly. Once Mom and I had moved beyond our initial hesitation with each other, we built a relationship based on an awareness of the other's hard work and family loyalty. Whenever I visited my in-laws, I always followed her into the kitchen to help out. Though there was a posse of servants to do her bidding, she was the director of this production. If there was a party, things were even more frenetic. Mom spent hours preparing a meal and even after guests had arrived, she was still in the kitchen, directing the flow of appetizers, making sure the food was heated to just the right temperature and garnished properly, and that hot puris or chapatis were being rolled, cooked and brought to the table quickly enough to feed everyone.

My sisters-in-law were not interested in cooking so their mother was happy to share what she knew with me. Over time, she responded more enthusiastically to my constant questions about Sindhi food, sharing recipes with me for Sindhi kadhi, a sweet-tart lentil soup which Sanjiv loved, twice fried potato chunks called tuk, and my personal favourite, dharanji kadhi, steamed lentil flour dumplings that are fried and dunked in a tomato-onion sauce.

28. Coming to America

We're coming over to y'all's house.

—Lawson Newman

On Indian Independence Day, 15 August 1996, Sanjiv left India. He was headed to Austin, Texas, to study for a Masters in Urban Design. I was to join him three months later once I had packed up our Bombay apartment, finished pending writing assignments and tied up loose ends. Mostly, I wanted my husband who'd gone from living with his parents to living with me, to experience bachelor life.

Sanjiv always says I pushed him to go to the USA, that he would not have left India had it not been for me. I thought he needed an interlude, a change, and an expansion of his horizons. We were young, energized and raring to go when we got married. I was completely under the spell of his charm, his talent for talking about architecture and design with passion and knowledge. I admired his aesthetic and our tastes seemed to coincide, even though he loved mid-century modern architecture and I was more of an Edwardian girl!

By the time I arrived in Austin that December, Sanjiv had settled into college life and made close friends with his classmates, Lawson Newman and Clarke Gernon, both Southern boys. The Masters programme included travel so Lawson, Clarke and Sanjiv had the opportunity to visit Taos and Santa Fe; Marfa, Texas; important architectural sites in Mexico; and the United Kingdom.

He was getting exposure to different facets of life, taking classes in music and history, working as a teaching assistant in the architecture school, and in his last semester, researching and writing his Master's dissertation on colonial Bombay. He was so busy that he often came home late at night and I was left to my own devices. This was no hardship. I have always been happy alone, content with my own company. And I was thrilled to be back in North America with the freedom it gave me to walk, to read, to experiment with ingredients I had only read about in Laura Ingalls Wilder's books and novels like *Little Women*, *To Kill a Mockingbird* and *Saratoga Trunk*.

Sanjiv and I had both bought utilitarian bikes to get around Austin and two of us got an education at UT for the price of one. As his wife, I had access to university facilities so I biked to the gym regularly and joked that I made more use of the libraries than he did. I will never forget the moment I walked into the multistorey Perry-Castaneda Library (PCL) for the first time. After being deprived of a good library since leaving Canada in 1982, I now found myself in paradise. Hallelujahs were ringing out in my ears and if anyone had taken a closer look, they would have seen a young woman with the broadest of smiles floating from the card catalogue to the stacks, a long list of call numbers in hand for books she had been waiting years to read.

My arrival in the USA coincided with the beginning of a food revolution in America and both the country and I were taking it all in. I found books on French and Italian food, naturally, but there were also Hungarian cookbooks, Thai, Vietnamese and Russian. I cooked my way through them and came back for more. And there was one book with no recipes that would change the way I thought about food forever. The first lines of Reay Tannahill's *Food in History* resonated, clarifying why I thought an understanding of food history was critical. 'It is an obvious truth, all too often forgotten,' she wrote, 'that food is not only inseparable from the history of the human race, but basic to it. Without food, there would be no human race and no history…In the late twentieth century, after 50,000 years of fully human intellectual and technological development…Food remains as essential—and as divisive—as it has ever been…'

I took Tannahill and the other books I'd borrowed back to our sunlit, ground floor apartment in Hyde Park, a quaint neighbourhood filled with mustard-yellow, sky-blue and rust-red painted Victorian houses, fragrant purple wisteria vines and magnolia trees, less than a mile north of UT. When I wasn't reading, I couldn't get enough of my newfound freedom to walk around without worrying about being poked, pinched or prodded as I used to be in India, nor about tripping on a stone or pothole and breaking my neck. I walked everywhere, stopping to fly on every park swing, exploring historic downtown Austin, and shopping for groceries, discovering a little Indian store for lentils, spices and papads that were not yet available in mainstream stores, and a wee co-op called Wheatsville that was to go on to greater things in the next decade.

When Lawson's wife, Andrea asked if I wanted to drive with her to run errands, I happily agreed. She and I got along well and enjoyed each other's company. We exchanged life stories and recipes, played Frisbee in the park and discovered the only farmer's market in town on Burnet, a road that was like a slice of the 1950s and appealed to my love of Americana. Andrea and I took time to understand each other, being culturally and socially worlds apart. I found it strange that she never seemed to express anger except to say, 'I'm frustrated' and rarely ever laughed out loud at something humourous, only remarking, 'That's funny.' I made it my mission to make her laugh. She thought it amusing that I used old English expressions like 'Let's push off' when it was time for Sanjiv and me to head out somewhere, and 'I'm going to the loo' when I went to the bathroom. We also spent time together as a foursome, having dinner at each other's homes, walking to Amy's Ice Cream for an after-dinner treat, or driving to Zilker Park to dip our feet in the cool water at Barton Springs.

Sometimes Lawson called and said in his slow Southern drawl, 'Hi, we thought we'd come over to y'all's house.'

'Of course,' I replied. 'Come on by. I just cooked.'

*

We spent hours in our book-filled living room, discussing politics, art and architecture. Lawson and Andrea were taken aback by how passionately and hotly Sanjiv and I debated, no matter what the subject. We soon realized that Americans, at least the ones we were meeting, did not discuss anything so heatedly in public. Political correctness was already well ensconced in the late 1990s American mindset.

The Newmans became our family in Austin and we spent two happy years together there and on the road. We traveled to Llano, a small town of three thousand people, to eat pit barbecue sold by the pound. We climbed Enchanted Rock—a pink granite pluton batholith—one hot, dry Texas day, and took a road trip across the southern United States, driving along the Gulf Coast past plantations and pecan trees on our left and floating casinos in the water to our right. We visited Andrea's family in Biloxi, Pensacola and Gulf Breeze before heading to a campground in Lower Alabama for her brother Tim's wedding.

It was at a rest stop in Louisiana that we arrived at a pivotal moment in our relationship. When Lawson pulled into a parking lot, Andrea turned to me and said, 'Shall we go to the loo?'

I blinked. When we were done, she said just as casually but feeling out the words to see how they fit, 'Let's push off.' I had never heard the nautical sense of the line before. We laughed and headed to the car, our friendship cemented.

The other lifelong friend we made in Austin was Rosemarie. She was Sanjiv's student in architecture school and at the end of the year she brought him a spider plant in a blue teapot and a book of ee cummings' poetry as a thank you gift. Rosemarie is a free spirit—a welder, a carpenter, an engineer, a hydrologist, a rower, a coffee shop manager, later president of the board at Wheatsville Co-op, and now a consultant to cities that wish to start their own food coops. She began as Sanjiv's student and ended up as our friend.

*

When we were not socializing, I had plenty of work to do and my soul cat, Enzo, to keep me company. Let's be clear, I am not a cat person and I am allergic to them. But Enzo, just past being a kitten when he moved into the apartment next door with a young student named Leslie, was beautiful. A tuxedo cat, short-haired, sleek black except for white paws and chest, very elegant. We met when Andrea and I returned home from Central Market in a Texas spring thunderstorm. There were loud crashes in the sky and bright flashes of lightning. I jumped out of the truck as the rain poured down and saw a bedraggled, frightened cat on the doorstep, unable to go in. I pushed the door open and let him onto the landing. Whenever he was out after that, Enzo made a beeline for my door, sitting with me as I edited *Temples of India: Circles of Stone* for publication, and then when I started collating recipes for the cookbook. I never sneezed around him, which meant that I wasn't allergic and the next time I was at the grocery store, I bought some cat food and treats to keep on hand for his visits. Enzo and I could be quiet together, we understood each other implicitly, neither asking for more than it was possible to give. He brightened my days and I longed to take him with me when we moved. Alas, Leslie didn't want to give him up and I couldn't blame her. Enzo is still with me though, on my bedside table in a photo frame, memory of happy, carefree days.

Despite friends and Enzo, I was often homesick. Being away from Sameera, Jerry and my parents was difficult and I felt adrift.

I contemplated taking courses at UT but they were too expensive. Instead, I wrote long letters and learned to use a new computer tool called email! I also began to explore this funny thing called the Internet. And when I was tired of research and writing, I watched TV on our little black-and-white set. I listened to the news; Jon Benet Ramsey's death and Bill Clinton's Lewinsky scandal had the wires humming. I was amazed at how full of scandal and lacking in real information and analysis American television reporting was. I watched *M.A.S.H.* reruns and tried out late night shows like David Letterman and Jay Leno. On PBS, there was reporting of a still relatively nascent and fringe film and music festival called South-by-South-West. I also discovered a little-known, three-year-old, somewhat rudimentary channel called the Food Network. A Louisiana chef named Emeril Lagasse and a youngster named Bobby Flay hosted cooking shows on it. There were also some stalwarts: English chefs Graham Kerr and Jamie Oliver. Kerr's cooking show was one of the first I ever saw and, therefore, memorable. Oliver had inspired me with his fresh approach to food. The first *Naked Chef* series was light and fun, easy to watch. He considered cooking an enjoyable pastime, not drudgery. It helped too that the show's cinematography was gorgeous, making both ingredients and Oliver's London stunning.

In 1996, the Food Network was still building its brand. There were no big celebrity chefs as there are now, no game shows like *Iron Chef* or *Chopped*, and no competitions for *The Next Food Network Star*. The food world was still a pure and innocent place. I watched the channel because food fascinated me and I wanted to know what Americans were eating and how they talked about it, useful knowledge for when I would start my own food business someday. What I saw inspired me to explore culinary school. Fifteen thousand dollars seems a piece of cake now but back then it was a fortune I did not possess. Instead, the television station became my cooking school. I still tell students proudly when they ask where I learned to cut onions so finely, 'On the Food Network.'

The more I read and experimented with food, the more I thought about how to approach it, the more proficient and knowledgeable I became. In Austin, I discovered ingredients I had never used before—sweet, rich balsamic vinegar, artichokes, fresh mozzarella, smoky pasilla chillies and brisket. I gathered recipes from cookbooks and friends, putting them onto index cards I could use easily in the kitchen. I baked banana breads and cheesecakes, experimented with jambalaya and gumbo, cooked fragrant white grits and hearty black beans. I made Indian comfort food too and learned the differences between ingredients in India and the USA, adapting recipes for use in my new world. When we left our first American home to head west to California, I had two books under my belt and a wealth of accumulated food lore. We had enjoyed our years in Texas and as Californian as we became, I've never stopped using the phrase I'd learned from Lawson: 'We're coming over to y'all's house.'

29. God's Own Country

This ain't no disco. It ain't no country club either. This is LA.
—Sheryl Crow, 'Santa Monica Boulevard'

Los Angeles, California, never ceases to amaze, puzzle and captivate me. Combining the best of natural and architectural beauty with culinary and ethnic diversity, anyone can feel welcome or isolated, loved or marginalized in LA. It is the place of dreams and the place of disillusionment.

It is where you reinvent yourself. Here, I metamorphosed from woman to mother, writer to chef, cook to entrepreneur. In a town of fifteen million people, I could have felt lost. Instead, I see people I know wherever I go, whether it's on the freeway or far north in Sequoia National Park. I walk into an LA shop or a restaurant and spot friends. I walk into places where I know no one, but they know me. 'Excuse me, Kaumudi?' says a young woman. 'I'm so excited to see you. I came to one of your pop-ups. I *love* your food.'

This is where I belong. I first came here when I was twenty-nine to see Leena. Sanjiv had visited her in 1994 when she was at the University of Southern California (USC). He stayed with her just outside the downtown campus. Unfortunately, the most common sound he heard was gunshots so he came away with the impression that Los Angeles was unsafe, unfriendly, difficult to get around. When I came, Leena was working downtown but living in a town called Glendale. Then known as the second safest city in the USA, it nestled picturesquely against the San Gabriel Mountains, nine miles due north of downtown. I was smitten.

In Southern California, I noticed everything was larger than life and seen through a clarifying lens in the vivid Technicolour I had dreamed of as a child. Hollywood had influenced the look of the people, houses, streets and gardens. Everything was bigger, better, cleaner, more sparkling than anywhere else in the world. Roses; pale pink, flaming orange and crimson red, bloomed as big as my face; huge canopied trees studded with jacaranda flowers created a misty purple haze in the sky. Bougainvillea were brilliant shades of garnet and amethyst, magnolias were overblown, creamy white. I saw manicured lawns and carefully sculpted trees, punctuated with citrus ornaments of bright orange and pale yellow. The rolling hills were carpets of variegated greens and the skies electric blue like paper that's been shaded all over with pastels.

Art, cinema and music blend seamlessly and surreally into our lives in this town, creating an odd juxtaposition of reality and artifice. As much as I loved Hollywood movies, I was not enamoured of celebrity, but seeing actors, musicians and locations made famous on film became a matter of course. Even after seventeen years here, I have strange moments of déjà vu or deja écouté, without quite knowing whether the feeling comes from my life or the silver screen. Many of my friends are screenwriters, producers, actors or cinematographers, so two or three degrees of separation are not uncommon. We meet Anna Faris and Chris Pratt at a party or see Alexis Bledel of *Gilmore Girls* fame quietly waiting for a friend at Forage. Keanu Reeves is one of the donors to Keya's preschool and Timothy Olyphant regularly came to my pop-up in its early years. Molly Shannon from *Saturday Night Live* is a mom at Keya's middle school. Seeing Molly arrive to pick up her child always made me blink. I expected her to jump up and down with her big grin and do a *Saturday Night Live* skit for me right there on the sidewalk.

It's not just people who are famous in LA, but landmarks and cityscapes. When I first drove over the Hyperion Bridge to go from Glendale to the once grungy-now hipster neighbourhood of Silverlake, I said to Sanjiv, 'Why does this bridge look so familiar?' It's been the backdrop of innumerable scenes in movies and television shows. Nearby, the Griffith Park Observatory, indeed the entire park, brought out the same sensation. The observatory is a popular location and park roads and trails appear as themselves or other locales in countless productions, from James Dean's iconic *Rebel Without a Cause* to TV shows like *NCIS* and *Criminal Minds*. And why did I feel so comfortable in the Santa Monica mountains the first time I hiked there? Turns out I'd been seeing them for years as South Korea's terrain on my all-time favourite sitcom, *M.A.S.H.*

In this town, film and television in-jokes and references make sense in a way they cannot anywhere else in the world. How can I drive down Sunset Boulevard without thinking of Billy Wilder's 1950 eponymous classic starring William Holden and Gloria Swanson? On a camping trip, I see the San Andreas Fault. It stretches for 810 miles through California, rising out of the soil like a giant finger predicting catastrophe, and I hum:

> *San Andreas Fault moved its fingers through the ground.*
> *Earth divided, plates collided, such an awful sound.*
>
> *San Andreas Fault moved its fingers through the ground.*
> *Terracotta shattered and the walls came tumbling down.*
>
> *Oh promised land, oh wicked ground,*
> *Build a dream, tear it down.*

Natalie Merchant's lyrics speak not only of the precarious nature of California's landscape but of the fragile dreams of Hollywood fame-seekers. The song runs on repeat in my mind when I see the mentally ill and the homeless on Hollywood Boulevard, polishing stars on the Walk of Fame, cursing loudly or rocking back and forth in some private agony. What are their stories, what brought them to California? How fickle fate is, to choose certain ones for glory and cruelly discard the rest. Yes indeed, the silver screen is everywhere and our little town is a small but consequential part of this construct.

*

One of the wealthier cities in Los Angeles County, with a population of 350,000, Glendale is well run with high quality public services. The Disney Company offices are at one edge of the city limits and a huge outdoor shopping centre called the Americana draws people to a city otherwise considered fusty. I don't care. I loved what I saw of it in 1997—clean, well-lit, walkable streets; a large public library; a downtown YMCA; well-stocked Armenian markets; banks, bookshops and parks all within easy reach. To me, Glendale combined the best of urban and suburban. As I walked from the library on Harvard and Louise Street, and peeked in the glass at the YMCA at people swimming inside, I thought, this is where I want to live. But something happened that first weekend that could have turned me off the city for good.

I had arrived on a Thursday and Leena and I spent the next two days together. 'I have a business trip to Tennessee,' she said late Friday evening. 'I'll leave tomorrow and be back on Monday after work.' I said I'd be fine. I had no car and cell phones were still rare. In any case, I knew no one else in Los Angeles so I planned to spend my time alone having a mini-vacation, watching classic Hollywood films, drinking coffee, sleeping in and relaxing. Leena showed me where the spare key was stored.

'It works, right?' I asked.

'Oh yeah, my friend used it recently when she visited,' Leena replied.

She left the next morning and I turned over and went right back to sleep, like a young, healthy woman with no cares in the world. When I awoke again, it was eleven so I made tea and started a black-and-white movie marathon. It wasn't until four that I roused myself enough to step out of the house. It was hot so I wore shorts and a tank top, with a thin cotton shirt and carried a small purse with my credit card, driver's licence and cash. I locked the door of her apartment on Milford and walked the two blocks to Brand Boulevard. The wide main street was a mix of high-rises and one-storey shops, most of which were shuttered or vacant. There were only a handful of people out. I'd only been in the US for seven months and the emptiness still felt strange. Nevertheless, there was a lot to see. In the distance, parallel with Brand, was downtown Los Angeles, skyscrapers erupting out of an otherwise low-rise cityscape. Behind me were mountains I would explore later. Across the street, a ring of police officers stood outside a bank, guns drawn, foiling a robbery. A police helicopter circled noisily above. I blinked. This really was America!

I walked on, peering into store windows as I made my way towards Porto's, the Cuban bakery that Leena had raved about. As devoid of people as the street had been, the bakery was humming with life. My eyes grew larger and larger as they took in the delights in the display cases. I needed a voucher to be served, because there were so many customers waiting for their Cubano sandwich, cortadito and guava cheese pasteles! I chose Porto's classics for dinner: potato balls; mashed potato stuffed with a spiced meat filling, breaded and fried; ham croquettes; and cheese rolls, narrow, sweetened cream cheese-filled pastries, light as air so you ran the risk of inhaling them. Then I made my leisurely way back to Leena's place, enjoying the characteristically cool Southern California summer evening. I was glad of my shirt and I learned that layering was always needed in this desert climate, where high and low daily temperatures differ by fifteen degrees or more.

I was even more glad of the shirt half an hour later when Leena's door wouldn't open. I waited for a few moments and tried it again.

No luck. I settled down on a step and pondered my options. I had no other clothes with me nor much money; no car; and I didn't know a soul in Southern California because Leena hadn't introduced me to her friends yet. If I disappeared off the face of the earth this weekend, no one would be the wiser. What could I do? Find a hotel? Without a car, I was limited. I had not been in Glendale more than forty-eight hours so I had no knowledge of the city apart from my recent walk. I could spend the night on the landing outside the apartment, but what then? Leena was not back till Monday evening so I had another night and two days to get through after tonight. Then it came to me. I would ask a neighbour to use their phone and request Leena's landlord to let me in. A stout Latina answered my tentative knock and I explained my situation. 'May I call your landlord on your phone?'

She kindly agreed and I dialled the man. A gruff voice answered. I told my story again, stating which tenant and which building I was talking about. And then I had my first interaction with American detachment and litigiousness. 'Are you on the lease agreement?' he asked, knowing full well I was not.

'No, I'm visiting from Texas.'

'If you're not on the lease, I can't let you in.'

A flicker of anger ran through my brain. I told him my passport was in the house. 'I can show it to you if you unlock the door. My friend's hotel number is there too. You can call her and check. Or you could let me in to get my things and I can leave. I have a key, it's just not working.'

'No. I'm way out in Tujunga. I'm not driving out there.' He hung up. Fuming and powerless, I put the phone down, thanked the sympathetic woman and went back to my staircase.

'Now what?' I muttered, rueing the fact that I'd left the apartment without testing the key. After a few moments, I sat up straight. I'd inherited Mom's amazing memory for names, faces, phone numbers and birthdays. What about Leena's friend from

USC? Melkon. Melkon Khosrovian. I'd heard about him and Litty Mathew for several years but we hadn't met. Would he even be aware I was coming to visit Leena? I shrugged. Calling him would be my last resort.

'May I use your phone book and phone again, please?' I requested the kind neighbour. I thumbed through her white pages till I got to the letter K. At that point, I did not know that the population of Glendale was largely Armenian. To me, Khosrovian was an unusual name. In this town, it was not. What were the chances of my finding the right Melkon Khosrovian? I didn't even consider that as I ran my finger down a page of Khosrovians, till I saw the first name, Melkon. Address: 1105 Louise Street. And a home number. I looked no further, I just dialled.

I've always been fortunate that no matter what predicament I find myself in, a way out presents itself serendipitously. So it was now. I breathed deep, calmed myself and waited for someone to answer. I would later realize there were many reasons why my plan could have failed. Melkon usually went from the public relations firm where he worked to his girlfriend Litty's or to his parents' place. The chances that when his phone rang that evening, he would answer were not high. But lucky for me that day, he had stopped home for a few moments to change from his business suit into jeans and a shirt.

After two rings, a soft voice said, 'Hello.'

'Uh hello, Melkon?' I replied hesitantly. 'You don't know me. My name is Bunny (I used my nickname, hoping Leena had used it when talking about me) and I'm a friend of Leena's…'

'Bunny!' he said in the warm manner I would hear him use over the next two decades. 'Of course I know who you are. How are you?'

'Not so great,' I answered, telling him of my jam.

'Oh no. I'll be over in five minutes. Don't worry, it'll be all right.'

As I waited, breathing a sigh of relief, I marvelled again about the goodness of people. Before I knew it, a man with a big smile and a look reminiscent of Andre Agassi (also of Armenian descent) was climbing the stairs towards me. 'I'm so sorry you got locked out,' he said, patting my shoulder. 'Let's go to my place and we'll get this all sorted out.' I felt myself relax.

Melkon's apartment on the corner of Dryden and Louise streets was in an old building once owned by Hollywood royalty, Mary Pickford and Douglas Fairbanks. They bought the building as an escape from Hollywood and their Beverly Hills home. In the late 1920s, Glendale was twenty miles east and offered a cool, quiet retreat, nestled against the mountains. The couple supposedly furnished large studios and one-bedroom suites to accommodate their friends on leisurely weekends away from the hot, dusty city. We walked up to Melkon's furnished second-floor studio. The evening light was diffused by old wooden shutters and dark, polished wood was everywhere. Antique, plushly upholstered, exquisitely carved couches and settees and tarnished gilt framed mirrors filled the rooms. I had stepped back seventy years into old Hollywood.

Melkon asked if I wanted to try calling the landlord in case he'd had a change of heart. I did, in vain. Hanging up after the man refused again to help, I was close to tears. 'Bunny,' exclaimed Melkon, aghast. 'Don't worry. I know a locksmith. Here sit down and I'll make tea.'

I sank into the couch and Melkon made a call, speaking to someone in Armenian. Then he disappeared into the kitchen, emerging with two glass mugs filled with clear, sweet tea, the rich colour of amber, and an exquisitely assembled tray of pastries, figs and grapes. Melkon doesn't cook, but since that day I always joke about his skill at 'assemblage.'

When I was calmer, we returned to Leena's where Mihran, a burly, blue-eyed giant, was waiting for us. I gave him my key and after trying it unsuccessfully, he filed it down and tested it again. The door opened and he made me a duplicate, just in case. 'Thank you *so* much,' I said, 'I am so grateful.' It was years later that I found out two things: Mihran was Melkon's cousin, and not a locksmith but a businessman! I still thank him for his kindness every time we meet.

And Melkon has had my undying friendship ever since that day.

30. Mi Casa...

It's a long day living in Reseda, there's a freeway runnin' through the yard...
And I'm free, free fallin', yeah I'm free, free fallin'.
—Tom Petty, 'Free Falling'

They say if you've lived in California for three years, you're a native.

Once Leena returned from her trip, she showed me the LA sights. From the Observatory in Griffith Park, the grid pattern of the city designed around cars was evident. Roads stretched north to south for miles into the South Bay, further than my eyes could see, streets ran east to west across dozens of townships that made up Los Angeles County. I soon learned that if someone gave me an address on Sunset Boulevard, I had to ask which city it was in. Sunset is 21.75 miles long so the location might be in Malibu, West Hollywood or east in Echo Park!

Next June, Sanjiv and I moved to Southern California. He'd finished his Masters and wasn't ready to head back to India. 'I'd like to work here for a year and learn more about architecture in LA. That's where one should be as a designer.' So he applied for jobs and was hired at a small, well-respected firm called Koning Eisenberg.

'Sure,' I replied, thinking of my writing career in Bombay dwindling to nothing. But I was game for an adventure, with one caveat. 'If we have children here, Sanjiv, I don't want to move back to India.' I refused to let my child feel displaced as I had in 1982, returning to India from Canada. 'Then we're going to stay in the US, OK?'

Just a year after I had admired Glendale, we found ourselves there, landing at Leena's. Ironically, she moved to Toronto the following week so we stayed with Melkon after she left.

'*Mi casa es su casa.* My house is your house,' he said graciously and we took him up on his offer because finding a rental had proven difficult. Glendale was twenty-five miles away from Sanjiv's Santa Monica office. With public transport infrequent and time-consuming, we needed at least one car. Since I was going to work from home, we also needed to live somewhere safe, walkable and pleasant, with access to shops, a library, and parks. We rented a car to house-hunt. In 1998, Santa Monica was already unaffordable and with rent control being recently done away with, apartments were at a premium, Venice was unsafe, West Hollywood expensive and far from a freeway. Finally, we found an apartment in a Los Feliz neighbourhood that had not begun to gentrify. Since there was a gurudwara across the street and we'd gotten engaged in one, I took it as a good omen.

For once, my instinct was wrong. We moved in, transferring all our belongings from a storage facility only to discover that the basement bedroom window opened onto the parking lot. We realized on our first night that we were breathing in car exhaust and that the new carpeting the landlord had laid was infested with little cockroaches. Covering ourselves from head to toe with bedsheets, we spent a restless night imagining, if not really feeling, the insects crawling all over us. The next morning, I refused to unpack. We asked for our deposit back and looked for another place immediately. We drank tea and ate cold cereal for breakfast for a week, unpacking only as few supplies as necessary. I spent days looking for rentals and at night, we ate at a rustic Indian restaurant called Electric Lotus or at The House of Pies across the street. We'd been in LA almost two months and were beginning to feel the frustration of being unsettled. But for now, back it was to Melkon's. He made us feel very welcome and we got to know his parents and extended family. We also discovered Armenian food.

Melkon's parents, Vanik and Shake, had moved the family to the USA when Melkon was eleven but they were able to maintain their culinary traditions in Glendale, which houses the greatest number of Armenians outside Armenia. The Khosrovians' large dining table was invariably hidden beneath platters of delectability. Every Armenian meal includes plates of tarragon, parsley, green onions, radishes and cucumber, pickled turnips, string cheese studded with nigella seeds, hummus, to eat with pita bread or lavash, thin, flaky swathes of bread, designed for wrapping around kebabs or chunks of meat. If Vanik was grilling outdoors, he made kebabs from pork or ground beef, and roasted peppers and aubergines for salads and muttabal, a dip I adored.

Shake spent hours shaping kufte (dome-shaped wheat and ground meat dumplings), kibbeh (egg-shaped meat and grain dumplings), sarma (rice stuffed cabbage leaves) and dolma (grape leaves stuffed with meat and rice). The garlicky aroma of thin slices of basturma, cured beef, wafted up from the table. Sometimes there was heavily spiced beef sausage known as soujouk that Melkon cut into thick pieces and toasted on an open flame till the fat dripped off and the outside got deliciously crusty. Thanks to him, we also discovered lehmahjun, a thin, soft bread topped with a thin layer of ground beef, tomato and spices, and tahn, a yoghurt drink very much like Indian buttermilk. Our eyes widened as more and more food emerged from Shake's kitchen. This was very much like India, we thought, the hospitality, the sumptuousness, even some of the flavours, reminiscent of North Indian cooking.

The many meals and celebrations we attended at the Khosrovians were my introduction to the Armenian language, people and culture. Soon I was comfortable enough to offer my help and I helped Shake out in the kitchen over the years. There were many parallels between the food of Melkon's home and ours, which made sense given the proximity of Armenia to Afghanistan, Pakistan and northwest India. The Armenian word for cheese is 'banir' like paneer; their generic term for bread is puri, like our fried bread. Armenians also make desserts very similar to jalebi and gulab jamun, and a common love of dates, aubergines and chickpeas runs across the Central Asian region.

When we reached a point in the meal when we couldn't swallow another bite, plates were cleared, giving us a moment to breathe and contemplate before a round of sumptuous desserts and hot drinks was set before us. There were ornate demitasses filled with finely ground Armenian coffee brewed in a traditional coffee pot or soorj, or clear tea without milk, sweetened with young walnut jam or rock sugar. There were delicate pastries; nut-filled and honey-sweetened, and platters of luscious figs, grapes, raw green almonds and crunchy persimmons.

*

While our little neck of the LA woods was Armenian, the county was a strange hotchpotch of ethnicities: Vietnamese and Korean, Filipino and Chinese, European and Mexican, Persian and Canadian, alongside native Californian. This meant we could eat any kind of food we wanted any day of the week. During our first few years in the city we did just that, driving miles to taste the much acclaimed beef braciole at Salerno Beach, an Italian restaurant we'd read about in *LA Weekly*, discovering a taqueria in east Los Angeles that served huit la coche or corn fungustacos and drinks like Mexican horchata and tamarindo, and finding quite by accident a tiny restaurant in Monterey Park that served Chinese-Muslim cuisine. Every outing was an exciting adventure, frequently in the company of Melkon and Litty and other friends we gathered over time.

For now, we were still homeless. After a disappointing weekend spent house-hunting, we headed back to Melkon's one Sunday evening. As we turned onto his street I said, 'Why aren't we looking in Glendale, Sanjiv? Since you have to buy a car anyhow, why not live in a town we like?' Instead of parking and going back to Melkon's apartment, we decided to look for more 'For Rent' signs. We didn't have to go far. One hundred yards from Melkon's, we saw a man putting a sign into the lawn of a very well-maintained, small grey Craftsman.

I got out of the car. 'Hello,' I smiled. 'Could you tell us what the rent is?'

The man's name was John and though the front house was more than we could afford, he and his wife Hasmig showed us a one-bedroom cottage around the back. It was quiet, clean and well-maintained unlike our Los Feliz dive. When John proudly showed us the bedroom, Sanjiv and I looked at each other and agreed wordlessly that this was it. The landlord waived our credit check because he liked us, so we could move in immediately. The best part was that we were a stone's throw from Melkon and some of my first LA friends—Irene, Melissa, David, Uta—were made in this neighbourhood or at the YMCA nearby.

California may be associated with Hollywood, it may be called God's own country, it is certainly the land of beaches and mountains, exquisite sunrises and sunsets, a place where surfing and hiking and skiing and biking are within two hours' reach. There are blue skies, wildflowers, mountain trails, discos and nightclubs, down-to-earth folk and over-the-top industry insiders. It is a land of good fortune and the land of broken dreams, a place of extreme poverty and incredible wealth. But for all that is good, bad and ugly about it, to me California is simply one thing.

It is the place I call home.

31. Mama

I love you forever, I like you for always. As long as I'm living, my baby you'll be.

—Robert Munsch, author of *Love You Forever*

When I was ten, it struck me how much I loved babies. After Sanjiv and I got married, I daydreamed about having a family cottage like Jerry and Beth's on Lake Michigan, or in Maine or on Nantucket. It was not so much the physical space that interested me as the thought of little feet pattering in and out, bringing in Hansel lines of sand from the beach, and as they got older, gathering there for Christmas or weddings or special birthdays.

We were ten years into our marriage when I woke up on New Year's Day in 2001 with the absolute certainty I was pregnant. A blood test soon confirmed this. Unlike many women who don't know that they are going to have a baby until after their first trimester, thanks to my eagerness and excitement that I was finally having the baby I had wanted, it was the longest pregnancy ever.

My in-laws, excited that their son was finally going to be a father, arrived from India to stay with us for three months. 'Couldn't we have them come when the baby is born?' I asked.

'They're excited. They want to come now,' Sanjiv replied.

My in-laws had waited a decade for their son's child. But never having been pregnant before, I was not sure how my mind and body would react. I would have preferred my privacy but that was not to be. The in-laws visited from February to the end of May. By Memorial Day weekend, I was beginning to tire of being pregnant and could not wait for my baby to arrive. I didn't know if I would have a boy or girl but I didn't want to find out. I had no desire for buying blue or pink baby clothes or preparing a gender-appropriate baby's room. I also had a deeper interest in not knowing.

Every morning, my father-in-law asked me, 'How's my grandson?'

Every time I replied, 'Your grand*child* is fine.'

When the doctor asked if I wanted to know my baby's gender, I emphatically shook my head. I didn't want the debate or judgments that would ensue if the baby was a girl. What I was delighted to get from an ultrasound was a picture of my baby's face as clear as a photo of a newborn. You could see the sweet, heart-shaped face, the eye sockets, the curve of the forehead and cheeks, and the wee pointed chin. My father-in-law stared at the ultrasound image intently.

Three days after he and Sanjiv's mother returned to India that June, he had his third major heart attack and passed away. His death changed everything and I was glad that he got to 'see' his grandchild. Sanjiv boarded a plane to India for his father's funeral. I could not accompany him because I was close to six months' pregnant. He had to grieve alone. I was left behind to wonder and think and regret.

I was beginning to push my belly around more and getting myself out of bed took an effort each morning. I imagined what my child would be like and was devastated that he or she would never meet their paternal grandfather. There were also practical matters to take care of. I had to cancel the last vacation Sanjiv and I were to have as a couple before the baby arrived. To add to my stress, our landlord had asked us to move out. The geriatric component of our apartment building did not want a family with a young baby there, even though I'd told them when we signed the lease that I was pregnant.

I spent hot summer days driving around Glendale looking for apartments. When Sameera arrived for a visit mid-June, she came along too. I also took her to the places I had been writing to her about for years—Bay City Italian Foods in Santa Monica, where we argued the relative cooking merits of Indian masoor and Egyptian green lentils as we ate humungous Italian sandwiches; the Hollywood Bowl to hear Cesaria Evora sing, a gift for Sanjiv that he never got to enjoy; Porto's Bakery for Cuban indulgence. We saw the newly released *Bridget Jones' Diary*, had coffee at my favourite coffee shop, Buster's in South Pasadena, walked through the Huntington Gardens and sat down to a proper English tea there. We crammed as much fun and conversation into her short visit as possible, knowing that motherhood was to change our lives forever.

My daughter was born in September but I first heard her voice during Sameera's visit. I was six months' pregnant. It was two o'clock on a muggy, still June morning in the first year of this millennium. Sameera and I had just lain down on cool sheets after taking showers to wash off the day's sweat and grit. We both lay silently on our sides, staring out at the lights on the Brand Mountains.

In the stillness, a voice cried, 'Mama.'

It was not my voice. It was not Sameera's. No children lived nearby and none who were awake at that hour. I had felt the sound emerge from my belly but I told myself I was hearing things. I lay very quietly as if the stillness would undo the sound. My friend's body looked frozen. First, I thought she had fallen asleep. Then I realized that she was lying still and listening.

Very softly Sameera whispered, 'Did you hear that?'

'Yes,' I whispered, shaken.

'I did too,' she continued, still turned away from me. 'It came from your stomach.'

My relief was unbelievable. So I wasn't hallucinating. Then, we heard it again. Clearly, distinctly, a baby's voice said, 'Mama.'

Sameera turned toward me. We stared at each other. I think we fell asleep that way, somewhat mystified but certain that something rare had just happened. To me, it was a portent that I was going to have a girl, and this child was going to be a talker! That night I dreamt I had given birth to a baby who emerged from my body fully-grown like Athena, ready to take on the world.

Months earlier, when my friend, Uta, moved to New York, she had given me a cardboard cutout of a jaunty little girl with windswept hair and a flounce in her skirt. It had been in her living room window for years and I saw it every time I walked past her building where Sanjiv and I now lived. I wasn't pregnant when she moved to the East Coast but she knew how much I longed for a baby.

'I want you to have this, Buni,' she said, using her name for me. 'She always brought me good luck so I hope she brings you some too. And a happy baby.'

Then there was Melkon. He was the person we had known the longest in LA and Sanjiv and I counted on his knowledge and friendship. 'I want our child to have godparents,' I told Sanjiv one evening. 'So if something happens to us, he or she will be looked after.' Who would these parents be? 'One in India and one here, I think, don't you?' I said.

Sanjiv shrugged. 'Sure.'

Sameera, who was married but had no children yet, agreed immediately when I called her in India to ask. Then I called Melkon one night in August. Litty, his soon-to-be wife answered the phone.

'Helloo,' she trilled.

'Hey Litty. You two free for dinner this Saturday? There's something I want to ask Melkon.'

'Of course, dah-ling,' she replied.

So Melkon and Litty came to dinner. I made pork meatballs with coriander chutney to start off the meal. For the main course, there was a Basmati pulao with chicken marinated in yoghurt and cooked with onions in a silky coconut milk sauce. I also lightly sautéed asparagus, seasoning it with cumin seed and finely minced garlic. Grated beets in yoghurt were my raita. For dessert, there was soft, chocolate-whiskey bread pudding. When we sat down to eat, I turned to our dearest friend and said, 'So Melkon…We wanted to ask you something.'

'Yes,' he said, smiling.

I blinked.

He continued, 'Yes, I will.'

This important matter settled, we arrived in September. Till after we went to bed late on the 10th, the world was the one I, and everyone else, had always known. At 5:30 the next morning, everything changed. My phone rang. Uta calling from Brooklyn where she and her sister, Bibi, had been jogging around the track. Along with millions of other New Yorkers, they witnessed a surreal and unbelievable sight.

I answered the phone groggily. 'Hello?'

'Put on your TV, put it on right now, Buni,' Uta shouted. 'Something is happening. Oh my God…I'll talk to you later,' she yelled, hanging up abruptly.

What on earth? I jumped out of bed and ran as fast as I could to the living room. Sanjiv followed, rubbing his eyes.

'What's going on?' he asked, sinking onto the couch. The television was on now and a newscast was in progress. But it was all chaos, reporters and anchors sounding almost as puzzled as we were. We could see a smoking building on the screen.

'It's one of the World Trade Center towers,' whispered Sanjiv disbelievingly. 'What on earth happened?' There was a huge, gaping hole many storeys high in the building. 'That's the North Tower,' he exclaimed, louder now.

Reporters were announcing that a plane had crashed into the World Trade Center and all the on-screen pundits were trying to understand what had caused it to veer so radically off course and head to New York City.

As we listened and watched, confused and horrified, something even more startling happened. Now there was another plane on the screen and we watched it travel inexorably towards the World Trade Center. 'OK, wait, what? Wasn't it an accident? This doesn't… what's the pilot doing? Oh my God, oh my God, what is he doing?' I screamed as the plane headed directly for the South Tower.

And then, as millions of us sat, frozen, breathless, speechless, the jumbo jet impacted with the high-rise in silent, deathly slow motion. The images had the realism, efficacy and panorama of a disaster movie. After a seeming lifetime of silence, came the storm; a fury of shrieks and sirens and yells and rumbling noises as the world came crashing down, with a collective scream of agony and pain and disillusionment heard thousands of miles away.

Nothing, nothing would ever be the same again. Then came the tears. For the people who had died, for the loved ones left behind, and for all our children who were entering a place that had lost irrevocably its last vestiges of innocence.

In my little world, the upshot of 9/11 was that my mother could not get to me. Already en route to LA from India, she was stranded in Hong Kong that day. Mom worried that if the shock induced my labour, she wouldn't be on hand to help me, but I wasn't worried. My due date was 24 September. I really wanted a Virgo baby, which meant she would have to arrive before the 22nd. So when Melkon called on the 19th to tell me he was heading to San Francisco for a day and that I should call him if I went into labour, I told him not to worry.

'The baby's not coming till the 21st.'

'How do you know?'

'I just do. You'll be back.'

Mom arrived in Los Angeles on 16 September and we spent four days catching up. On the 20th, I made a dinner of spicy jambalaya especially for Mom and we went to bed around eleven. I woke up at two in the morning feeling like a Daseri mango being squeezed for juice. It took me a few seconds to realize I was in the beginning stages of labour. Not wanting to disturb Sanjiv or my mother too soon, I lay in bed, timing my contractions, clicking my digital clock on when I needed to check how many minutes had elapsed. I thought I was being quiet so when Sanjiv said grumpily, 'Could you stop making that noise?' I was taken aback.

'Oh sorry,' I said, laughing. 'I didn't think you could hear it.'

We lay together in the darkness a little longer till the contractions speeded up. It was the last time there would only be two of us in our family. Less than twelve hours later, at 1:57 pm on 21 September 2001, our baby was born. For months, everyone we met had told us we were going to have a boy so Sanjiv was somewhat surprised.

'It's a girl,' he told me, astonished, holding her in his arms.

The baby was blue because her umbilical cord was so long it had begun choking in the womb. When Sanjiv picked her up and put her on my chest, her cord was still attached!

'I've never seen one so long,' said Dr Selena Lantry, measuring it. 'One metre,' she called out. 'No wonder she was all tied up inside.'

The baby turned pink quickly and we were caught off guard with no girl's name picked out! For a boy, our plan had been clear. We would call him Neel, which means blue in Sanskrit, for we were certain our child would have green or blue eyes like mine, and the name would work both here and in India. I wanted his middle name to be Manohar after the grandfather he would never meet.

As I held my little girl's slippery, resilient, tightly packed little body, she instantly rooted for my breast and started suckling. This child is going to be just fine, I thought. As she nursed, I did a quick check to make sure she had all her fingers and toes and smiled with delight when I saw that she had her father's broad shoulders and strong calves. And a voice. When they finally took her away to do a heel-prick test for phenylketonuria, she howled so loudly that people heard her all the way down the hall.

In my room in the maternity ward, with its view of the Verdugo Mountains and the American flag, Sanjiv and I discussed girls' names so our daughter's could be officially recorded before we left Glendale Adventist Hospital. We finally agreed on a first name but I decided I wanted a more traditional middle name too. What I had never intended was for her to have my last name but when I held her in my arms, it seemed the right thing to do.

'Do you mind if I add my last name to yours?' I asked.

He was as easygoing as when I told him ten years before that I didn't plan to change my maiden name when we got married. 'Not at all.'

So the six-and-a-half-pound little baby with the grey-green eyes whom we took home two days later, had a name to grow into. Keya Vaidehi Marathé-Bajaj.

*

When we reached our home on Louise Street, I put her on my bed to change her diaper. I talked to this big-eyed wonder before me as I worked and she seemed to listen intently, already familiar with my voice. Once I'd changed her, I casually gave her my fingers to hold. She grabbed them with her little hands and before I realized what she was doing, pulled herself up to standing. She stood, balancing on strong quads for ten seconds till I gently eased her back down.

'Whoa, can babies so young do this?' I asked Sanjiv, incredulous. 'Look how strong her legs are. This girl could be a dancer!'

In her first few days on earth, Keya showed us everything she was going to be—gregarious, outspoken, sharp, driven, enthusiastic, confident, cussed, strong, happy. Her first word at the age of six months was 'Hello'. At one, she looked at a page in a book we were reading together for a few seconds and announced that there were five Es, ten As and three Ws on it, but she would not read till she was good and ready to at the age of four. At eight months old, she had skipped crawling and was standing on her own. Then at ten months, she felt that it wasn't time to walk yet and decided to crawl instead, crying bitterly whenever she did so, whether because it hurt to crawl or because she was mortified at herself, I would never know.

When she was a year-and-a-half old, our friend Kairav was reading *The Little Prince* to her and asked, 'Keya, do you know what a coquette is?'

'Yes,' she answered unhesitatingly. 'Every week Mama and I go to Porto's and I get a ham coquette.'

Food has always been a significant part of her life. In America, I had no help with cooking or cleaning and wanted to engage her while I worked. When she was three months old, I put her in the baby seat by the kitchen door when I made dinner. I told her what I was cutting, sautéing or seasoning as I did it. We kept each other company and I shared my love of cooking with her.

*

Unlike some parents, we had no desire for our child to pursue a particular career. We just wanted her to be happy. I had made a conscious decision many years before to never ask children what they wanted to be when they grew up. So when the subject came up, it was because Keya raised it. First, she wanted to be a garbage collector and drive the big truck she saw every Monday. Then she wanted to be an architect like Daddy or a typer like Mama. She soon moved on to wanting to work at Trader Joe's because she thought her favourite grocery store was the happiest place on earth. For a while, she toyed with the idea of being a pediatrician, and when she was nine, Keya told me that she wanted to be a ballet dancer. She had been taking ballet lessons for six years. 'Mama, I will go to college,' she assured me. 'It just might have to be when I'm a little older, after I've had a career as a dancer.'

She drew a pyramid in her dance journal and listed on it all the steps she had to take to become a professional. Five years later, she is climbing that pyramid determinedly, having already performed with the Joffrey Ballet at the Dorothy Chandler Theater in downtown Los Angeles, and trained at prestigious ballet schools. During the academic year too, our life revolves around her dance schedule at the Colburn School downtown, the Juilliard of the West Coast. It's our home away from home, our family away from family. Being there six evenings a week is no hardship though for I carry my work with me or go for a long run through downtown Los Angeles, and nothing gives me more pleasure than peeping through the one-sided glass in the dance studio and watching my daughter make her graceful way across the room.

Whatever she did, she always enthusiastically gave it her all. Whether it was homework, an art project, or a plié, Keya couldn't be rushed. She was going to take her time and make sure she did it well. I did not have that kind of dedication or endurance or enthusiasm till I was much older, and I admire those qualities in her. Keya exceeded any expectations I might have had of what having a child would be like. Her responsiveness was just what my maternal soul needed. For her first three years, my full-time job was raising her and I enjoyed every moment. We walked, played, talked, painted, read together. I made up songs for whatever she was doing and also sang her all the songs I knew in English, French, Hindi, Marathi and Sanskrit. I also made up tunes for the songs in storybooks she liked, like *Love You Forever*, and when I was reading, I did the appropriate accents for a story—English, Indian, Southern, French—making her double over with laughter.

When she was older, we cooked together in our little, yellow-tiled kitchen. She did not watch much television but her favourite show was *Thirty Minute Meals with Rachael Ray* so when we cooked, Keya imagined we had a show called *Mommy Ray & Baby Ray*, and did the commentary like a pro.

My baby was born being who she was always going to be. She might have learned from her parents and she might resemble them, but whenever people said to me, 'She looks like you' or 'She's just like you,' I had to smile.

'No,' I said. 'She doesn't look like me. She looks just like herself. She looks like…Keya.'

32. Un-Curry

Do you know the only real 'curry' there is, is a little green leaf?
—Kaumudi Marathé

'Are you Indian?' they asked. 'We love curry.'
I was tired of hearing that question wherever I went in North America. There are only so many times you can smile politely and say thank you. I began asking people what they meant when they said curry. 'A spice blend, a sauce, my country's food?' They looked confused.

So I decided to set the record straight, doing what a journalist does best, research. In 2005, I studied the phenomenon of curry through the ages and wrote an article about it on spec for UC Berkley's journal of food and culture, *Gastronomica*. This is how I ended:

> I hope that in this age of global kitchens, Westerners will discover the true diversity of flavours that make up the great Indian culinary spectrum. And I hope that in doing so, they will also begin to utilize the traditional names of Indian dishes the way they do those of French or Italian origin. Part of the answer lies in Indians using them as proudly as the French use theirs.
>
> For now, as I look at my fragrant curry plant, I believe I've discovered the real meaning of 'curry.' It is the exotic that everyone is seeking, the hunger for an experience far from the ordinary. It is the desire for something mystical, hidden in that country where mysticism flavours all.

What I didn't know was that my research was laying the groundwork for my approach to Indian food as a collection of culinary traditions. I was about to birth two more babies: another cookbook and my own catering company; and this article helped define their direction. For the time being, there was rejection.

Darra Goldstein, then editor of *Gastronomica*, told me she loved my piece but the review panel decided against it. A book about the history of curry had just been published in England so it was too much of a good thing to publish my story too. Like so many opportunities in my life, however, I didn't think this one had been pointless.

When Keya and my friend Irene Borromeo's son, Julien, were three years old—they were born six weeks apart—Irene and I thought we should go into business together. We had always worked well together and we had complementary skills to make a business succeed. We communicated well, had inordinate trust in each other and possessed the kind of energy needed to start a new venture.

My interest in food had obviously made itself known in our circle of friends. They enjoyed eating it and told me over and over that they had never tasted Indian food like mine. 'Why don't you open a restaurant?' they asked. 'You would do really well.'

'Why don't we?' we wondered.

Irene and I spent many enjoyable hours discussing the kind of restaurant we'd like to have and came up with two great ideas. The first was a café that served coffee drinks and snacks from all over the world. We were going to call it World Café and we spent months doing our pleasurable research, visiting cafés: the French-Moroccan Casbah in Silver Lake; Café Literati in Santa Monica; a Hollywood coffee shop called Espressa Mi Cultura that hosted poetry readings; Groundworks on Venice Beach, which served organic coffee, roasted in-house. We learned everything there was to know about the coffee business.

The other was a restaurant that served quick, healthy, delicious

Indian food. I even came up with a great name: Un-Curried. It was catchy and expressed my position about what was wrong with the way Indian food was marketed in the West. In India, the seventh largest country in the world, there is a great diversity of cooking styles but all that non-Indians knew about was the food from one small, northern region, the Punjab. The reason was that Punjabis were entrepreneurs and they were the ones who first went abroad and started restaurants in England, cooking the food that came naturally to them. Their rustic flavours of onion, garlic, tomato, and cumin were easy on English palates, unusual without being too foreign.

The consequence, however, was that Punjabi food began to be equated with Indian food, with rest of the subcontinent being ignored both in India and abroad. Even in India until very recently, most people ate Punjabi or Mughlai party food when they went out for a special meal. There were also generic South Indian fast food restaurants that offered inexpensive fare that was worlds apart from Northern Indian. It has only been since the 1990s that an awakening of interest in regional food has burgeoned in my country, and I am proud that I played some role in this awakening by documenting for the first time, Maharashtrian cuisine for English-speaking audiences. In the West, the changes have been much slower. That my country's plethora of culinary traditions should still, in the twenty-first century, be lumped into an ignominious, non-descriptive catch-all term like curry was intolerable.

Unfortunately, Irene's and my plans went nowhere. Her husband refused to help out financially or with childcare, and we had a much more insurmountable problem. I was still waiting on my green card. Without it, I couldn't work in the USA, and my immigration attorney Kevin told me there was no way around this obstacle. We just had to be patient and wait.

Soon, I started work on my second cookbook, *The Essential Marathi Cookbook* for Penguin India. Keya was now four and my time was limited because I also volunteered at her school. So I made the best use of my day by serving the recipes I tested as our breakfasts, lunches and dinners. Kind neighbours and friends also tested some after I had done the first round. Every night, after Keya went to bed and I had cleared up the kitchen, I crept into her room where our desktop lived. I made sure she was sound asleep so I wouldn't disturb her and turned it on, facing the screen away from her. From 10:30 pm to 2 am every morning I wrote, finally falling into bed for a few hours before my hungry daughter woke me at six the next morning with these important questions: 'Pancakes? Waffles?' Good morning world!

*

In September 2007, Sanjiv called me unexpectedly from work to give me some good news. We had been granted work authorization, which meant we were another step closer to getting permanent resident status. It also meant I could now apply for jobs or start my own business. I was ready. This is what I had trained myself for since we'd come to the USA eleven years earlier. I'd put myself through my own cooking school. Most of all, I'd had the luxury of being a full-time mom, without having to worry about earning a living. For this gift, I will be eternally indebted to Sanjiv. Now it was time for me to do my part. I was thirty-nine years old and full of energy and ideas.

I imagined a three-pronged business, tapping into all my skills and my love of food and writing. I would be a caterer and personal chef cooking organic Indian food, I would also teach people how to cook, and I would write about food. Once my goal was defined, I went into overdrive, planning menus, creating a business plan, doing a course in safe food handling, writing text for my new website and discussing with Sanjiv how it should look to reflect my food's look and flavour—clean, modern, refined.

I wanted people to move past the idea of Indian food being

greasy, spicy-hot food you got for cheap in a dive. I wanted them to explore beyond samosas, tandoori chicken, naan and tikka masala, which were all delicious but only represented a tiny portion of India's rich culinary diversity. I needed Americans to know what I knew; that Indian food was varied and sophisticated and textured and nutritious. I described my cooking as exotic but familiar, comforting but adventurous. It was easy to cook, once you had the basic techniques, and it could fit beautifully into American lifestyles.

My dream was for India's cuisine to attain the place that Italian, Chinese and Thai food had attained in the American psyche. To that end, I pondered a name that would be appealing, catchy and appropriate. After two weeks, I remembered an old idea I'd had. 'Irene,' I called her one morning. 'Would you mind if I used Un-Curried for the new business?'

'Not at all,' she replied in her characteristically generous fashion. 'You came up with it. You should use it.' But the more I thought about it, Un-Curried seemed too long. After a few days' contemplation, I had a brainwave.

'What do you think of Un-Curry?' I asked Sanjiv.

'Perfect,' he answered, and my new company was born.

My friend Uta, a talented cinematographer, offered to take professional photographs of my food and of me. I never wore make-up so Uta played make-up artist too. We spent a happy day shooting at the Hollywood Farmers' Market and then at her friend Jennifer Lane's home. I styled my own food and Uta's magic did the rest. Sanjiv built the Un-Curry website and designed business cards, using Uta's beautiful, sunlit photographs for both.

In two months, on 7 November, with an investment of $500 and the gift of an Apple laptop from my husband, I was ready to launch Un-Curry. Our friends Alicia and Jack offered us their home for the launch party and about fifty people converged in Mount Washington to taste my cooking and send me off on the adventure of a lifetime. I cooked up a storm, serving up treats like chivda, santosh, coriander shrimp, beef chilli fry, and my surprise fudge—potato vadi reimagined.

Cooking for pleasure is a choice, even a fancy; running a food business a completely different beast. A simple love of food or a desire to cook will not suffice. Love, while critical, slips down the ladder of priorities that make for success. In fact, I smile now when I hear people telling good home cooks that they should cater or start their own restaurants. The food business requires biceps and a strong back, the ability to stay awake through long days and work on weekends when clients want to party. And cooking? The moment when I actually start cutting onions and making seasonings is the culmination of a long process that includes interacting with clients about their needs, designing a unique menu and costing it once they've approved. Then it's time to increase recipe quantities based on the number of people I'm cooking for. There are lists to be made: of groceries and supplies; of what I need to pack to take to a job site; of what dish I will make when and what its various components are; of what I need to do and cook at the venue; of timelines for myself and my staff at events. Then I shop. And prep. Running a food business needs you to love cooking but also to accept hard work.

*

For the first five years, all I thought about awake or asleep was how to make Un-Curry work, how to keep track of clients and keep them happy, how to constantly reinvent my recipes and find new ones. I've made mistakes and learned from them, I've developed speed and whittled away at jobs that seemed unending, lifting hundreds of pounds of groceries and bins full of pots and pans, breaking down meat, peeling shrimp by the score and chopping onions for hours on end. I've cooked a romantic Valentine's Day dinner for a couple in the comfort of their own home and I've cooked for 225 lawyers at the courthouse downtown, cutting fifty pounds of lamb into cubes, dissecting cauliflower, stuffing aubergines, rolling hundreds of pastries, frying enough puris to make anyone's head spin, serving it all and cleaning up afterwards.

I've been asked to cook Marathi, Gujarati, Punjabi, Tamil, Chettinad, Malayalee, Bengali and Hyderabadi food. I've also been asked to cook Romanian, Filipino and French dishes and I never refuse. I am my own shopper, prep cook, sous chef, baker, weightlifter and dishwasher. I often put in fourteen-sixteen hours a day for several days leading up to a job because, even after almost eight years, I am usually the only person in the kitchen. This is partly because my business is too small for me to hire a full-time employee and even when I have help, no one I work with knows Indian food like I do, so I cannot delegate cooking tasks. Whenever he can, Dean helps me with groceries, heavy-lifting and dishes, but it is still only me who does the seasoning, cooking and flavouring of food.

The first big catering job I was given was by Sanjiv's boss, Aleks Istanbullu, and his wife, Anne Troutman. Both architects, they had recently converted a beautiful old church into their home and wanted to throw the company Christmas party there. My server, Melissa Hanson, and I decorated a long table in the large open space, placing square vases filled with water and cranberries or red and silver ornaments along its length. We passed appetizers while the guests had cocktails and then everyone, including myself, was invited to sit down. To my surprise, Aleks asked me to say a few words.

'I first learned all there was to know about food from my grandmothers and mother,' I said. 'The tomato-coconut soup you are about to have is my grandmother Vahini's recipe. It was my favourite dish growing up and I hope you enjoy it too.'

Aleks raised his glass of Pinot Noir. 'To Kaumudi's grandmother. You are 10,000 miles away but we toast you.'

And as everyone said, 'Hear, hear!' I thought of all the

wonderful people in my life who had brought me to this moment and thanked them wordlessly. Since then, there have been moments when I've wanted to throw it all up, sit down at my desk and have someone pay me to write. I recently tried a full-time gig for a few months and realized it was not for me. I like the variety of my work, the people I get to meet, what I learn from them and share with them, and the wonder I see on their faces when I explain Indian food in a way they have never considered before. I've cooked for movie stars, artists and writers, for Supreme Court judges, college students and terminally ill patients who just wanted one last good supper. I have cooked chicken tikka masala if it was asked for but made it the best avatar of the dish. I've also put Marathi food on the Western map and consciousness for the first time and this is one of my greatest satisfactions. Each catering menu is unique, designed for the client's specific needs and tastes. And they return the love, coming back again and again.

There was the woman who, as she ate a dinner I had cooked, confided, 'I've never eaten Indian food before but if this is what it is like, I love it.' And the Gujarati diner who took second and third helpings and told my staff, 'These are the best pani puris I have ever eaten.'

My cooking classes allow me to share stories, history, folklore and a good meal with people who want to learn about Indian food. One of the first things I ask students is what spices they associate with the cuisine. Chillies? I tell them that they came from the Americas and have only been used in Indian cooking for the last six centuries or so. 'It's a myth that all Indian food is spicy. Before we had chillies, we used black pepper and ginger.' This is a revelation to many.

I pick up a jar of commercial curry powder and ask them to smell it. 'If you have this in your spice cupboard, save it for the curried chicken salad or curried puff pastry recipes from *Sunset* or *Good Housekeeping*. Please don't use it for Indian cooking.

Traditionally, no one in India uses curry powder.' There is a collective gasp as people try to wrap their minds around this idea.

Then I pick up a branch of fragrant dark green leaves. 'Take a leaf, rub it between your fingers and smell its distinct aroma. Taste it. Isn't that beautiful and unique? Do you ever get that taste from curry powder? No. This leaf is from the karivepillai tree, otherwise known as the *Murraya koenigii* or the curry leaf tree. It is native to South India, and it is what unknowingly gave its name to the cooking of India.

'This?' I wave a branch of kadi patta in the air. 'This is the only curry there is.'

33. The Shared Table

The time will come
when, with elation,
you will greet yourself arriving
at your own door, in your own mirror,
and each will smile at the other's welcome,
and say, sit here. Eat.
You will love again the stranger who was your self.
Give wine. Give bread. Give back your heart
to itself, to the stranger who has loved you

all your life, whom you ignored
for another, who knows you by heart.
Take down the love letters from the bookshelf,

the photographs, the desperate notes,
peel your own image from the mirror.
Sit. Feast on your life.

—Derek Walcott, *Love After Love*

My grandmother Veerbala died when I was twelve but when she looked at me from her photograph on my computer screen, I heard her words loud and clear. 'Tell the stories you've been gathering all your life. Say the things I never got to say.'

Everything had pointed me towards writing this book: hearing family stories, documenting the past, cooking traditional Marathi food from recipes shared by older generations to revive flavours not often tasted today. Whether in the bedtime tales I shared with Keya or anecdotes I included in my cookbooks and classes, my message was the same: We need to remember before we forget forever.

I did not have this clear sense of urgency in 1999 when I was thirty-one years old, with my life fanned out before me. My husband rightly said that we needed two salaries to survive in California, to save for a house, and to live the American dream. Other Indian wives were doing it, getting work as techies, going back to school, making it possible to buy the requisite duet of Honda sedan and Mercedes coupe and the 3-bed, 2.5-bath house in Cerritos—good school district and large Indian community—or suburban Valencia (outside Los Angeles but with affordable tract housing). These were the outward trappings of first generation immigrants who had 'arrived.'

I too thought of the USA as the land of milk and honey, but I did not come to it for the large house, expensive car, or conventional suburban lifestyle. My tastes did not run to suburbia and I had never gravitated towards my own 'community' just because we shared a nationality. I followed the path of work and passion that fulfilled me and sat right with my conscience. For me, the tempting milk and honey of America was freedom, adventure and big possibility. I came here to get away from the parochialism (which seems like an irony now!), corruption and pollution I had never gotten used to in India. In the USA, I had sidewalks to stroll down without worrying for my life or safety, I had libraries and parks and museums where I could indulge the interests my parents had fostered, and I had a place that matched my notion of a home in which to raise my child.

Though I didn't have a paying job, I was busy. Apart from researching food history, I was writing a book of children's stories, doing freelance journalism, and applying for reporting jobs whenever something interesting popped up. But it finally dawned on me that I was not going to be considered for my ideal writing jobs unless I had studied in the USA (there was no money for that) or changed careers, and how could I do that without an American education? I was an English-writing foreign journalist on a spouse visa, ineligible to work unless a special permit was issued to me by an employer, in a country where in the late 1990s, even American reporters were finding it difficult to get work.

So I told myself, I should do what Sanjiv said and try for a corporate writing job that paid well. I could do that kind of writing, I was sure I could. I was elated when a casual application to an audit firm resulted in a phone conversation and an in-person interview in Los Angeles. My meeting must have gone well, despite my lack of business experience, because I was invited to New York as the next step in the interview process.

That was how I found myself in the city, 3,000 miles from my home in Los Angeles and 7,000 miles from India, my birthplace. New York was hot and sticky, like an inedible cinnamon bun. It was raw and crowded and exciting, everything I had imagined it would be, a Western sister of Bombay; a string of reclaimed islands on which civilization was packed into a few square miles of exclusiveness, untethered to their mother nation.

I stepped out of the taxi cab that muggy June evening in front of the Hotel Benjamin, nervous, excited, and innocent all at once. Once in my room, I peeked into the bathroom and promised myself a soak in the tub after dinner. I looked over at the bed. On the pillow, instead of a mint, was a small card that read: We are the hero of our own story—Mary McCarthy. I sat, looking out the large windows, as the violet light of dusk settled on skyscrapers, and thought about those words.

I did a three-hour-long test for the firm, I schmoozed with various company bigwigs over fancy lunches I could hardly swallow from nervousness, and I knew I was all wrong for that job, I was certain I would not get it.

What stayed with me from that trip was the card with the

McCarthy quote. It has lived on my bulletin board ever since. The words became part of a larger revelation that living in America was to bring me, a growing to a full-fledged sense of the individual. Despite having my fair share of self-centredness, I had never before given myself the importance of being the axis of the network of people and events that make up the story of my life. I had never thought of myself as the Heroine.

*

Another decade went by. On 6 September 2008, my fortieth birthday, I was a mixed metaphor; the proverbial happy clam, the world my briny oyster. Everything was just right. I felt alive. I was fitter than I had ever been, I had just returned from a fabulous birthday trip to Amsterdam with two of my best friends, Sameera and Jagruti. Un-Curry had begun its second, very successful year, a literary agency in New York had asked me to sign on with them, and the Food Network was about to call, interested in what I was doing with Indian cuisine. Maybe I am not such an unlikely chef after all, I thought.

It was not all a jar of rose petal jam. My marriage was on the rocks. I had spent two years hunting for a home we could finally afford and the day we were to hear if our offer had been accepted, Sanjiv lost his job. He got another quickly enough but we had to set aside the idea of buying for the moment. I had absolutely no inkling of what awaited me in my forties—separation, single parenting, increased work to pay mounting bills and the resulting anxiety and stress. Trying to make a go of life when my peers were settling into pleasantly satisfied middle-agedom? This was what the new decade would hold. Contrary Mary after all!

In 2011, five months shy of twenty years, Sanjiv and I untied the knot we had tied on on 12 December 1991. We had attempted till death do us part. The year my marriage died was one of many other deaths in my life, from the passing of Beth Bentley to the death of Vahini whose love affair with Anna had survived fifty years of marriage and twenty-three years of widowhood.

In 2010, I travelled to India to shoot a video of home cooks in Maharashtra. My mother-in-law and I were making saffron rice in her kitchen when she turned unexpectedly to the camera and said proudly, 'Of all my children, Bunny is the only one interested in Sindhi food.' The following year, just after Sanjiv and I had decided to go our separate ways, I was slated, in a somewhat ironic twist of fate, to travel to India again, this time to research a story on Sindhi food for *Saveur* magazine. I found myself in the odd position of working on a feature about Sanjiv's family and having to interview his mother and relatives and cook while dealing with the newness of our split. It could have been uncomfortable but it ended up being a beautiful bonding time for Mom and me and added unlooked for poignancy to my article. While I was in India, Mom kept the news to herself so none of the relatives plagued me with questions. When an aunt or uncle asked if I knew about some Sindhi dish or the other, she told them, 'She already knows. She knows a lot more than we do about our culture.'

Her high praise tasted bittersweet because it came when my marriage was on the brink of collapse. I confided in one of my close friends, Jagruti, telling her how I hated breaking up our family and Keya's life, how moments such as the ones with my mother-in-law made me doubt my decision. 'Bunny, just because your life is changing, it doesn't mean you will lose your family. You are so good at bringing people together and keeping them around you,' she said, trying to comfort me. 'You'll keep your in-laws and Sanjiv close. You'll make a new kind of family. If anyone can do that, it's you.'

Yes, Ganesha, Krishna and Annapurna had all done their best for us. The rest was up to me.

*

That is another story. Right then, on that day in 2008 when I turned forty, I was content and blissfully ignorant of the future. I stood in the middle of Viet Noodle Bar in Atwater Village to celebrate life, love, good friends and food. For a change, I was not cooking. Irene had planned this evening at my favourite restaurant and the room was filled with people dear to my heart.

Plates of tightly wrapped Vietnamese spring rolls and spicy banh mi decorated the large communal table, with glasses of house-made soymilk, sake and wine. In the refrigerator, a gigantic carrot cake waited, a gift from Stacy who was glowing and beautifully pregnant with her much-awaited third child, Odin Jacob.

We had just sat down and ordered dinner—as always for me, tender turmeric fish on rice noodles topped with crispy fried onions and coriander, the most satisfying meal apart from my mother's cooking—when my cell phone rang. I would not have answered except that it was Rajeev.

'Hi-i!' I sang, stepping out into the cool dusk.

'Happy Birthday!' his voice melted into my eardrum. 'Old girl!' he drawled. 'Now you're my age!' Since his birthday was on the 8th, we were the same age for two days each year and he liked to rub it in.

'Thank you,' I said, laughing. The day had been filled with cards, letters, emails and phone calls. This one capped my delight. I twirled happily in my black-and-white dress, slowly coming to a stop in front of Viet's large glass front. I inhaled. And though I continued telling Rajeev how beautiful my day had been, I was captivated by what I saw through the window. An entire table occupied by friends of mine, talking to each other, laughing, nibbling on shrimp and jackfruit, enjoying themselves. I had brought them together.

My eyes moved down the long wooden table, resting on each smiling face. Melkon and Litty. Stacy and Alicia and Jack from Keya's magical preschool, The Garden. Irene whom I had met along with my friend Melissa at the YMCA in Glendale years before. Dean, whom Melissa had introduced me to because we had both spent our childhoods in Canada. Sanjiv, whom I had known since I was twenty-one, was throwing his head back and laughing at a classically off-colour joke of David's. And Keya, shimmering in her grey sequinned dress, my little Keya flitted about the room like a sparkly butterfly, bringing smiles to everyone's faces.

My phone call ended, I walked back into the restaurant eagerly. For once I was not just an outsider looking in, wishing I could be at that party. This was *my* feast, *my* story.

I would savour it at leisure, at a Shared Table of my very own making.

RECIPES

List of Recipes

Marathe Clan: Konkanastha Braised Okra with Tamarind & Jaggery	277
Sirsikar Clan: Saraswat Pan Fried Pomfret	278
Spinach Stew with Peanuts	279
Contentment or Tomato-Coconut Soup with Ginger	281
Coriander Chicken	283
Comfort Lentils with Hot White Rice & Homemade Ghee; Mom's Green Beans with Coconut	284
Sautéed Fenugreek Greens	290
Cheese Fondue with White Burgundy & Compté	291
Hyderabadi Biryani & Mint-Garlic Raita	292
Sanjiv's Best Scrambled Eggs	296
Greenbar Cilantro Martini	297
Rose Petal Jam	298

About These Recipes

These recipes reflect different stages and aspects of my life. I hope you will enjoy making them and tasting a few of my favourite flavours. The recipes for okra and pomfret pay homage to my roots. They are dishes that my two families, the vegetarian Marathes and the fish-loving Sirsikars, adore. The spinach stew with peanuts was my grandfather Anna's special farmaish. I learned to make it from his wife, my grandmother Vahini. She also taught me how to make my favourite, santosh (contentment; a tomato-coconut soup with ginger). Even now, eating it takes me back to those summer days of utter innocence. Vahini also made coriander chicken for parties and I have successfully adapted her recipe. At Un-Curry events, pan-fried 'cilantro shrimp' is a frequently requested appetizer.

But if you asked what I would like to eat on any given day, I'd be torn between two meals: santosh on hot rice, or comfort lentils on rice with homemade ghee, and Mom's green beans with coconut. Sautéed fenugreek greens are delicious too, instead of the beans. I detested fenugreek as a child and it is certainly an acquired taste, but if your kids are willing, give them a chance—they are bittersweet and 'addicting', as Keya says.

By the time I was a teenager and had become more experimental about food, we lived in Hyderabad, where I fell in love with Nizami cuisine and culture. Nothing reminds me of those halcyon days more than an aromatic plate of Hyderabadi mutton biryani and its accompanying garlic-mint raita or boorani.

When Sanjiv and I got married a few years later, he was not a cook and since I gravitated to the kitchen, I became the one who usually cooked our meals. There was one dish that Sanjiv made really well, however: creamy scrambled eggs—and I learned his technique. This scramble is fabulous for a Sunday brunch with sautéed potatoes in cumin and bacon, alongside a cup of hot coffee.

If an alcoholic beverage is what you're looking for instead, try Greenbar's cilantro martini. Litty and Melkon invented this cocktail, using their vanilla vodka, for an Un-Curry party. It's been on my menu ever since because it pairs beautifully with Indian food, and the coriander, ginger and lime juice make for a refreshingly perfect drink for a hot summer night.

Finally, when you reach the last chapter of *Shared Tables*, you'll read that when I turned forty, I was still happy, optimistic and eager to live my life even though life was not a bed of roses. I contemplated what recipe to pair with that notion, which co-existed in my mind alongside my ability to be joyful and enjoy 'la vie en rose'. I chose gulkand or rose petal jam. It is easy to make and good for you, sure. But what I love is its fragrance and complexity, its floral notes and the scented sweetness that overwhelms your senses. With one spoon, you are immediately transported to a rose garden in full bloom, one that you can savour at leisure.

Marathe Clan: Konkanastha Braised Okra with Tamarind and Jaggery

Serves: 2-4, Time: 30 minutes

My great-aunt Susheela Marathe shared this unusual Konkanastha recipe for okra with me when I was researching my first cookbook.

Ingredients:

1/4 kg okra/bhendi, washed, well-dried & stemmed
1 tablespoon vegetable oil
1/2 teaspoon mustard seeds
pinch of asafoetida
pinch of turmeric
2 tablespoons tamarind pulp
2-inch lump of jaggery, grated
2-3 tablespoons water
3/4-1 teaspoon salt
3-4 sprigs coriander leaves

Method:
- Chop okra into 3/4-inch long pieces.
- Heat oil in a medium wok.
- Pop mustard seeds. Stir in asafoetida and turmeric.
- Sauté okra over medium-high heat for 2-3 minutes.
- Stir in tamarind, water and jaggery.
- Reduce heat and cook covered, stirring occasionally, 12-15 minutes.
- Add salt and cook uncovered 2-3 minutes to evaporate most of the water.
- Serve hot, garnished with coriander leaves.

Sirsikar Clan: Saraswat Pan-Fried Pomfret
Serves: 2-4, Time: 30 minutes marinating + 30 minutes cooking

The Saraswats love fish and I am no exception. Vahini's fried pomfret makes a delicious appetizer. If pomfret is not available, try it with thin fillets of firm, white fish like tilapia, cod, or turbot, even shrimp.

Ingredients:
1/2 kg pomfret OR other firm fleshed white fish fillets, washed & patted dry
2 teaspoons salt
3 teaspoons turmeric
50 grams fine rice flour
2 1/2 teaspoons red chillie powder
1/4 litre vegetable oil
lime wedges for garnish

Method:
- Rub fillets with salt and turmeric 30 minutes before frying.
- Spread rice flour in a small plate.
- Heat 2-3 tablespoons oil on the griddle till very hot, 4-5 minutes.
- Sprinkle some red chillie over each fillet and transfer it to the rice flour, pressing down to coat both sides evenly.
- Shallow-fry 6-8 coated fillets at a time, 3-5 minutes per side.
- Drizzle a little oil around them as they cook.
- Turn fillets when the first side is firm and golden brown. Replenish oil as needed.
- Drain well before serving hot with lime wedges and sliced onions.

Spinach Stew with Peanuts
Serves: 4, Time: 30 minutes

My grandfather Anna loved this stew so Vahini made it for him often. He liked eating it with chapatis but I love it on hot white rice.

Ingredients:
1 tablespoon split Bengal gram
2 tablespoons peanuts
6 tablespoons water + 1/2 litre water
1/4 kg OR 2 bunches spinach, cleaned, washed & finely chopped
1 tablespoon besan
1 cup yogurt OR 2 cups thin buttermilk
2-3 tablespoons vegetable oil OR ghee
1 1/2 medium onions, minced
1-1 1/2 teaspoons salt
1 tablespoon slivered dried coconut (optional)
3/4 teaspoon mustard seeds
1/2 teaspoon turmeric
1 teaspoon ginger, grated (optional)
2-3 green chillies, sliced
4 small cloves of garlic (optional)

Method:
- Soak Bengal gram and peanuts in 6 tablespoons of water 30 minutes before cooking.
- Cook them in their soaking water, 3-5 minutes. Drain.
- Blanch the spinach in 1/2 litre boiling water, 2-3 minutes. Drain well.
- Mix besan and yogurt/buttermilk till smooth.
- Heat half the oil in a saucepan and sauté onions till translucent, 4-5 minutes.
- Add spinach, lentils and peanuts.

- Sauté over low heat, 2-3 minutes.
- Add the besan-yogurt mixture. Raise the heat to medium and bring the sauce to a boil.
- Reduce heat and simmer, 3-5 minutes.
- Add salt and coconut. Turn off the heat.
- Heat the remaining oil in a seasoning wok.
- Pop the mustard seed. Stir in turmeric, ginger, chillies and garlic.
- Cook 15-20 seconds till aromatic and golden.
- Pour the seasoning over the spinach, stir once and cover the pan, 2-3 minutes.
- Serve hot with hot white rice/chapatis.

Contentment: Tomato-Coconut Soup with Ginger
Serves: 2-4, Time: 60 minutes

My all time favorite dish is Vahini's tomato-coconut soup, delicate, subtle, so satisfying. She always made it for me on the first day of my summer vacation when I arrived in Dehu. I had a pattern of eating santosh—first I scooped it up in a chapati. For my second course, I ate it mixed with hot rice and ghee. And since it was my once a year treat, I then drank a bowlful of it, neat! It was pure heaven.

Ingredients:
1 lb. tomato purée from 2 lbs. washed tomatoes (see below) OR 2-28 oz. cans whole tomatoes in juice
2 tablespoons clarified butter OR canola/grape seed oil
1/2 red onion OR 1 small shallot, minced fine
1 teaspoon ginger, grated
1 1/4 teaspoons cumin seed
3/4-1 teaspoon red chillie powder OR cayenne
1 1/2-2 teaspoons salt
2 cans thick coconut milk OR 26 ounces milk made from the flesh of a fresh coconut
1-2 tablespoons rice flour OR Bengal gram flour (besan)
pinch of sugar
5-6 sprigs coriander, washed & finely chopped

Method:
- Blanch tomatoes in 8 cups boiling water till they soften and the skins split, 3-5 minutes. Cool tomatoes slightly and skin them. Squeeze the skins for juice and discard.
- Purée the tomatoes and strain the pulp to remove seeds.
- Heat the ghee in a deep pot over low heat. Sauté ginger and cumin.
- Add onions and sauté till they turn 'gulabi' (pink), 4-7 minutes; do not brown them.

- Stir in the tomato purée, chillie powder and salt. Simmer 5-8 minutes.
- Gently stir in coconut milk, adding 1 cup at a time so you don't dilute the tomato flavor. Taste the soup occasionally and stop adding coconut milk when the taste of tomato and coconut are balanced (neither too sweet nor too tart).
- Raise the heat slightly. If the soup seems too thin, slowly stir in a tablespoon rice flour/besan to thicken it. If it is tart, add a pinch of sugar.
- Bring the soup just up to the boil but do NOT boil it because coconut milk can curdle if it gets too hot.
- Serve with hot white rice and ghee. Enjoy a good nap afterward!

Coriander Chicken

Serves: 4-6 as a main course, 10-12 as an appetizer
Time: 2-8 hours marinating + 45 minutes cooking

I remember Vahini making a huge kadhai of chicken drenched in a coriander chutney marinade when she threw a party for Anna's army buddies. I make it more often with shrimp, marinating and then pan-frying them as an appetizer for Un-Curry gigs.

Ingredients:

1 kg chicken OR fish (like kingfish, monkfish, tilapia or halibut), washed & patted dry
350-400 grams fresh coriander, washed & stemmed
4 green chillies or to taste
6-8 small cloves of garlic
4-inch piece of ginger
juice of 1-2 limes
1 1/2 teaspoons cumin seed powder
1 1/2-2 teaspoons salt
2 medium onions, minced
2 tablespoons vegetable oil

Method:

- Cut meat into 2-inch chunks or 4-6 single serving pieces.
- Grind coriander, chillies, garlic, ginger, lime juice, cumin powder and 1-1 1/2 teaspoons salt into a chutney.
- Marinate the meat in the chutney, 2-8 hours.
- Heat the fat in a large pan till bubbling hot. Brown the onions, 7-10 minutes.
- Add the meat and sear it over high heat. Stir in the remaining marinade.
- Reduce heat to medium-low and cook, stirring occasionally, 15-20 minutes.
- Thicken the sauce over slightly lower heat, 2-5 minutes. Taste and add more salt if needed.
- Serve hot with chapatis or rice.

Comfort Lentils with Hot White Rice and Homemade Ghee
Serves: 4, Time: 20 minutes

This is my comfort food, what I would want to eat for a last supper—hot lentils and rice topped with fresh ghee, with a squeeze of lemon and a pinch of salt. Any vegetable dish and raita are delicious on the side but Mom's green beans evoke happy memories of my childhood.
Turichi dal (yellow lentils/split pigeon peas) is probably the most commonly cooked lentil in Maharashtra. Many even eat varan with sugar/jaggery, scooped up in bread! This is the basic recipe.

Ingredients:

1 cup yellow lentils (tur dal), cleaned & rinsed
1/4 teaspoon turmeric
pinch of asafoetida
1 teaspoon vegetable oil
2 1/2 cups water
1 teaspoon salt
pinch of sugar
¼ teaspoon cumin seed powder
1 1/2 teaspoons vegetable oil
1/2 teaspoon cumin seed
1/4 teaspoon red chillie powder

Method:
- If possible, soak lentils in water, 30 minutes. Pressure-cook them with asafoetida, oil and turmeric in a shallow pan, covered with water (7-10 minutes, 3 whistles) or on the stove in 2 1/2 cups water (medium heat) till very soft (30-45 minutes).
- If cooking on the stovetop, stir occasionally and add more water if needed.
- Mash the cooked varan smooth, adding warm water to make the desired consistency.

- Stir in salt, sugar and cumin powder. You can now serve the varan but if you would like to season it, follow the method below.
- Heat oil in a small wok. Pop the cumin seed. Add red chillie powder, if you like and mix the seasoning into the varan.
- Serve comfort lentils with hot white rice, ghee, and your favorite vegetables.

Rice

Serves: 2, Time: 20-30 minutes

Ingredients:

1 cup short OR long grained rice
2 cups water

Method:
- Pick the rice grain over for debris if necessary. Rinse well to remove excess starch and dirt.
- Drain rice and put it into a deep pan. Add water.
- Cook half covered (medium-low heat) till the water comes to a boil and reduces to about the level of the rice.
- Lower the heat and cook covered till the water is nearly absorbed (10-15 minutes). Check if the rice has cooked and turned from translucent to opaque.
- Add more water if needed and depending on whether you like your rice grains distinct and separate or soft and mushy.
- Pinch a grain of rice between thumb and forefinger to test. It should be firm but mash easily.
- Keep rice covered till serving time.

Homemade Ghee
Makes: 1/3 pound, Time: 30-45 minutes

Clarified butter gives food a rich flavour and is actually good for your skin, bones, digestion and weight, when eaten in moderation. Ghee solidifies easily. If you use it frequently and the weather is cool, store it in a cool, dark spot in your kitchen. For occasional use, refrigerate it, 2-3 weeks.

Ingredients:

½ kg homemade or store-bought unsalted butter

Method:
- Place butter heavy bottomed pan that seems too large for the purpose, to prevent the ghee from boiling over.
- Heat gently, with a metal spoon in the pan, checking often to prevent burning. Do not stir the butter. Reduce the heat if the butter is warming up too quickly. It makes a rattling noise as it boils.
- When the noises slows down and reduces, the butter is clarified. The liquid fat rises to the top, the milk solids settle to the bottom.
- To test if it is done, put in a drop of water. If it sputters instantly, the ghee is ready.
- Turn off the heat. You will be left with about one-third or half the weight you started with. The milk solids will be crisp and pinkish-brown.
- Allow the ghee cool to room temperature before straining the liquid into a glass jar.
- Cover tightly only when completely cool.

Mom's Green Beans with Coconut
Serves: 2-4, Time: 25 minutes

Mom's green beans were the first vegetable I ever liked eating! She sliced them finely, lightly sautéed them, mixed in goda masala and topped them with fresh scraped coconut! You can cook gavar, papdi, and long beans in the same way.

Ingredients:

1/4 kg French beans OR other beans, washed & strung
2 tablespoons vegetable oil
1 teaspoon mustard seeds
1/4 teaspoon turmeric
1 medium onion, minced (optional)
1/4 cup water
1-1 1/2 teaspoon salt
1 teaspoon jaggery OR sugar
1 teaspoon goda masala
2 tablespoons fresh coconut, scraped
2 teaspoons lime juice (optional)
4-5 sprigs coriander leaves, washed & finely chopped

Method:

- Line up 4-6 beans at a time and chop them fine (break papdi/gavar into 3-4 pieces).
- Heat oil in a medium skillet. Pop the mustard seed and add turmeric.
- Sauté the onion, 2-3 minutes, over high heat.
- Add beans and stir-fry, 2-3 minutes. Stir in up to 1/4 cup water, reduce heat to medium and simmer covered, 10-12 minutes.
- Uncover, stir and reduce the heat to low. The beans should be bright green and most of the water should have evaporated.
- Add salt, sweetener and goda masala. Cook uncovered, 5 minutes, stirring occasionally. Add more water if needed.

- Mix in 1 tablespoon coconut and steam the beans, 1-2 minutes.
- Sprinkle lime juice over the beans and serve hot, garnished with coriander and the remaining coconut.

Sautéed Fenugreek Greens
Serves: 2, Time: 20 minutes

This vegetable dish was my bête noir growing up. Now I long for fenugreek bhaji as part of a traditional Marathi meal. The greens are very bitter—an acquired taste—but they are delicious with yogurt-rice or chapatis, and a simple salad or koshimbir.

Ingredients:

1 1/2 tablespoons vegetable oil
3/4 teaspoon mustard OR cumin seed
1/4 teaspoon turmeric
pinch of asafoetida
3-8 small cloves of garlic, minced
1 onion, minced (optional)
1 large bunch fresh fenugreek OR other leafy greens, washed & chopped
pinch of sugar
1/4 red chillie powder (optional)
3/4-1 teaspoon salt

Method:
- Heat oil in a medium wok/skillet till almost smoking.
- Pop the mustard/cumin seeds. Stir in asafoetida and turmeric.
- Sauté the garlic till aromatic and golden brown, 1-2 minutes.
- Brown the onions, 3-5 minutes.
- Raise the heat and sauté fenugreek till wilted, 3-5 minutes. Cook covered over low heat, 7-10 minutes.
- Sprinkle a pinch of sugar and chillie powder.
- For slightly tough leaves, add up to 1/4 cup water and simmer, 2-3 minutes.
- Add salt once the bhaji is cooked and serve hot.

Cheese Fondue with White Burgundy & Compté
Serves 4—6; Time: 30 minutes

Jerry Bentley likes to have a fondue supper a few times each summer at his cottage. Keya fell in love with it there and when we visited Jerry's daughter Sarah and her husband Alan Kahan in Paris in 2011, Sarah made it for us one evening. She cooked it with one of the loveliest wines I have ever drunk, a white Burgundy, and fresh Compté from their neighborhood farmers' market, located under the bridge just south of the Eiffel Tower. This is Sarah and Alan's recipe and it calls for compté, a kind of gruyère. If you cannot get it, use another gruyère.

Ingredients:
3 cloves garlic
1 1/8 cup dry white wine (white Burgundy is best)
5 cups (1 kg) compté, diced or grated
3/8 teaspoon nutmeg
3/8 teaspoon black pepper
3 tablespoons kirsch
1 baguette, cut into bite sized pieces

Method:
- Rub pot with garlic.
- Heat wine until it barely simmers.
- Over low heat, add cheese slowly, stirring until melted.
- Stir in nutmeg, pepper, kirsch, and take to the table.
- Serve hot with cubed baguette to dip into the pot.
- Enjoy the deliciousness, accompanied by the same kind of wine you cooked with.

Sarah's friend Fabienne also suggests some cheese alternatives to go along with the Compté but both Sarah and I just like using Compté.

165 g Vacherin de Savoie (1 ¼ cup)
220 grams compté (2 cups)
190 grams Tome de Savoie or Abondance (1 ¾ cups)

Hyderabadi Biryani
Serves 8-10; 4 hours

On New Year's Eve in 2003, I made a huge pot of Hyderabadi biryani from Bilkees I. Latif's The Essential Andhra Cookbook, *part of the same series that my* The Essential Marathi Cookbook *would join a few years later. It was a full day's project to assemble the biryani in that attempt but the result was worth it. Its intoxicating fragrance filled the house, my meat-eating guests devoured the dish, and it provided a delicious counterpoint to the passionate political conversation in the room. Biryani has been on Un-Curry menus ever since. I've adapted the recipe considerably, and I've also innovated a really satisfying vegetable version. I accompany both kinds with my spin on boorani, a traditional mint-garlic raita.*

Ingredients:
2 teaspoons ginger paste
2 teaspoons garlic paste
salt
¾-1 kg lamb, in 2-inch cubes
1 bunch of mint
1 big bunch coriander leaves
2 green chillies, minced
1 cup yogurt
2 tablespoons grated coconut
1 teaspoon poppy seeds
12 cashewnuts
1 tablespoon chironji
1 teaspoon royal cumin (shah jira)
8 peppercorns
½ kg Basmati
5 onions, finely sliced
1 cup ghee
2+2 bay leaves
4+4 green cardamoms

4+4 cloves
1+1 cinnamon sticks
1 teaspoon turmeric
1 teaspoon red chillie powder
¼ + ¼ teaspoon saffron
juice of 2 limes
water
2 tablespoons milk

Method:
- Combine ginger and garlic pastes with 1 teaspoon salt. Marinate the lamb in this mixture.
- Mix finely chopped mint, coriander and chillies into the yogurt. Set aside.
- Briefly toast coconut, poppy seeds, cashews, chironji, shah jira and peppercorns on a griddle, for 30-40 seconds, till aromatic. Transfer to a spice grinder and blend into a fine powder. Set aside.
- Wash and soak rice in water with 1 teaspoon salt for 20 minutes.
- Meanwhile, slice onions finely with a mandolin.
- Heat ghee in a deep pan and add the onions. Cook, stirring occasionally, till caramelized, 15-20 minutes. Drain well and set aside to cool.
- Pour half the ghee into a glass cup and set aside.
- Heat the remaining ghee in the pan and stir in 2 bay leaves, 4 cardamoms and cloves, 1 cinnamon stick. Add turmeric, red chillie powder, half the caramelized onions, ¼ teaspoon saffron, and the lamb. Sauté for 3-5 minutes till aromatic and browned.
- Stir in the herbed yogurt, coconut-spice powder and ½ cup water.
- Cook lamb covered, stirring occasionally, 20-30 minutes, till tender. Mix in lime juice and set aside.
- In another deep pot, heat 9 cups of water with the remaining cinnamon, cardamom, cloves and 2 teaspoons salt.

- Bring to a boil, remove the whole spices, and stir in the rice.
- Cook rice for 15 minutes till almost tender.
- Drain and cool rice in a large platter without handling the grains excessively.
- Heat the milk briefly and stir in the remaining saffron. Set aside.
- To assemble the biryani, use a heavy bottomed, deep pot.
- Spread ½ the remaining ghee on the bottom and sides of the pot.
- Spread a layer of Basmati over the ghee. Cover with a layer of cooked lamb.
- Add another layer of rice, topped with a layer of lamb.
- Add a third layer of rice. Poke holes in it and pour the saffron milk into them to keep the rice moist as it cooks.
- Pour the remaining ghee over the rice and arrange the caramelized onions over it.
- Cover the pan tightly, adding a layer of aluminum foil under the lid or sealing it shut with some dough.
- Heat in the oven for 30-35 minutes at 250 degrees Fahrenheit.
- Remove from oven and keep covered till ready to serve.

Mint-Garlic Raita
Serves 8-10; 4 hours

In California, I make boorani with heirloom tomatoes because I like their color and taste. I blend the yogurt with garlic and mint instead of just mixing the herbs into the raita. This heightens the garlicky-mint flavor.

Ingredients:

3 cups full-fat yogurt

1-2 tablespoons milk

2 cloves garlic

½ bunch fresh mint, washed and drained + 1 tablespoon finely chopped mint

1-2 green chillies

4-5 sprigs coriander + 1 tablespoon finely chopped coriander

1 teaspoon cumin powder

1 teaspoon salt or more to taste

¾-1 teaspoon sugar (optional)

3 ripe tomatoes, sliced finely and drained of liquid

1-2 small, mild onions, finely sliced

Method:
- Combine all ingredients in a blender jar, except the chopped herbs, tomatoes and onions.
- Blend till the mint, garlic and chillies are combined with the yogurt.
- Pour the mixture into a serving bowl and add the tomatoes and onions.
- Garnish with chopped mint and coriander and serve cool or at room temperature.

Note: the recipe can easily be halved to serve fewer people.

Sanjiv's Best Scrambled Eggs
Serves 4; 15 minutes

When Sanjiv and I were first married, I cooked scrambled eggs for breakfast the way my mother had done; an Indian style burji or akuri in which the eggs are firm. Sanjiv preferred his mother's technique. So one Saturday, he made them for me—soft, fluffy scrambled eggs, more French than Indian. Twenty-five years later, this is still how I make them.

Ingredients:

4 eggs
¼ cup whole milk
salt and pepper, to taste
1 tablespoon unsalted butter

Method:

- Break eggs into a mixing bowl and beat till fluffy. Whisk in milk, salt and pepper.
- Heat butter in a skillet till almost smoking.
- Pour in egg mixture and reduce heat to medium. Cook without stirring for 30 seconds till the eggs begin to set slightly.
- Gently move a spatula through the eggs once to prevent them sticking to the skillet.
- Fold eggs over but do not keep stirring or they will break into smaller, firmer pieces.
- Finish cooking for 30-60 seconds more over low heat, without stirring.
- When eggs are not liquidy, run the spatula through once more and flip the scramble to turn over parts of it.
- Cover briefly to keep in heat. Serve hot, with bacon and toast on the side for Sunday brunch.

Greenbar Cilantro Martini
Serves 1; Time: 5 minutes

In 2004, Keya's godfather Melkon and his wife Litty started a company that made infused organic spirits. Today Greenbar Distillery is located in downtown Los Angeles and offers the biggest portfolio of organic spirits in the world. It's been a thrill observing and taking part in Melkon and Litty's journey. Some years back, Un-Curry clients asked me to serve specialty cocktails at a party I was catering. I asked Melkon for ideas and he came up with this martini. I now offer it frequently at events and it's always a big hit. If you can't find Greenbar products, use any good quality vodka and gin!

Ingredients:
2 oz. TRU organic lemon vodka
1/2 oz. TRU organic gin
1/2 oz. simple syrup (or to taste)
Juice of 1 organic lime
Pinch of freshly grated ginger
Fistful of fresh cilantro/coriander leaves
Fistful of crushed ice

Method:
- Combine all the ingredients in a cocktail shaker.
- Shake hard.
- Strain liquid into a martini glass.
- Garnish with a sprig of cilantro and serve chilled.

Rose Petal Jam
Makes 1 jar; 1 hour + preserving time

The roots of this jam are probably in Persia but it has long been made in India too. Roses are said to be cooling and this jam is used to cool the body, purify the blood, aid digestion, prevent acidity and sunstroke. Whenever I visited Appa, he gave me a spoonful of the sticky, chewy substance that smelled like roses. I washed it down with a tumbler of cool water from Appa's copper water pot.

Ingredients:

1 cup tightly packed Damask roses
3-4 tablespoons sugar
1 wide mouthed canning jar

Method:
- Collect the fresh and fragrant rose petals.
- Gently wash them and air-dry on a clean cloth.
- When they are completely dry, spread a layer of petals in a dry glass jar.
- Sprinkle a layer of sugar evenly over them. Repeat till you have used all the petals.
- Shut the jar tight and set it in the sunlight for 7-10 days.
- Mix the gulkand every other day with a clean spoon.
- Store the jam in an airtight container and refrigerate it for use as needed.

Acknowledgements

I was lucky to grow up with male and female heroes. Women figure largely in my story but having dedicated earlier books to them, I use the word hero as masculine in this book's dedication to acknowledge some of the men I admire.

My deepest thanks to Sudhakar and Meera Marathe for making my childhood absolutely perfect and for cheerfully rerouting my story when it had detoured or meandered or derailed, and to Janie McLeod who understood and believed in my dreams even when I didn't.

I am so grateful to Jerry Bentley for his love and for teaching me how to embroider a tale, and to his family; Beth, Julia, Sarah and Alan, for decades of friendship and for the generous invitations to stay at Dutch Boys Landing for as long as I want, when I want. This book was written, in large part, at the cottage there.

Thank you to Sanjiv Bajaj for growing up with me and helping build a Falling Water of shared memories, food exploits, and stories; to our daughter, Keya for being the heroine of my best story ever; to Ever for being my eternal baby and writing companion; and Franklin who is the more strong, silent type.

I cannot thank Dean Douglas enough for making my life more fun and full of laughter than I could have imagined; for listening to my stories, oft-repeated; for understanding that I am most fulfilled when I write and providing me the space to do so.

My sisters Sameera Khan, Irene Borromeo, Stacy Lauren Kon, Rosemarie Klee, Jagruti Gala and Leena Pandit believe in me blindly and wildly. Gracias for celebrating me when I'm up, picking me up when I'm down. And to Sameer, ever my baby brother, for always looking up to me and for sharing my love of family.

Melkon Khosrovian and Litty Mathew, you are my guardian angels in Los Angeles, please stick around. I admire you and I count on you for so much.

Thank you to Jerry Pinto, dear friend and honest critic. Merci beaucoup to Anne-Sophie Moore-Jones for her notes and her unstinting belief that I had a good idea, and to Terry Fuller and Dileep Gupte who read the finished manuscript.

Catherine Schofield introduced me to my writing group, Book 'Em. The entire group, led by Mark Hague and including Lois Osborne, Willow Healy and others, has been an invaluable source of critiques and encouragement.

The 'rock stars' in my women's entrepreneurs' group, Mind Our Own Business: Vanessa McGrady, Libby McInerny, Quynh Nguyen, Charlotte Eyerman, Annie Wharton & Kathlyn Albright Lewis have been individual and collective sources of strength and loud, cheerful support.

People have taken me to culinary heaven on plates of kringle, semlor, haleem, fatoush and more. Others accompanied me on journeys of self-discovery, from learning to ride a tractor in a Michigan asparagus field to building a straw bale house in Texas! I thank them all.

In Canada: Cory, Simon & Evan Davies, Nain & Taid Bieman, Grandma and Grandpa Reinhart, the Bikkers, Jock McLeod, Marlyn Loft, Renee Silberman and Dick Holt, the Jamesons, my teachers Mary Southcott and Grant Boland, and my friends Clare Menzies, Andrea Lehnhoff, Veronika Blokker, Fiona Somerset and Karin Micheelsen.

In the UK: Gwyn and Emrys Edwards, the Duftons, Dorinda & Peter Hulton, Patricia and Ian Crangle, Daniel and Satya Roberts, Peter and Chandrika Amin.

In India: Maya (Kale) Laud, Reena Sirsikar, Jyoti & Sheetal Joshi, Shanta Bai, Adela Moa Pongener, Achyut and Savita Gokhale, Elizabeth Kassim, K.F. Mathew, Shakeela Khanam, Shridhar Shrimali, Rajeev Lingam, Mondira (Mona) and the Jaisimha family, the Pandit clan and their wonderful cook Ratna Bai, the Khans and Kapasis, P. Sainath, Jeroo Mulla, my in-laws: Tribhovan, Savitri (Bada Mummy), Manohar and Madhu Bajaj, my amazing and beloved Asha, Kamala Lulla, Sharada Dwivedi and Bal Mundkur, Anuradha Samant, Sualeh Fatehi, Father Terence Quadros, Pravesh Bhardwaj, Shamu & Anuj Thapar, Padmaja (Agte) Vora who died too young of ALS and Alzheimer's, Mohsina Mukkadam, Ajay Noronha, Vinay and Sarita Chilakapati, the Jains, the D'Penhas.

In the USA: Martha Tolman and Martha B. Northrup, Jessie Fleming, Lajja Aunty and the Jumanis, Pooja Lulla, Lawson and Andrea Newman, Danilo Udovicki-Selb, Kairav-Jaya-Amitabh Sinha, Carolyn (forever Cory to me) Juris, Vanik and Shake Khosrovian, John and Hasmig Geucherian, Alexis Moore-Jones, Marilena Rambaldini, Sam Flores, Melissa Williamson, David King, Rachel Mathew and family, Nadia Fakhreddine, Julien and Manon Labarsouque and the Borromeos, Yadira Rojas, Grandma Florence Coco, Caroline and Sean Harmer, Sarita Vasa, Deepali Panjabi and Justin Ziegler, Anita Sood and Abhijit Mankar, Garnet, Robert and Ian Basile, Christopher Tree, Alicia Gold & Jack Paulson, Laura Cooper and Nick Taggart, Danny Kon, the Arangurens, Cynthia Watros and Curt Gilliland, Soo Kim Choi, Hakim Iqbal, Valentin Babakhanian, Carrie Stein and Jim Ricci, Jacqui Biery, Baxley Andresen, Kevin Levine, Christy and Greg Dold, the Karsemeyers, my large and loving Colburn School family including Aimee Garvey and Brenda Lapchinski-Matthews, my Facebook writers' groups and my real life group—Christi Minarovich, Hilary Kaplan and Sara Mortimer-Boyd, Alexandra Burton, John Pitblado and the Surfas crew, Clemence Gossett and the Gourmandise School crew, and Teri and John Valentine and Joe Forristal of The Perfect Bite Company where I teach my cooking classes.

I am also grateful to my students, readers and Un-Curry clients who, by their curiosity and interest, inspired me to share what I love about my country's cuisine.

To everyone who gave me permission to tell their stories, thank you. I have tried to record memories faithfully but I enjoyed embellishing where I thought it was warranted. Any misrememberings or misinterpretations are mine alone.

How can I thank my publisher, Ravi Singh of Speaking Tiger for taking a chance on me with this book? I feel fortunate to tell this story to so many! Renuka Chatterjee of Speaking Tiger, and my editor Aruna Ghose helped get the manuscript ready for publication, providing sensitive, thoughtful notes and being that near-impossibility: delightful editors! Many thanks to Maithili Doshi for her book design that reflects the emotions of my stories. My thanks also to Shalini Krishan and Radhika Shenoy for helping get this book ready for print.

Finally, I am infinitely grateful to grandparents, parents, brothers, aunts, uncles, cousins, friends, colleagues, icons and heroes who played a role in my life story and whose presence in it provides me with the happiest of possible endings.

www.ingramcontent.com/pod-product-compliance
Lightning Source LLC
Chambersburg PA
CBHW061932220426
43662CB00012B/1885